The COMPLETE *book of*
PERFORMANCE
CYCLING

The COMPLETE *book of* PERFORMANCE CYCLING

PHIL LIGGETT

CollinsWillow

An Imprint of HarperCollins*Publishers*

First published in 1992 by
CollinsWillow
an imprint of HarperCollins*Publishers*
London

Second edition 1994

© P and P Promotions and Luke Evans 1992, 1994

A CIP catalogue record for this book
is available from the British Library

ISBN 0 00 218473 7

Designed and produced by
The Cooling Brown Partnership, Hampton, Middlesex

Printed and bound in Great Britain by
Butler and Tanner Ltd, Frome, Somerset

INTRODUCTION

Cycling is infectious, and once you have become infected I'm afraid there is little you can do about it. But – and here the similarity with other illnesses ends – you will never want to find a cure. For you will have entered a world of like-minded people who, using the most basic form of transport, have discovered the sights and sounds, the eloquent silence and the stunning beauty of places that others simply pass by.

I caught the cycling bug more than thirty years ago, having realized that I was not made for the sports that were played at my school. Instead I went fishing – by bicycle – and from that pond I began to venture over the nearby Welsh mountains. Later, after seeing my first professional cycle race, I dreamed of travelling the world cycling for money. But it was a few years before I found out how hard it was to win a race, even as an amateur.

No matter, for I had taken the first steps, and even if my dedicated training on dark evenings, and the lying awake at night analyzing how I lost the race (usually every race), did not improve my performance, I still could not give it up. To echo the title of the late Tom Simpson's book, cycling had become my life.

Nowadays, every year I fly thousands of miles to meet others like me who long ago decided that the car need not rule your life. Whatever their nationality, their cycling stories and experiences are the same. Everyone has a favourite roadside café, a dreaded climb, a story of pain or pleasure and a memory of one great ride, whether their preference is long-distance touring or racing.

Even the great Eddy Merckx, undoubtedly the finest competitive cyclist who has ever lived, still enjoys riding for pleasure and fitness. Each year he calls old friends and former team mates and they get together for a few days in Montpellier, France, to reminisce, ride more than 100km (62 miles) a day and in the evening dine on the best wine and food. I'm sure the tales of how the legendary Belgian won Milan-San Remo seven times and Liège-Bastogne-Liège five, mature like the wine!

Cycle racing, from club to professional level, usually grows out of simply enjoying

riding a bike. But, as any top rider will tell you: 'If you don't enjoy cycling, don't try racing.' Many cyclists, of course, never race. They discover the other side of this fascinating pastime: wandering freely across country, exploring hidden places that the motorist rushes by. Youth hostelling, meeting people on the road and feeling the sheer exhilaration of standing atop a high pass, having taken two hours to climb it and knowing it will take only twenty minutes to descend it, are memories only cyclists can savour. At night, after a long day's ride, welcome sleep comes naturally and dreams are sweet. And the next day you can do it all again, with just as much pleasure.

In *The Complete Book of Performance Cycling* Luke Evans and I have done our best to make sure you discover the same enjoyment and success as we have. Every one of our carefully chosen contributors from Britain and America was as enthusiastic as us when we asked them to help produce this comprehensive look at both the sport and pastime of cycling. Whether you want to race, tour, get fit or just learn more about a

sport that is stronger than ever after more than a century, then this book is for you.

In the first chapter, La Petite Reine, or the Little Queen, as the bicycle is affectionately known in France, the functions and features of six widely differing bikes are

considered, ranging from a high-tech time-trial machine and mountain bike for professional competiton to a track bike used for six-day racing.

An Injection of Pace is aimed at the fan in all of us. All the great competitive disciplines of cycling are covered by acknowledged experts, two of whom at present compete at top international level.

Cycling for Real is a comprehensive practical section, with advice on choosing and maintaining a bike as well as a detailed look at amateur competitive cycling and other forms of the sport.

The final chapter rounds the book off with a quick-reference guide to the results of the world's top races, a glossary and a list of the major cycling organizations.

All the branches of cycling develop over the years, but the rapid evolution of mountain biking since the late 1970s has been particularly spectacular. It is the latest welcome addition to the cycling scene, and as we all become more environmentally conscious this form of transport can only grow, to give thousands more the pleasures that others have been enjoying for many years.

There is nothing to beat the sense of achicvement and well-being that riding a bike brings. You will feel the same inner satisfaction after achieving your own goals, whether touring or racing, as Greg LeMond felt when he became the first American to win the Tour de France. That's the great thing about cycling: everybody feels equal. Have fun.

PHIL LIGGETT

CHAPTER ONE

LA PETITE REINE

a specialist tool

Road bike

The Eddy Merckx Motorola team machine is a rugged performer, capable of tackling a full season of racing with little more than routine maintenance. It is neither unique nor expensive.

Framed in steel

Despite an ever-increasing choice of frames made from alternatives to alloyed steels, the conventional steel frame is still the most popular choice among European professionals. For sheer versatility and longevity it cannot be matched.

Eyecatching team colours are instantly recognizable.

Over the years major advances in gearing systems, frame materials and many minor detail changes have all contributed to faster average speeds and closer racing. But long races, up to seven hours, over every road surface imaginable and in similarly varying weather conditions, still prevail, and that ensures that the top priority for most riders is to have a bike that lasts the course. Not necessarily the season, for even here lightweight carbon-fibre, aluminium and titanium framesets are increasingly used in preference to steel-framed bikes during the summer, leaving the more traditional machines to carry teams through the spring classics.

The Belgian-built Eddy Merckx bicycle pictured is a typical example of an early-season campaigner, combining a no-nonsense frame and wheels with the latest gear shifting and braking levers from Shimano and an eight-speed block. Tailor-made to fit tall (6ft 2in/1.88m) US professional Frankie Andreu, it may not be the most elegant of bikes, but professionals' bikes must fit them, pretty or not.

Merckx, the most prolific winner cycling has ever known, has been supplying frames to the USA's top pro team since 1989. Built in a self-contained factory in Meise, near Brussels, all the bikes are hand-crafted to fit each indi-

brazed-on boss for race number

computer

combined gear and brake levers

close-ratio eight-speed block

dual pivot brakes

EDDY MERCKX

vidual member of the team. A perfectionist during his racing career, the great Belgian still takes a personal interest in the riders and their bikes. In the case of Tour de France specialist Andy Hampsten, the search for the perfect position resulted in numerous frame changes during the 1989 season. There is nothing radical about the materials or angles of a standard-issue Team Eddy Merckx bike – the frame is strong and reasonably lightweight, it offers a comfortable pedalling position and the machine's steering is neutral.

Many steel-framed road bikes used by professionals now feature shallow 72-degree seat tubes, an angle that a touring rider might specify, though for quite different reasons. The Eddy Merckx bike is no exception and although every frame is different the majority of frames built for average-sized riders have a laid-back riding position of 72-3 degrees with a correspondingly innocuous 73-degree head tube. With taller riders, who require a long top tube, the temptation is to build a frame with steeper angles in order to keep the wheelbase at a normal length. This can affect stability, however, and a set-up based on conventional angles is advised. Yet many riders will not be told and in the case of Belgian professional Benny Van Itterbeck, who rode an Italian-built Basso (23¼in/59cm) frame in 1990, a seat tube of 75 degrees was specified. He still insisted on having his saddle pushed as far back on the rails as it would go and was reported as being quite satisfied with the set-up.

The geometry of today's road bikes is evidence of the steady improvements since the turn of the century in road surfaces and refinements in the position of the cyclist. It may be only by degrees, literally, but the overall trend has been towards a more upright bike with less emphasis on the shock-absorbing qualities of the frame and more thought put into the riding position and handling. In the 1950s, for instance, a typical road bike would have had a 70-degree seat tube, a 71-degree head-tube angle and generously

raked forks. A couple of degrees were added over the next twenty years, mainly in response to improved road surfaces, until the late 1970s, when a French-built Mercier team bike was built with angles of 74 degrees parallel. In the 1980s, when attention turned to the cyclist as athlete, thought focused on the position of the rider on the bike, particularly on the spatial relationship between the points of contact (saddle, bars and pedals). This led to a relaxation of the seat angle, a reflection of how the stronger, fitter rider of the modern era was able to push a bigger gear as well as adopt a more aerodynamic, stretched-out position. Forks have become less and less raked, inevitably resulting in the recent, rather extreme, adoption by Italian frame maker Colnago of straight forks.

A laid-back seat tube, with a long top tube and moderately raked forks contributing to a stable, comfortable ride has been the style in Europe for a good ten years. US racers, including Greg LeMond, climber Andy Hampsten and sprinter Davis Phinney all came over to Europe on bikes that put them too far over the bottom bracket and too upright because of short top tubes. LeMond's coach in the early 1980s, Frenchman Cyrille Guimard, put him on a bike with a more relaxed seat tube, a longer top tube, a higher seat and longer cranks – a position he has kept ever since. Phinney came over to Europe in the mid 1980s riding a frame suited more to short-circuit criterium racing than long-distance classics. It did not take him long to realize that a bike with a 75-degree seat tube was contributing to an upright, unaerodynamic position and painful shoulders after several hours in the saddle. Over the years he knocked a degree off his seat tube and lengthened the top tube by 2cm, giving himself the advantage of a more relaxed and aerodynamic pedalling position.

Merckx noticed virtually the same problem with Andy Hampsten in 1989 – the American was sitting too far forward and too high in the saddle. After several attempts Hampsten ended up

Wonder stuff

Titanium is a material that has excited bicycle manufacturers for about twenty years. In the early 1970s titanium frames were used by 1973 Tour de France winner Luis Ocaña of Spain. Problems with the grade of titanium used, however, saw them disappear until more recently, when Greg LeMond and mountain-bike racers started using lightweight, corrosion-proof titanium frames.

Spokes first

Spoked wheels, as opposed to tri-spoke wheels, are still the preferred choice on the road. A spoked wheel with thirty-two spokes and a small-flange hub is light and more comfortable to ride than a rigid tri-spoke. A skilled wheel builder can build a wheel that offers a variety of 'spring' rates, and that is something a solid wheel, either a disc or tri-spoke, cannot match.

with a bike that not only matched his effortless riding style but also offered improved stability compared with his original bikes. Aerodynamics and the search for a more efficient position encouraged even the great Bernard Hinault to elongate his bike at the end of the 1984 season, when the Frenchman returned from injury to win the Tour of Lombardy and the Grand Prix des Nations.

Frame materials have also come a long way since the days of Eugène Christophe, who lost the Tour de France twice, in 1913 and 1919, because of frame failures. Frames were heavier and weaker until the introduction from the mid 1920's of lighter, stronger tubes that featured butted ends and could be brazed at lower temperatures. British-made manganese-molybdenum Reynolds 531 double-butted tubing, which was thinner in the middle and thicker at the ends, was widely used until the late 1960s, when tubing manufacturers like Columbus of Italy introduced their SL range, followed a few years later by the first frames in aluminium and titanium.

More advanced steel tubing, with its innate ability to soak up vibration from the road, also added considerably to the comfort of the pre-war racer and accelerated the development and use of narrower tyres. Brazed seat stays further reduced weight, and did away with the cumbersome method of securing the stays with a lug and pinch bolt. In 1928 it was possible to build a track-racing bicycle, using steel-butted tubing with light lugs and brackets, that weighed a scant 15lb (6.8kg). Alloy was used for all the major components and the wheels, shod with 1-in (2.5cm) tyres, ran on wooden rims. In 1950 a ten-speed British-built Claud Butler road-racing bicycle, with a steel-butted frame and forks weighing 6lb (2.9kg) and equipped with the latest alloy equipment and derailleur gears, weighed in at 24lb (10.9kg). Between then and now the weight of a quality road bike has come down by approximately 1lb (0.5kg) per decade.

Today the modern frame builder can select tubing to suit every road condition. Lightweight tubes like Reynolds 653/753 and Tange Prestige, not a great deal heavier than the lightest composite and aluminium frames, can be used for time trialling, mountain climbing or smooth roads. Heavier tubes like Columbus SLX, used for Andreu's Eddy Merckx frame, are ideal for the day-to-day pounding inflicted on a bike used in the spring and autumn classics. It has always been possible to build a light bicycle, but today's bikes are light and strong. For instance, in 1990 a frame built by Basso for German professional Andreas Kappes using Columbus EL oversize tubing weighed 5lb (2.3kg) and had the same stiffness as the 6lb-3oz (2.8kg) Columbus SLX/SPX Basso Loto team frame.

Modern components work better, and are lighter. Gear systems have come a long way since the days when riders had to stop, whip out the back wheel and put it back the other way round to make use of one of just four fixed sprockets either side of the hub. Freewheels, allowing faster descents, were in universal use before the First World War but race development of a derailleur-type gear-changing system was held back until 1937 when the Tour de France finally relented and allowed the racers to use rudimentary derailleur gears. Derailleurs had been in useful existence since the 1920s but thanks to the technophobia of the Tour de France's founder, Henri Desgrange, professionals in that race, for once, lagged behind ordinary cyclists in terms of equipment. After the Second World War development continued apace with Campagnolo's Corsa (later called Paris-Roubaix) gear, while the French made Simplex and, soon after, versions of the derailleur system as we know it today.

Since then the basic function of both the rear and front derailleurs has remained the same and concentration has focused on the number of gears available, the position of the shift levers and the accuracy and ease of the shift itself. Narrow chains and stronger wheels have increased the capacity of gear blocks from five, to six, seven and currently eight sprockets, giving a maximum of fourteen usable gears. A narrow Shimano hub, some 3mm slimmer than a standard hub, is used to accommodate the eight-speed block on Andreu's Eddy Merckx. The derailleur is Shimano's top Dura-Ace model, operated by their latest innovation – combined brake and gear levers. Motorola, formerly the 7-Eleven team, were involved with the development of the STI levers right from the prototype stage and after they were launched in 1990 they were a common sight on many professional team bikes. As a brake lever the device works as normal, braking occurring when the lever is pulled back in the direction of the bars. To change gear the same lever is pushed inboard, clicking the rear derailleur up one sprocket. A smaller catch behind the lever is clicked to move the chain down the block, in one go or sprocket by sprocket. The second lever operates the front derailleur in the same way.

Like the frame, the wheels on Andreu's bike were built to withstand a season of hard racing and the mechanics on the team do not believe in cutting corners, especially with light rims. Wolber Profil 18 rims, which have a V section and are anodized grey, are built on to thirty-two-hole Shimano hubs with DT Swiss stainless spokes. Tyres are Wolber Champion de France SP1 Soie (Silk), team issue. Thirty years ago professionals rode thirty-six-spoke wheels and although thirty-sixes are still used on occasion, most teams favour thirty-two-spoke wheels built with plain-gauge spokes to give a softer, more lively ride. Motorola are one of the few teams to build special wheels for the Paris-Roubaix classic, part of which goes over some of the worst cobbles in northern France. These are loosely built wheels with plenty of spring in them and square-section Wolber rims (thirty-two holes) that are not as rigid as aero V rims. With large-profile Wolber tyres they provide a less bone-jarring ride as well

as some important impact resistance.

Andreu's bike is fitted with a gel-filled saddle and his hands rest on imitation-cork bar tape. Clamped to the bars is an Avocet 30 computer informing the rider of speed, mileage, time elapsed, the time and total mileage. Fatter tyres, especially the new breed of clincher tyres that can be pumped up hard without blowing off the rim, have also helped to improve the ride of the modern road bike.

The Look company, manufacturers in 1984 of the first quick-release pedal system, supply the Carbon Pro pedals, which represent the latest in low weight, strength and ease of use. Only a few professional riders still use toe clips and straps, so popular has the clipless system become. The pedals are screwed into 175mm Shimano Dura-Ace cranks to compensate for Andreu's long legs. Finally the brakes are Shimano's dual-pivot Dura-Ace calipers, which provide excellent stopping with a secure bolt-on fitting that cannot be pushed out of alignment by clumsy wheel changes.

'Hell of the north'

For cobbled classics like Paris-Roubaix team mechanics might fit wider-section tyres, a straight-through block and lightly tensioned wheels. In the past, forks with a longer rake, padded handlebar tape and even heavier components were fitted. Following cars on the race have their hub caps removed!

Shimano, Campagnolo and SunTour have produced combined gear and brake levers. On the Campagnolo and SunTour systems the cables are concealed.

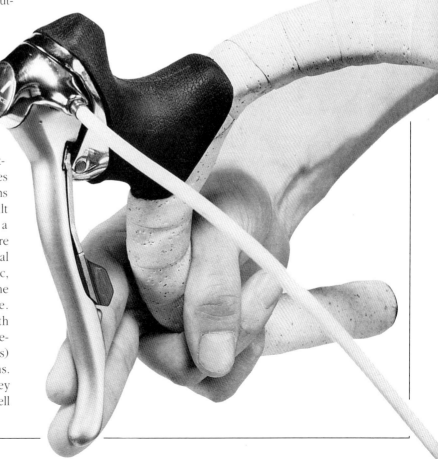

Time-trial bike

Designed to cheat the wind and shave seconds from every kilometre, today's modern time-trial bike is uncompromisingly pure in purpose and function. Like the modern car, it is a product of the wind tunnel.

Fight the drag

Inspired by the skier's tuck position, the modern time trialist cuts through the air with a flat back and hands clenched in front of the face. This position serves to channel the wind above and below the body – not into the chest.

A low frontal area and a ski-tuck riding position are vital.

At the end of every year *Miroir du Cyclisme*, France's venerable cycle racing magazine, produces a special issue to celebrate the past season. The 1984 edition of this 'Golden Book' featured three cover shots: the grinning face of Francesco Moser, poking out from an astronaut-style helmet; Harvey Nitz in a rubber-ized skinsuit clambering aboard a wafer-thin track machine; and Laurent Fignon in the yellow jersey, bending over his Gitane Delta, sporting a bright yellow helmet in the shape of a shark's tooth. Above the three photographs were the words 'L'Année des Mutants'.

The 'mutant' bicycle had arrived, aerodynamics were in, and on the evidence of the succeeding years, they are here to stay. From 1984 no bicycle designer, especially those looking for a performance edge in solo rides against the watch, could afford to ignore the race-winning advantages offered by a steadily growing armoury of wind-cheating aids.

Without question the first mutant bike of the modern era was the machine that Francesco Moser used to break Eddy Merckx's long-standing

disc rear wheel

aero bars

padded elbow supports

tri-spoke front wheel

(1972) hour record in January 1984. Moser, who at thirty-two was widely considered to be past his best, prepared like a boxer in the four months before the scheduled attempt in Mexico. Constantly monitored by a team of experts in nutrition and physiology, the great Italian champion was coaxed to top form at a time of year when most racers were taking a well-earned rest. No aspect of the record attempt was overlooked and the record bike, designed by Professor Dal Monte, got the full treatment.

It was sensational. Tested in the Pininfarina wind tunnel, it featured a long, swooping, low-profile frame, solid disc wheels weighted at the back to produce a flywheel effect, titanium components, upturned bars and a solid chainset. Even with the relatively heavy wheels it weighed just 16½lb (7.5kg). The track itself was coated in a resin to reduce the rolling resistance. The bike was fast, Moser was fit, and when he completed 51.152km (31.784 miles) in one hour on 23 January 1984, the record of Merckx, bettered by 1.72km (1.07 miles), was consigned to a bygone era – an era when such a mechanical advantage would have been inconceivable. Tests made after the record showed that Moser had used less energy to go faster than Merckx, and that had Merckx used such a bike he would have done more than 52km (32.3 miles) in the hour. There was much grumbling about the validity of the new figure, and even Merckx turned his nose up at the ride. Nevertheless, it went straight into the record books, marking the official start of the 'drag wars'.

Rejuvenated by the record, Moser went on to win the first classic of the year, Milan-San Remo, and a few months later, the Tour of Italy – both for the first time in his career. Incidentally, the final time trial of the Tour of Italy, where Moser, riding a low-profile, twin-disc replica of his hour-record bike, beat race leader Laurent Fignon, was the first of two cruel blows to the Frenchman, who estimated that he lost two seconds

every kilometre because of the Italian's superior machinery. Five years later Fignon again suffered at the hands of technology, losing the final time trial, and the overall lead of the Tour de France, to Greg LeMond, who was using triathlon extension bars.

Later that year the Olympic Games were held in Los Angeles and although Moser's bike was well on the way to being accepted by the cycling community, the world was to see how much cycling had changed since the previous Olympics. Cyclists from the USA led the way, riding aluminium 'funny bikes' with disc wheels made from Kevlar and composites, 24-in (61cm) front wheels and monocoque handlebars and stems. Riding futuristic track and road machines, and wearing rubberized skin suits and aerodynamic helmets, the American racers were a potent and unmistakable symbol of the new high-tech, rarefied world of international competition.

The shot of Laurent Fignon in a bright yellow aerodynamic helmet might not have looked very significant, but the story behind his blue Delta bike precedes Moser and the Los Angeles Olympics by some seven years, and marks the true start of the development of the modern time trial bike. Research started in 1977 at the Institut Aérotechnique de Saint-Cyr-

The bike is not the only aerodynamic aid – body-hugging one-piece skinsuits and teardrop crash helmets also contrive to further reduce drag.

Tips from the saddle

'The faster you go, the more difference they make,' says Ian Cammish, referring to the narrow clip-on aero bars on his Team Raleigh. His advice to riders using 'tri-bars' is this:

'The idea with tri-bars is to stay in the tuck position for as long as possible. You could lose out on a twisty road if you keep having to change your position, or reach for the gears more than usual.

'The rider's position should resemble the tuck of a downhill skier, with the elbows in and hands in front of the face. Whatever you do, the position should feel comfortable.'

Francesco Moser's hour-record bike stunned the public when the Italian used it to break the hour record in 1984.

The indoor hour

In 1988, four years after capturing the world hour record at altitude and two years after taking the sea-level record, Francesco Moser improved the world indoor record for the hour. The thirty-seven-year-old champion used a bicycle with a huge rear wheel of 101cm (39.8in) in diameter. It was heavy, too, but Moser got it rolling fast enough to set new figures of 50.644km (31.469 miles).

l'École, near Versailles, where an impressive wind tunnel, normally used for testing cars and larger vehicles such as the high-speed TGV train, was hired by the Renault-Gitane team. As Renault was a regular visitor to the wind tunnel, it was natural that the company's cycling team, in particular the young Bernard Hinault, his manager Cyrille Guimard and the technical director of Gitane cycles, should take advantage of the opportunity to explore a few ideas. Within two years Hinault was to test the first Gitane Delta time-trial bike in the 1979 Tour de France. Compared with later creations it was a modest machine, with concealed cables, aerofoil section tubes, drop handlebars and spoked time-trial wheels.

Close observers of Hinault, however, could see that it was not so much the bike, but a change in the Frenchman's position, that was the most significant aspect of the Delta. Drawing on their experience with skiers, the Renault team came up with a position for Hinault that was both athletically and aerodynamically perfect. By contrast with his position in 1978, Hinault rode the 1979 season on a bike that had him sitting 2.4cm (0.9in) further behind the bottom bracket, 2.8cm (1.1in) further

away from the handlebars and 0.9cm (0.35in) higher in the saddle. The stem was also set 0.8cm (0.3in) lower. In 1984 another centimetre (0.4in) was added to Hinault's stem, with the seat set a further 0.5cm (0.2in) back for the Breton's race-winning ride in the Grand Prix des Nations.

Throughout the 1980s Guimard and his team continued to develop the concept of the Delta bike, with later versions incorporating 'flying wing' handlebars and even a spoiler behind the seat. Undoubtedly they made some advances on the machinery front, but those innovations were eclipsed by Moser's disc wheel and, later in the decade, the triathlon extension bars. However, one thing they can take credit for is the riding position now favoured by most professional road racers, which matches physiology with wind-tunnel technology.

Triathletes, Greg LeMond and the 7-Eleven team are to thank for ushering in the most revolutionary time trialling aid of the modern era. Devotees of the swim, bike and run discipline were familiar with Boone Lennon's ski-racer-inspired clip-on bars long before the conservative cycling establishment gave them a try. Fittingly, the breakthrough was made by riders from the USA – traditionally outsiders in the insular sport of European cycling. When Greg LeMond used the U-shaped bars during the 1989 Tour de France they had already been seen earlier in the year when the 7-Eleven team tried them out on their low-profile time-trial bikes. If few were convinced then, they became converts in the space of 26 minutes and 57 seconds on the final day of the 1989 Tour, when LeMond covered the fastest 24.5km (15.2 miles) in his life to topple Laurent Fignon from the race leadership. The American won the race overall, in the closest finish ever (eight seconds), and said later that the bars had been worth between 10 and 20 seconds to him.

After that, no one could dispute that the aerodynamics of a time-trial bike had a crucial effect on performances at racing speeds of 30mph (48kph) plus, where drag accounts for 90 per cent of the rider's energy output. Tyres and the weight of the machine were now secondary in the search to reduce the frontal area. Time-trial bicycles were well developed by 1989, but tri-bars were the first major breakthrough in reducing the drag of the rider, which can account for up to 80 per cent of the total. Tests in the USA have shown that tri-bars reduce drag by 12 per cent more than upturned standard-width time-trial bars. It is not just the elbows that contribute to the lower drag - a more stretched-out position flattens the back without adverse effects on breathing or comfort.

A typical example of the modern time-trial bike is the titanium Raleigh Dyna-Tech, a machine built specially for English time trialist and record-breaker Ian Cammish. The Nottingham company put the bike together for a series of record attempts by the thirty-five-year-old professional during the 1991 season. Apart from recording more than fifty time trial wins in the 'home' of time trialling that year, Cammish also smashed the straight-out 25-mile (40km) and 50-mile (80km) records by riding at speeds well in excess of 35mph (56kph). As the straight-out records are ridden mostly on downhill and flat stretches of road with a strong following wind, gears ranging from 56 x 11 to 64 x 12 (top gear on the bike pictured) can be used.

Reynolds titanium 2325 tubes are used for the main triangle of the frame, with the tubes inserted and then glued into aluminium alloy lugs. According to Raleigh, this method of joining tubes ensures that their tensile strength is not affected by brazing and results in a very true, stiff frameset. That is just as well, because few would describe

the lugs as pretty, nor the frame particularly light when compared with a conventional lugged frame. Angles are 74 degrees for the head and an unusual 64 degrees for the curved seat tube. Wishbone stays help to smooth out the airflow over the seat stays and vertical dropouts make wheel changing a simple affair. Both the stays and the forks are made from Reynolds 753 tubing.

Equipment on the frame, apart from the 64-tooth chainring, is mostly by Campagnolo, again not the lightest around but beautifully finished and reliable. Rear changes are made by Campagnolo's click system, with a seven-speed block, while the front changes are made by a SunTour Superbe mechanism. Cinelli bars and stem and bolt-on tri-bars with foam-padded armrests complete the compact front end.

Composite wheels, a Campagnolo rear disc and a US-made Zipp tri-spoke on the front, keep the weight within reasonable limits. The tri-spoke has been found to be just as slippery, or more, than a disc wheel and has the added advantage of being far less susceptible to cross-winds when used on the front. Both types of wheels offer less drag than the most sophisticated aero-spoked standard wheels. Tyre choice is important too, with narrow tyres offering less resistance than conventional sizes. Vittoria 18-mm Crono Seta CS 150 tubulars keep the resistance low and the demon drag to a minimum.

Aero additions

Gear shifters mounted on the aero bars and even a single brake lever have appeared on team time-trial bikes. The brake lever allows the rider to make small adjustments in speed while staying in the tuck position. Water pouches under the saddle, with a tube running to the bars, also allow the rider to maintain his position while drinking without disturbing the airflow.

Who would have thought that a U-shaped bar on the front of a bike could have such an effect on performance?

Track bike

Track bikes range from the sleek, aerodynamic lines of the pursuiting machine to the more upright, robust sprinting bike. But for the ultimate track workhorse, you need look no further than the six-day track bike. If ever there was a timeless machine – this is it.

Marathon machine

Six-day track racing is one of the oldest branches of cycle sport, dating back to the Victorian era, when long-distance indoor marathon events were contested by men on high ordinaries.

This six-day machine is the workhorse of track bikes.

Looking at the track bikes that have aroused the most interest over the last ten years or so, one might be forgiven for thinking that the days of the minimalist, diamond-frame, conventional track bicycle were over. Carbon-fibre, monocoque droop-snoop machines with miniature front wheels and solid rear discs have made the track series the high-tech highlight of the world championships and Olympic Games in recent years. However, these specialist speed machines, used in the individual and team pursuit, have more in common with the modern road time-trial machine than the all-round track racer. The track bike, almost in its original form, lives on unobtrusively in the other championship disciplines and on the winter indoor six-day circuit.

It is the simplest, most versatile bike of all – capable of performing at top level in every track event except pursuiting and the motor pace. It is simple in both design and operation, with a single fixed sprocket on the rear wheel driven by a chain run off a single chainring at the front. There are no

seat brace

laid-back
seat tube

large-flange hubs

single fixed gear

brakes and no gears.

Of course, not all track bikes are built with the same angles or the same components, but they are all constructed on similar lines, with perhaps minor alterations to gearing, frame geometry or wheels to suit a particular discipline. A machine used for a season of racing on the winter six-day circuit will be expected to survive about twelve meetings, covering many thousands of miles on the punishing, steeply banked wooden tracks of Europe. Distances for each 'six' are of minor stage-race proportions and when several run concurrently, a not uncommon situation in the past, an effort on a Tour de France scale is required. Add to that the stresses put through

the bike from hand slings between racing partners, the G forces from the near vertical bankings and the fast and furious racing and you have a recipe for the ultimate do-it-all track bike. It is no coincidence, then, that a six-day bike is two machines in one: a long-distance stage racer and a track greyhound.

Tony Doyle is Britain's best-ever six-day racer. The two-times world professional pursuit champion has won more than twenty 'sixes' since he started racing the winter boards in 1981. In his early thirties, with nearly ten years of his six-day career still to run, he is one of the senior professionals on the circuit and knows everything there is to know about the twilight world of six-day racing. Naturally, he knows his bikes inside out. Two new bikes plus one spare machine accompany him to every winter engagement, along with seven or eight pairs of wheels and an assortment of tubular track tyres. Doyle's bikes are built for Halfords, a UK chain of bicycle and car accessory shops, who use their Carrera badge on

the frame. Most track frames, and certainly a six-day frame, will be built by a specialist builder to the exact measurements of the rider.

A shallow-angled seat tube combined with a steep-angled head tube is the most unusual feature of Doyle's Carrera bike. Compare a seat angle of 71.8 degrees and a head angle of 75.6 degrees with those of Doyle's world championship track bike (72.4 seat/75.2 head) and you can see that the six-day bike is at the same time more laid-back yet steering faster than the points-race machine. On the Carrera, Doyle will be sitting lower and further back, pedalling a relatively modest gear of 52 x 16 (87¾in/223cm). A shallow seat tube also promotes stability at the back end, allowing Doyle to give and take hand slings without having to shift his weight too far back on the saddle. Hand slings are used in the important 'madison' races that usually decide the outcome of a six-day race, taking place every two laps or so, when a resting partner is literally thrown into the chase by his

Tony Doyle throws Danny Clark into the chase in the Munich Six. His left hand grips the centre of the handlebars to stop the bike twitching during the hand sling.

Star attraction

Apart from the six-day regulars like Doyle and Danny Clark, stars from the road are a big attraction. Some, like France's Gilbert Duclos-Lassalle and Belgium's Étienne de Wilde ride the whole season but riders like Gianni Bugno of Italy, Olaf Ludwig of Germany and Axel Merckx of Belgium treat six-day racing as a one-off training event for which they are handsomely rewarded.

Bracing action

When the pace goes up the rider will often move along the saddle for a more vertical position over the pedals. The extra stress this puts on the nose of the saddle, especially on the banking, can break the rails or cause the saddle to point down. A brace prevents this happening.

racing partner. With perhaps twenty riders on the track (ten teams), half of them hurtling round the bottom of the track and the other half circling slowly above them, there is no room for error, especially during the hectic change-overs. This type of racing calls for one of the most responsive front ends in cycling, an ultra-steep steering head angle that allows the rider to make split-second steering changes.

While the frame geometry may be designed to perform a dual role, the frame itself is put together with the sole purpose of staying in one piece throughout a season of six-day racing. Reynolds 653 tubing is used for the main triangle and forks of Doyle's bike, and venerable 531 tubing is deployed in the rear triangle. That makes for a rigid and strong frame – compared to strength, low weight is not a priority, and most six-day racers would gladly trade a little extra weight for peace of mind on the boards. Steel is still preferred to other frame materials, although aluminium frames and the occasional carbon-fibre have made an appearance. Experience with carbon-fibre frames suggests that they perform

The seat brace holds the nose of the saddle securely when the rider is sitting forward over the pedals.

well at first but suffer from a loss of rigidity over time.

The solid feel to the frame is reflected in the components, which are finished in smooth alloy unmarked by drillings, slots or grooves. Even the transmission is heavy-duty, using a 3-mm chain compared to a normal 2.25-mm chain and running on a single fixed sprocket at the rear with a Shimano Dura-Ace chainset with 165-mm cranks at the front. Doyle is one of the few six-day riders still using toe clips and straps. He prefers the security when leaning away from the bike during a hand sling, for other riders using quick-release pedals have become disengaged in such situations.

A plain alloy seat pin (post), not the lightest by any means, supports Doyle's Cinelli saddle. Lodged underneath is a thick wedge of foam rubber, put there as a final buffer against the top of the seat pin should Doyle bounce the saddle when cornering or during a hand sling. A sprung-metal support bolted to the nose of the saddle braces the nose against the top tube to prevent the saddle from tilting or even breaking when Doyle is sitting forward during a hard chase or when motor pacing.

Like the frame, the wheels are designed primarily to withstand the

G-forces on the near-vertical banking can cause the rider to bounce in the saddle. A thick sponge prevents a painful landing.

punishing G forces meted out on a small six-day track. Built with twenty-eight spokes, which are tied together with wire where they cross and then soldered in place, they are extremely rigid, especially when used with large-flange track hubs. Doyle's best wheels are rather special as they use rare Italian-made Gipiemme hubs with a

higher flange on one side to cope with the one-way stresses of anticlockwise racing. The rims are anodized and aero-dynamic for extra strength, and the light cotton or silk track tubulars are carefully stuck on with shellac (pure alcohol and shellac crystals mixed together) to prevent them from rolling off. Years ago bandages, wrapped around the tyre and rim and glued into place, were used to prevent tubulars from rolling or sliding off the rim.

Cotton tyres are favoured for much of the racing, especially German-made Continentals, which can take up to 12 atmospheres of pressure and weigh 5⅓-6¼oz (165-175gm). The best wheels, with silk tyres such as Wolber Piste, are used for the important madison chases. Tyres are changed if they are badly scuffed or cut, and double-checked after every spill, however minor. Wheel preparation is the most time-consuming job of the six-day mechanic, who will spend much of his time during the six nights building, gluing and truing wheels.

At around 21lb (9.5kg) Doyle's six-day bike is certainly no featherweight, but for him and the other six-day pro-fessionals it is a trusted tool.

Dual small and large-flange hubs are unique to six-day race bikes. They are designed to handle the stresses of a steeply banked track.

Foot brake

There are no brakes on a track bike – riders slow down by easing off the pedals and applying a small amount of back-pedalling pressure on the rear fixed wheel. Ringside mechanics 'catch' the riders when they reach a safe speed.

A no-nonsense fork crown with round fork blades create a rigid front end.

Mountain bike

Tim Gould's Peugeot is a no-frills racer built to the English rider's exact dimensions. In the fast-changing world of mountain-bike racing it stands out as the purist's choice.

Leading the way

Road riders have a lot to thank mountain bikers for – the boom in popularity of the fat-tyred off-road machine in the 1980s revitalized what was a technologically sluggish market and resulted in a number of major improvements.

Gould uses telescopic front forks for bumpy courses with tricky descents. Pictured is his standard racing bike.

With his light build and supple riding style Tim Gould is a natural climber. He is in his element on courses that feature long, steady climbs and to prove it he took a bronze medal at the 1990 world mountain bike championships in Durango and has had numerous wins in Europe and the USA. Gould has a background in cyclo-cross and holds the record for the most wins (six) in the gruelling Three Peaks contest in the UK – one of the toughest long-distance cyclo-cross events in the world. Cyclo-cross riders are a pragmatic lot, and there is no room for frills in this dour sport. In keeping with the starkly functional role of the cyclo-cross bike, Gould's Peugeot mountain bike reflects the

cyclo-cross rider's instinct for a gimmick-free machine. It is a bike that puts reliability above the mechanically risky pursuit of high performance.

But in spite of the impression of indestructible simplicity given by a cyclo-cross bike, the truth is that a top rider will use three machines during a one-hour cyclo-cross race. That means twenty minutes for each bike, while the others are being hosed down ready for the next change-over. A mountain bike is often expected to endure a three-hour race over much rougher terrain, with no outside mechanical assistance. Mechanical problems and breakages are common and when a mountain bike emerges unscathed from a three-hour off-road ordeal, that says a lot for the

lugless frame

soft compound competition tyres

quick-release pedals

quality of the machine. Given also the fact that there is a constant search for lighter materials, it becomes clear that there is a fine line between function and failure.

Unlike road machines, where the last decade has seen the wind tunnel take over from the scales, mountain bikes have no call for a slippery profile. They do not go fast enough and besides, some aerodynamic components actually add weight to the bike. Low weight is, and always will be, the key to off-road competence. A light, nimble bike can be carried for longer and manoeuvred more easily in tight situations. As always, the starting-point is the frame.

Gould's frame was built at the lightweight unit of Peugeot Canada, based in St Georges Beauce in French-speaking Quebec. The tubes are Ritchey Logic, a Taiwanese-made derivative of Tange Prestige marketed by Ritchey in the USA. Tange Prestige is one of the lightest tubes on the market. Ritchey Logic is lighter still and the tubes are made from wafer-thin chrome-moly 0.5mm thick in the middle and 0.9mm thick at the butted ends. As frame tubes rarely fail in the middle Tom Ritchey designed a tube with a thicker-butted section at the ends, where most of the stresses are concentrated from both riding and welding. Weight is further reduced by keeping the length of the butted ends short, thus extending the thin area of the tube. Using these specially drawn Tange tubes Peugeot are able to build one of the lightest framesets in the world. Gould's frame was TIG (Tungsten Inert Gas) welded with a silver brazing material that was also used to attach the braze-on fittings. The forks are supplied by Ritchey. They feature a head tube that is thicker down the leading and trailing edge, and thinner down the sides, as well as triple-butted chrome-moly fork blades with a 27-mm diameter.

With such exotic frame materials one might expect the angles to be similarly radical. They are not. Peugeot has wisely desisted from straying too far from the now popular 74-degree seat, 71-degree head tube angles favoured

by many mountain-bike racers. A steep tube over the bottom bracket, similar to a road bike, improves response from the back end by ensuring a stiff rear triangle. Up front Peugeot have gone for a slightly steeper head angle, which guarantees sharp though not unstable steering. With a 1⅘-in (4.6cm) rake to the fork there is a much-needed shock-absorbing element, not afforded by straight forks, on this quick-steering bike. The extra rigidity from straight forks often results in an uncomfortable ride and frame failure is not unknown as a result of the extra stresses exerted on the front of the bike. Peugeot have

Suspension systems, front and rear, have been developed to give a smoother ride over rough terrain and more control on descents.

Transmission components have a hard life and certain parts, like chains, are replaced regularly.

Soft-sell cycling

The key to the success of the mountain bike is not just its off-road ability, but the ease with which it can also be ridden on the road. For newcomers to cycling the fat tyres, wide bars and user-friendly gear-changing system all contribute to a bike which appeals as an accessible, fun machine. It's the soft-sell approach to cycling, and it works.

also stayed faithful to a conventional dia-mond-shaped frame that can be picked up and easily shouldered when the going gets really tough.

The seat tube is short at 19in (48cm) but Gould's long upper body and road bike position dictates a long top tube of 22⅓in (56.6cm). Add to that a specially made 6⅓-in (16cm), 90-degree ITM stem and you can see how stretched out Gould likes to be. Handling is said not to be affected by the long stretch to the bars and every attempt has been made to replicate Gould's position on his road bike. Finding the correct length can be difficult when comparing the distance from flat bars to drop han-dlebars and Gould's manager, Simon Burney, takes a measurement from the tip of the saddle to the ends of the 'tops' on Gould's road bike to find the correct distance from the flat bars of a mountain bike to the saddle. The ITM bars are cut down at the ends to 21in (53.3cm) and, in keeping with the mini-malist theme, he does not use bar extension hooks. Seat height, 28in (72.4cm) on Gould's bike, is the same as on his road bike.

Gould has experimented with the various front-fork suspension systems on the market and in certain conditions where sure handling is important he will use a British-made Pace fork. Unlike other, heavier models that rely on conventional air and oil damping, forks like the Pace and the US-made Manitou use an elastomer damper that can be used in various soft and hard settings. Carbon fibre and light alloys keep the weight low, although they are nowhere near as light as a traditional lightweight fork.

Italian-made Campagnolo compo-nents are used on the Peugeot. They are not as light as other top-end custom and production groupsets but the extra strength has enabled Gould to finish events where others have suffered mechanical breakdowns. This some-times over-engineered approach adds a few pounds to the weight of the machine and compared with bikes with the lightest titanium and aluminium equipment the Peugeot is more of a performance middleweight. As Gould has been one of the few top mountain-bike racers to receive backing from Campagnolo, they have taken a special interest in his comments and have developed their off-road groupsets accordingly. One area where they have had to improve has been in the transmission and gear-shifting system, which until recently lagged behind the slick-changing gears from Shimano of Japan. With a new eight-speed block fitted to Gould's bike, Campagnolo are hoping to take a significant step in the right direction. A new thumb shifter, with Campagnolo's own block (12-28/30) with angled teeth, and a German Rohloff chain together produce a faster, more precise gear change than before. During the racing season Gould would have a new chain every three weeks to keep the transmission working smoothly and to prevent premature wear to the stainless-steel rings (26-38-48) and steel block.

Campagnolo's top of the range Thorr rims are used for the wheels, which are built with DT stainless double-butted spokes on thirty-two-hole Campagnolo sealed hubs. At 22.8mm the Thorr rim is not the narrowest, nor the lightest, but tyre changing in a race situation is much easier on a wider rim. Tyres are Ritchey Megabite Z-Max WCS 26 x 2.1 Kevlar, a soft compound super-grippy tyre that weighs 18¾oz (530gm) and can be pumped up harder than normal. Gould would not expect a pair of these to last more than a couple of hard races, so soft is the tread. Campagnolo also provide the cantilever brakes, derailleurs, cranks (175mm), pedals and toe clips, seat pin, and lubrication of the bearings and chain. The saddle is a standard racing Selle San Marco Rolls, Elite make the bottle cage and Gould also races with an under-saddle pack by Local Motion. Carried in the pack during all events is a spare tube, a CO_2 adaptor with two canisters, a chain riveter and two tyre levers.

After taking several years to find the right combination of materials, Gould is happy with the current Peugeot. Every year he has a new one built before the important second half of the season following the often wet and muddy races of the spring, which play havoc with soft alloy components and leave the bike completely worn out.

Campagnolo's alloy equipment is more durable than most, but in off-road racing the attrition rate is high and the same goes for frames. A used bike may be passed on to an amateur racer or used as a training bike. It is a tough life for a mountain bike on the professional off-road circuit and annual replacement is a luxury only the truly dedicated competitor can afford.

New components and the never-ending quest for lightness make mountain bikes the fastest-changing machines in the cycling world. Each year new materials and design innovations shave weight from the lightest bikes and it is now possible to buy a fully equipped racing mountain bike weighing less than 20lb. Suspension systems, once bulky and relatively heavy, move closer to the weight of a standard fork every year. Road riders have taken notice and Greg LeMond has already experimented with telescopic front forks in the Paris-Roubaix classic. Bikes of the modern era are changing faster than ever before – and mountain biking is largely to thank.

The mountain bike is very much a latecomer, but the meteoric growth of interest in it augurs well for its long-term survival. Not that the machines themselves will stay the same for long, as the changes of the last few years have shown. The most notable of these is the move towards ever greater lightness, by contrast with the road bike, where aerodynamics currently dominate.

Gear controls can be reached without moving the hands from the handlebars, which are also narrower than standard.

Cyclo-cross bike

At first glance the ALAN cyclo-cross bike looks like a standard road bike. However, a closer look reveals that the classic 'cross bike is a very unusual machine.

Cycling on foot

A cyclo-cross bike is lighter than a mountain bike, the wheels are bigger and it has fewer gears. Cyclo-cross racers spend more time running with their bikes than mountain bikers and a cyclo-cross course will often have hurdles added to make riders get off and jump over them.

Spot the difference: scores of minor details make the 'cross bike an individual machine.

Six-times British national cyclo-cross champion Steve Douce is a regular face on the world off-road scene, with five placings in the top twenty of the world cyclo-cross championships between 1985 and 1991. For years Douce has campaigned throughout Europe's cyclo-cross heartlands of Switzerland, Belgium and Holland. He knows what makes a good cyclo-cross bike and it is no coincidence that the bike pictured, an ALAN aluminium with Campagnolo components, is virtually identical to that used by numerous top 'cross' riders and world championship medal winners. Indeed the ALAN aluminium frame has hardly changed in twenty years. Many of the components on Douce's bike

have been in production even longer and there can be no better proof of reliability than that.

It is reliability that so often plays a major part in deciding the outcome of a cyclo-cross or off-road event, where conditions regularly conspire to cause machine failure. No matter how well prepared the rider, if the bike fails or is damaged in a crash, the chances of returning to the front in a road-race-style chase are slim. Unlike mountain-bike racing, where the rider must effect his or her own repairs on the same bike, cyclo-cross riders can shoulder their machines, run round the circuit to the pits and receive a spare bike. During muddy or wet races helpers will wash spare bikes and hand them up

aluminium frame

knobbly tubular tyres

radial spoked front wheel

every twenty minutes or so, but a damaged machine in a one-hour race often spells the end of a winning ride.

In contrast to mountain bikes the components that suffer the most abuse on a cyclo-cross machine are the wheels. Mountain bikes were designed for going downhill fast and as such they are put together with extremely robust 26-in (66cm) wheels with fat tyres that afford greater control, traction and impact absorption. As mountain-bike courses tend to favour riding over rough terrain the bikes are built to withstand sustained brutal treatment. Cyclo-cross bikes approach the off-road battlefield from another angle, putting finesse before force.

Instead of ploughing through mud in a tiny gear, or inching up a steep incline, a cyclo-cross rider will dismount, shoulder his machine and run with it. Over short distances running is faster and a light bike is therefore essential. The wheels

must be as strong as possible, rigid, and light. The rims can take a hammering during a cyclo-cross race. Douce's ALAN is equipped with twenty-eight-hole Campagnolo Sigma Pave Hardox, a rim developed for professional use over rough and cobbled surfaces. Normally a twenty-eight-spoke rim is reserved for super-light time trialling but laced with stainless-steel plain-gauge spokes on the front, the radial pattern, with the spokes going straight out from the Campagnolo C Record hub to the rim, keeps the weight down

and greatly improves stiffness in the front wheel. A radial wheel is also less likely to snag on the undergrowth and is easily cleaned. At the rear the butted spokes cross each other once on their way to the rim, giving the wheel extra strength to cope with the twisting forces coming through the transmission. Tying and soldering the spokes where they cross gives extra rigidity to the rear wheel and holds spokes in place if they break at the hub.

Tyres follow established practice: on the front is a fine-toothed pattern

A cyclo-cross bike must sometimes be carried as well as ridden, as 1982 world champion Roland Liboton demonstrates.

Lightweight cantilever brakes are powerful, easy to clean, and cheap to replace when damaged.

Off-road cross-overs

Mountain bikes have influenced cyclo-cross machines recently, and fatter tyres, giving better control on slippery descents, and quick-release pedals are two important cross-overs. Shimano, Campagnolo and SunTour all offer combined brake and gear-changing systems and these are already popular.

Barum tubular with the tread running backwards, giving good control in soft conditions, and on the back a Clement Grifo Neve with the arrow-patterned block tread running forwards. Compared with clincher rims and tyres, tubulars and sprint rims still offer greater strength, lower weight and less chance of an impact puncture when running at lower pressures. There must be no skimping on the glue when sticking knobbly tubulars on, as they have been known to roll off, often with embarrassing consequences.

For proof that cyclo-cross is a tinker's paradise you need look no further than the wheels. Despite experiments with many different types of wheel and tyre combinations over the years, mechanics and riders are still searching for the ultimate wheel. Braking in wet conditions has always been a problem and one solution has been to cut grooves into the side of a rim to help water escape. Tyres are constantly changing and fat-section tubulars are currently in vogue. Before Wolber's new wide-section tubular, riders were having their standard cyclo-cross tyres modified in France by a man who cut them open, inserted a fatter

inner tube and then stitched them back together with a wider base section.

Like the wheels, the pedals are also in the front line in terms of vulnerability. However, the approach here is quite the opposite to wheels, where the best builder and the finest materials are some guarantee of a trouble-free ride. If there is one area where you can save money it is on pedals and as can be seen on Douce's bike they do not come much simpler than the universally used French-made alloy-and-steel Lyotards. There is no point in having expensive pedals on a bike that is routinely dragged over obstacles, and through mud and running water. A strong, basic pedal with double-sided rat-trap back plates that can be pedalled on both sides and replaced cheaply when damaged does the job perfectly well. Few parts escape modification on a 'cross' bike though, and tell-tale welding blobs where the ends of the alloy backing plates meet the end plates show that some after-market strengthening has occurred.

Even the toe clips and straps do not escape the mechanic's eagle eye. Double metal toe clips are used, one laid over the other to prevent them from bending. Thick Binda leather toe straps are bolted to the sides of the pedals to allow mud to pass straight through the pedal and the sides of the straps are bound with insulating tape to hold them in an open position. Some riders pass a spoke through the back plate and round the front of the toe clip to make it easier to slide the foot into the pedal.

A clipless version of the quick-release-style pedals now favoured by many road riders has been developed by Shimano in recent years and is being used by a number of professional riders. Featuring a recessed moulding in a specially made shoe, the pedal is engaged in a similar way to the road model, using a spring-loaded catch. The pedal is also double-sided, allowing a quick entry on either side.

Campagnolo, renowned for their over-engineered but high-quality components, are used for the transmission and it is no coincidence that the rear derailleur and chainset are both vintage Super Record, available from the Vicenza factory since 1973. The chain-set uses 42/48 rings to give a close range of gears and a slick gear change from the Corsa Record front changer. At the back the chain is moved up and down a Maillard 13-24-tooth block with a Super Record derailleur with titanium bolts. Gear cables are routed through the bars to SunTour handlebar-end shifters that work on friction. These are standard equipment on cyclo-cross bikes – they are solidly made and trust-worthy in every situation. Shimano's STI combined brake and gear-changing system has found favour with some cyclo-cross riders although others have their doubts about the speed of a one- or three-click changing system and given also the levers' additional weight and expense it could be a few years before an ideal solution is reached.

Black anodized Italmanubri bars with a 4¾-in (12cm) stem give the usual range of road-race positions and the ends of the 'hooks' can be used to steady the front wheel when the bike is lifted on to the shoulder. SunTour brake levers with concealed cables pull on Weinmann cantilever brakes. These German lightweight brakes are simple in construction and easy to clean. While the front is adjusted to come on with the lever pulled back halfway, the rear brake only starts to work when the lever is pulled right back to the bars. The back brake is useful for control but not for stopping – it is kept away from the rim to prevent rubbing against a damaged wheel.

The frame is the now venerable ALAN, an aluminium, lugged frame that has delivered world championship victories to countless riders over the last fifteen years. Apart from its supreme ruggedness and practicality, the Italian-made ALAN is above all light, at 5lb 6oz (2.45kg), and that counts for a lot with a cyclo-cross

rider who might have to lift the bike on to his shoulder several times every lap. Aluminium tubes are assembled using aluminium lugs with threaded inserts. The tubes are screwed in, then glued into place, creating a stronger join than other pressed and pinned frames. Brazed-on fittings and front and rear dropouts are all easily replaced in the event of a crash and the repair can be made by a mechanic rather than a frame builder. No respray is needed and the durable finish also makes the ALAN easy to clean and presentable even after a full season of 'cross'. A flat-tened top tube on Douce's Super frame helps when the bike is being carried. This was not ALAN's intention – they use the same shape tube on the road frame – but it is a happy coincidence in the cyclo-cross frame's favour. The forks and the rear triangle are different from those of the road frame, with wider clearances to allow fatter tyres to be used and to make allowances for damaged wheels and sticky mud. Angles are shallow at 72 degrees parallel and with a generous fork rake there are no handling surprises, which is just how it should be in a sport where the aim is to keep frights to a minimum.

Valuable training

A number of professional roadmen use cyclo-cross as a valuable way of training during the winter. Some, like Adri Van der Poel from Holland, are world-class performers. Van der Poel has never won the world title but the 'eternal second' of cyclo-cross has five silver medals to his name. Other riders, like Tour de France star Claudio Chiapucci of Italy, are happy to compete in the winter knowing that the extra fitness will stand them in good stead for the following season.

Toe straps are bolted to the pedals and double toe clips are less likely to bend when stepped on accidentally.

Touring bike

Touring bikes are the long-distance cruisers of the cycling world. These Gran Turismo machines, built to carry luggage and rider in comfort, were once heavy, cumbersome and slow. Times have changed.

Luggage option

With a front rack and handlebar bag the luggage capacity of a tourer can be doubled. On the other hand, stripped of racks and bags, today's modern touring bike is ideal for training rides and randonnées.

Longer than a racer and heavier too, when rear rack and full-length mudguards are fitted.

Of the bicycles featured here, the touring bike stands out as the only one that is not a slave to the demands of high performance. A touring bike is not a race winner. It does not have to cut through the air with a low drag coefficient, or bunny-hop over rocks on a vertiginous descent. It does not invite the rider to flick through a bunch of racers, nor does it put speed above comfort.

Many bikes are designed to galvanize the rider into action, but not the touring bike. For a small trade-off in performance it is possible to make a bike that floats over bumps, holds a rock-steady line around corners and offers a comfortable ride. Racing purists should think twice before condemning the touring bike as a flawed concept.

On the contrary, the originators of the safety bicycle back in the 1890s were trying to design a machine that was both safe and comfortable. Speed and unpredictable handling had already been explored to the full by numerous brave high-ordinary and penny-farthing riders, and the creators of the chain-driven safety bikes that succeeded these tried to address themselves to the practicalities of everyday cycling.

What they quickly realized, once the basic diamond frame, small wheels and chain-driven rear wheel had evolved, was that here was a beautifully simple but above all efficient machine. It has been found, for instance, that a cyclist uses only one fifth of the energy of a walker to go three times as fast. For the same energy output as a gallon (4.5l) of

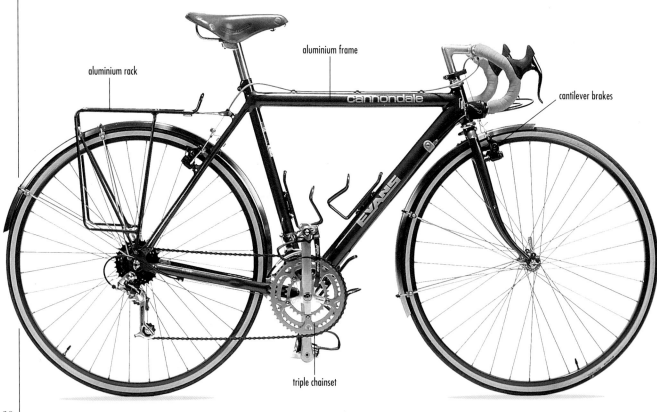

aluminium rack

aluminium frame

cannondale

EVANS

cantilever brakes

triple chainset

petrol in a car, a cyclist covers 1500 miles (2415km). Of all the machines and animals in the world, the cyclist is the most efficient. Bikes are by far the best converters of human energy into forward motion.

Racing has undoubtedly had a beneficial effect on utility cycling, with innovations in lightweight materials and components now evident throughout a wide range of cycle types. But it has also given the misleading impression to the general public that the cyclist must endure pain and suffering on every ride. For sure, some effort is required, but with gears, light components and high-pressure tyres overexertion can usually be avoided.

If you ignore the mudguards, racks and panniers that are the essential accessories on a touring bike, you will see that underneath it all a tourer looks remarkably similar to a racing bike. It may look a little longer and more spacious, but the fundamental elements are all where you would expect to find them. The extra length is no illusion, and there lies the main difference between a racing machine and its more leisurely cousin. The wheelbase of a tourer is longer than that of a racer, and although the wheelbase measurement itself has little bearing on the handling or feel of a bike, the steering-head and seat-tube angles and the chainstay length all contribute to the look and handling characteristics. Longer chainstays, 18in (45.7cm) on the US-made Cannondale ST1000, have the advantage of leaving plenty of room for mudguards, enough clearance between the back of the foot and panniers, and a little more room for lateral chain movement over a wide range of gears.

Apart from featuring a top-quality specification, the ST1000 is a fine example of tried and trusted touring principles married to a state-of-the-art aluminium lugless frame with an innovative gear-changing system. Frame angles on a 21-in (53.3cm) example are 73.5 degrees for the seat tube and 72 degrees for the head tube. The seat-tube angle, which is within half a degree of that of Cannondale's

Criterium racing frame, is in keeping with current thinking, which rates the position of the rider in relation to the pedals as more important than the supposed shock-absorbing properties of the seat tube. Tyre choice, fork rake and chainstay length have more bearing on ride comfort and with the long chainstays already mentioned, a 2.1-in (5.4cm) fork rake and 700c x 35 tyres, the Cannondale is suitably equipped for rough roads. Thanks to the 72-degree head angle – shallower than on most bikes – the steering should be neutral, and stable enough to keep the bike running straight when fully laden.

So far, everything is as it should be on a conventional touring bike with classic touring angles, designed to provide a comfortable, stable ride. But where the Cannondale parts company with convention is in the use of an unusually light and stiff aluminium frame, developed in 1983 in Pennsylvania, USA. There is nothing new about using aluminium to construct a bicycle frame – European frame makers such as ALAN and Vitus have been bonding together aluminium tubes for years – but Cannondale's welded frames with oversize tubes offer a number of performance advantages. Nearly ten years on, the Cannondale frame is still one of the lightest, stiffest frames around.

Its low weight makes aluminium an obvious choice as a frame-building material, despite the fact that it is not as strong as steel. While steel frames can be produced using tubes of conventional size with very thin walls, aluminium either has to be much thicker, for the same size tube, or at a thinner gauge as a fatter tube. Cannondale went for the latter option, which still offered a weight advantage and gave the additional bonus of increased stiffness, especially between the headset and bottom bracket. Using an oversize down tube to counteract the pendulum forces acting on the bottom bracket through pedalling, Cannondale created an instantly recognizable product.

After the tubes have been welded together by hand, the frame is then

Handle with care

Riding a heavily laden touring bike requires a different style from other bikes. Rapid changes of direction and out-of-the-saddle riding are to be avoided if possible, as the extra weight can have a disconcerting effect on handling. Extra weight should always be carried low on the bike – a high centre of gravity can induce a nasty attack of the wobbles.

Stability when loaded up is crucial, especially if the planned route includes some long, fast descents.

Tyres matter

Tyre choice is important on a touring bike and as a general rule it is better to err on the side of fat rather than thin. A fatter-section tyre provides a more comfortable ride and is less likely to suffer from impact punctures when the rim nips the inner tube. If some 'rough stuff' is also intended, a fatter tyre gives better grip and control. It's worth buying a top quality tyre with a reinforced bead - they last longer and can take more air without blowing off the rim.

A triple chainset gives a range of gears to suit every terrain, even when the bike is carrying luggage.

heat treated. This allows the aluminium brazing material to run into every joint, effectively fusing with the tubes to create a one-piece structure. The joints are smoother than on most hand-finished frames, with extra strength imparted by the heat treatment. On the road, especially when the bike is carrying luggage, this extra rigidity helps the Cannondale track a steady line where others might start to get out of shape. Reduced flex due to the stiff rear triangle also means that pedalling forces are transmitted more directly to the back wheel. Stripped of racks and bags, the ST1000 would make a deluxe training bike and the perfect mount for fast touring or randonnées. Rigidity does not always result in a harsh ride, and the damping effects of Kevlar banded Michelin Hi-Lite Tour 700c x 35 tyres and Cinelli cork handlebar tape, combined with the relaxed angles of the frame, make for smoothness.

A mixture of top-quality components are used on the ST1000, ranging from the British-made Brooks traditional tanned-leather saddle to the innovative

Grip Shift gear-changing system. The function of the Grip Shift system is much the same as the handlebar-end-shift levers used on cyclo-cross bikes, and that is to allow the rider to change gear without taking his or her hands off the bars. On a heavily laden tourer that counts for a lot. A more sophisticated system, combining the gear and brake levers, has been successfully developed by Shimano and is now in common use on professional racing bikes.

Cables run through to both ends of the drop handlebars on the Cannondale, on the right for the rear derailleur and on the left for the front changer. Both cable ends are attached to a circular cam that pulls or releases the cable along its length via a click system corresponding to single-sprocket changes on both derailleurs. Compared to other handlebar-mounted systems, including those used on mountain bikes, Grip Shift is relatively simple and trouble-free. All you need to remember is which way to twist the barrel to carry out changes up and down the gears. SunTour gears, with a seven-speed block and a SunTour triple chainset give a range of at least fifteen gears with a bottom gear of 28 x 30 and a top gear of 50 x 13. Braking is taken care of by powerful Dia Compe cantilever brakes and brake levers with concealed cables. Wheels shod with tough Wolber rims with thirty-six-hole Sansin sealed hubs, SunTour pedals with toe clips and straps and triple bottle cages complete this impressive and most practical of bicycles. The machine pictured makes it clear that the touring bike is better than ever and still evolving.

CHAPTER TWO

AN INJECTION OF PACE

the great races

Tour de France

When *l'Auto* magazine launched the idea of a race twice as long as its nearest competitor, with considerably more prize money and prestige going to the winner, cyclists in 1903 marvelled at such a daring challenge. The Tour de France was born and, despite a turbulent infancy, today it is one of the biggest sports events in the world. **Sam Abt**

The Auberge Réveille-Matin, the Alarm Clock Inn, is still there, just where the road from Paris enters Montgeron, a southern suburb of the capital. Here, at three o'clock in the afternoon of 1 July 1903, the first Tour de France began.

A plaque testifies to that beginning but fails to explain why Montgeron was chosen. The bartender in the Auberge Réveille-Matin is no help. 'I couldn't say,' he answers. 'I wasn't around then.' Nobody is left who was around then. At the offices of *l'Équipe*, the staff historian can say only that the prefect of police in Paris refused to permit the first Tour to start or end in Paris proper. Thus Montgeron at one end and Ville d'Avray, another suburb, at the other. But why specifically Montgeron?

All accounts agree on this: the Tour de France began as a gimmick to boost circulation for the newspaper *l'Auto*. Some accounts add that the Dreyfus Case, that turn-of-the-century scandal involving charges of treason and anti-Semitism, was really at the root of the Tour. Using the two newspapers he edited, *le Petit Journal* and *le Vélo*, Pierre Giffard was one of the few journalists to side with Émile Zola and defend Captain Alfred Dreyfus against the attacks of the Establishment. His impassioned articles in *le Vélo* especially ran-

Left: Miguel Indurain sets the pace during a mountain stage of the 1993 Tour. **Right:** Everything stops when the Tour comes to town.

Early Tour riders, like winner Romain Maes, had to carry their own spare tyre and plenty of liquids to combat thirst on the dusty roads.

Tour specialist

Some riders make a career out of riding the Tour. Dutchman Joop Zoetemelk tops the list of Tours ridden and finished with sixteen appearances and sixteen finishes between 1970 and 1986. Zoetemelk won the Tour once, in 1980, aged thirty-three, and was second six times.

kled Adolphe Clément, a major manufacturer of bicycles, and the Count de Dion, a financial supporter of *le Vélo*, who together helped set up a rival paper in October 1900. They chose for their editor Henri Desgrange, a former racer who set the first unpaced record for the hour in 1893 and later became a publicity agent for Clément's bicycles.

The new paper, *l'Auto-Vélo*, faced a difficult time in a field crowded with a dozen sports papers and magazines. *Le Vélo*, printed on green paper, had a daily circulation of 80,000 copies, a formidable position built on Giffard's flair in originating the Paris-Brest-Paris race in 1891, followed by Bordeaux-Paris in 1892. Under Desgrange, *l'Auto-Vélo* jumped right into the fight. Only six pages and printed on yellow paper, it attracted a fair share of advertising but could not get its daily circulation

above 20,000. No trick seemed to work, even when Desgrange staged his own Bordeaux-Paris race in 1902, running it a day after Giffard's and using the same route, if not the same riders, on the 373-mile (600km) course.

Giffard and *le Vélo* appeared to be unassailable, especially after they won a lawsuit for plagiarism that obliged *l'Auto-Vélo* to drop 'Vélo' from its name on 15 January 1903. That was bound to hurt in the circulation battle since bicycle racing was a major and mass sport while car racing was mainly a curiosity for the elite, who could afford cars and an interest in them.

Four days later Desgrange struck back. By today's standards, his one-column headline at the top of the front page was minimal display. 'Le Tour de France,' it said. Underneath, in small type in a reversed pyramid, it read: 'The greatest bicycling test in the world – a month-long race – Paris-Lyon-Marseille-Toulouse-Bordeaux-Nantes-Paris – 20,000 francs in prizes – Leaving 1 June. Arriving in Paris 5 July at the Parc des Princes.'

The article below, signed by Desgrange, noted that if the name of his newspaper had been changed, the announcement of the race proved that its coverage, 'which consists of not neglecting any sport', had not. Most of the article was given over to listing the prizes for each stage. The impressive total of 20,000 francs would be roughly equal in buying power now to 3.2 million francs (£332,000). The entire distance would be 1367 miles (2200km), covering three quarters of France, and riders could sign up either for the full race or for one or more stages. Further details would be made public before very long to the readers of *l'Auto*, Desgrange promised.

The announcement caused 'an enormous emotion in the sports world', *l'Auto* reported the next day in a front-page article signed by the paper's chief cycling correspondent, Géo Lefèvre. 'Naturally, champions of the road now in Paris paraded into our offices, enthusiastic about the idea and thrilled by such a manna of prizes,' Lefèvre continued, fuelling interest in the race.

To read *l'Auto* ninety years later, even discounting the self-promotion, it is easy to see that the idea of the race truly was a sensation. Sportsmen in cities to be visited sent letters celebrating the news. On the other hand, Desgrange reported on 25 January, many cities complained that the Tour would miss them. 'Perpignan, in a tearful letter, insists that it isn't far from the projected route,' he wrote. Albi, Cahors and Auch, 'with a touching unanimity', protested that they had not been included. Cognac, Niort and Limoges were to do likewise.

Desgrange had found the right formula: a race nearly twice as long as the record holder, Paris-Brest-Paris, and far richer and more prestigious than any other. As Lefèvre put it, 'the triumph of the winner will be that he did not win simply Paris-Lyon or Marseille-Toulouse or Bordeaux-Nantes, but the race of the Tour de France'.

The Tour had a difficult birth. Even Desgrange was forced to admit this early in May, when he wrote that he had thought of calling the whole thing off because barely more than a dozen riders had signed up. Without fifty riders, there would be no Tour de France, he warned. Realizing that a major obstacle was that few men wanted to be away from home for thirty-five days, Desgrange decided to reduce the race's duration to three weeks, as it is still.

The definitive plan listed six stages covering 1509 miles (2428km) with up to four rest days between stages. Racers could compete in the overall Tour or any number of stages, riding far into the night to finish. This new plan attracted to Montgeron sixty riders, of whom twenty-one finished on 19 July, led by Maurice Garin in 94 hours 33 minutes, an average speed of 15.9mph (25.6kph). Second, 2 hours 49 minutes behind, was René Pottier.

The thirty-two-year-old Garin, winner previously of Paris-Roubaix, Bordeaux-Paris and Paris-Brest-Paris, was exactly the prominent and colourful rider Desgrange needed to build interest in the Tour: a native-born Italian who had come to France as a boy and was traded by his father to a chimney sweep for a wheel of cheese. 'The Little Chimney Sweep', Desgrange dubbed him, the first in a line of Giants of the Road, as riders are still sometimes called in *l'Équipe*, the name *l'Auto* uses now.

Unmade roads in the high mountains were still a feature of the Tour in the late 1940s.

Italian star Gino Bartali **(left)**, Tour de France winner in 1938 and 1948, commandeers a bike from a team mate.

Longest and shortest

The longest Tour de France was held in 1926 when the winner, Belgium's Lucien Buysse, covered 5745km (3570 miles) in 283 hours, 44 minutes and 25 seconds. At 2388km (1484 miles), the 1904 Tour was the shortest and won by Henri Cornet in 96 hours, 5 minutes and 56 seconds.

With the first Tour a success, the paper's circulation began to rise. (*L'Équipe*'s usual 300,000 circulation increases by at least a third during today's Tours.) For the 1904 race, Desgrange made little change other than dropping the rule that a rider could compete in individual stages and adding one that eliminated riders arriving far behind the main field.

Eighty-eight riders left in the second Tour, which was conducted over the same course for 21,000 francs in prizes. The race was a disaster. The year before, cheating had been limited to some outdistanced riders hauling themselves and their bicycles on to trains to finish a stage. In 1904 cheating was rampant, with crowds of toughs blocking the roads at night, beating some riders and allowing their favourites through. Nails were strewn on the road, puncturing even the tyres on Desgrange's car as he attempted to return the race to control. Charges were heard that some riders had gained an advantage by travelling by car at night on difficult stretches of the road.

Maurice Garin was again the winner, followed by René Pottier, César Garin, Maurice's brother, and Hippolyte Aucouturier, the winner of four of the six stages. Four months later, after an investigation by the French cycling authorities, they were all disqualified and the first prize was awarded to Henri Cornet, at twenty still the youngest winner of the Tour. Pottier was suspended for life and Maurice Garin for two years. What their offences were has never been made public.

Publicly distraught, Desgrange was absolute in his declaration that this was the end of the Tour. 'The Tour de France is finished,' he wrote, 'and the second edition, I'm afraid, will be the last. It has been killed by success, by the blind passions it has unleashed, the injuries and filthy suspicions caused by the ignorant and the wicked.'

The Tour ended? In his heart of hearts Desgrange refused to believe it for a minute.

And he was right. Occasionally a stage would be interrupted and even halted by political demonstrations and rider strikes, including one in the 1991 Tour over mandatory helmets and a disqualified rider. But the Tour itself has only ever been stopped by war – there was no race from 1915 to 1918 and again from 1940 to 1946.

Desgrange, in fact, announced quickly enough that he would continue 'the great moral crusade of bicycle racing'. As part of that effort he made many changes in the 1905 Tour. The route was enlarged, adding excursions into Brittany, Normandy and Alsace, and the length grew to 1849 miles (2975km), divided into eleven stages. The stages themselves were shortened and night stages were eliminated. Overall time no longer decided the winner; in a system that was used until 1913 the winner would be chosen on the basis of points determined by the riders' times.

Finally Desgrange thought his race was ready to meet the mountains. The first climb was the Ballon d'Alsace and then came two in the Alps, the Laffrey Hill and the Bayard Pass. The public wondered if racers could ride up the mountains or whether they would have to dismount and walk their bicycles up. René Pottier answered the question by mounting the Ballon d'Alsace at a speed of 12.4mph (20kph) and adding to the legend of the Giants of the Road. That he had to quit the next day because of ten-donitis did not diminish the legend much.

Bit by bit, Desgrange was fashioning the Tour in its modern image. In 1907 the race was opened to other bicycle manufacturers besides Peugeot, which had enjoyed a near-monopoly after Garin's victory on a La Française model. At first manufacturers were allowed to sponsor individual riders and drive their team cars closely behind; by 1912 the manufacturers were allowed to sponsor teams.

Competition grew intense as each trade team laboured to produce the winner of the Tour for advertising reasons. Mistrusting the influence that the trade teams were having on the race, Desgrange could well understand the year when Octave Lapize of the La Française team suddenly quit in the Pyrenees to protest about what he said was a cabal of Belgian riders in different teams conspiring to help Odile Defraye and his sponsor, the potent Alcyon bicycle maker.

Eighteen years were to pass before Desgrange found a way to deal with sponsors. Although nothing could be proved, trade teams appeared to be strangling the race throughout the 1920s with their 'arrangements' of winners after long breakaways from unresponsive packs. Desgrange tried different approaches, including introducing time bonuses at the finish (1923) and sending teams off at different times in stages on the flat (1927), turning the Tour for days into a sort of continuous team time trial.

Late in 1929 he decided to revolutionize the race, ending competition by sponsored teams and introducing national and regional teams. For the 1930 race the 100 riders were divided

The all-time Tour greats

Not surprisingly Eddy Merckx heads the table for the number of stage wins in the Tour. His thirty-four victories total is seven more than another five-times winner of the race, Bernard Hinault of France. To find the third five-times winner of the race in the list of stage victories one must look further down the rankings before his compatriot Jacques Anquetil appears with sixteen stage wins. Some would say that Anquetil was the most calculating of the three all-time great Tour de France winners – his list of stage wins would appear to bear this out.

After a miraculous comeback win in 1989, the American Greg LeMond won his third Tour de France in 1990 with an impressive display of power.

Between 1969 and 1974 Belgium's Eddy Merckx won five Tours de France. In those days 'the cannibal', as he was nicknamed, was unbeatable in the world's toughest race – blitzing the field in time trials, mountain stages and bunch finishes.

into five teams of eight men, from France, Italy, Spain, Belgium and Germany, plus sixty riders representing the North, South-East, Ile de France, Champagne, Midi, Côte d'Azur, Normandy, Provence, and Alsace-Lorraine. By way of compensation for the loss of sponsors' fees, Desgrange added a publicity caravan of trucks and cars advertising everything from candy bars to cheese.

The system of national and regional teams helped reinvigorate the Tour during the 1930s and was continued after the Second World War until 1962, when trade teams were revived. In 1967 and 1968 the race again turned to national teams, but in 1969 the experiment was abandoned and trade teams have competed ever since. Now they are rarely sponsored by bicycle manufacturers, carrying instead the banners of electronics companies, carpet sellers, DIY franchises, clothing factories and storm-window suppliers. The arguments for trade teams include the dilemma of divided loyalties. A Belgian rider, say, who happens to ride most of the year for a Dutch team would find himself competing against his usual team mates in the most important race of them all. How should he respond to a breakaway by his habitual team leader, now on another side? This problem sometimes causes confusion in the one-day world championship road race, the only professional competition involving national teams.

In 1936 an ailing Desgrange, who was to die four years later, yielded his direction of the Tour to Jacques Goddet, the son of Victor Goddet, *l'Auto*'s original financial director. Goddet continued in that role for fifty-one years, sharing the responsibilities after the Second World War with Félix Lévitan, and allowing the race to benefit from continuity at the top for an astounding eighty-four years. The directors today are Jean-Marie Leblanc, who governs the race itself, and Jean-Pierre Carenso, who handles the complex commercial side.

Only in a few ways would today's Tour de France be unrecognizable to Desgrange. The man who created the leader's yellow jersey in 1919 and the 'King of the Mountains' classification in 1933 would not be surprised to see also the green points jersey (1953). From the first individual time trial (1934) it is not too far to the first prologue (1967) nor is it from the start in Montgeron to the first start outside France (Amsterdam, 1954). He would surely understand the change in the finish from a velodrome in Paris, either the Parc des Princes of

his day or La Cipale (1968) to the Champs-Élysées (1975) and its traditional half-million spectators.

Might Desgrange be amazed at the way the sport has become truly international? Not really, since he witnessed victories by the first riders from Luxemburg (François Faber, 1909), Belgium (Odile Defraye, 1912) and Italy (Ottavio Bottecchia, 1924). So Desgrange probably would have hailed the first team from outside Europe (Colombia, 1983), the first from America (7-Eleven, 1986), and the first from the Soviet Union (Alfa Lum, 1990). Less certain would be his reaction to the start of the Tour de France being located every two or three years outside the mother country.

The vastness of the race would be familiar. Limited now by international rules to 200 riders, usually divided into twenty-two teams of nine men each, the pack is no more than a quarter larger than any that Desgrange watched. In size, prestige and prize money, the Tour remains paramount.

The Tour of Italy is a fine race to win but the man who finished first in 1990, Gianni Bugno, admitted, 'The Tour de France is the summit. The fans, the attention, the pressure – everything is bigger.' The world championship is another splendid victory, but as Allan Peiper, an Australian, said of the Tour de France: 'This is the real world championship. The other just shows who's best for one day.'

Tommy Simpson was sixth overall in the 1962 Tour but his career was tragically cut short when he collapsed and died in the 1967 Tour. He is pictured on the Lyon-Nevers stage of the 1962 race time trial.

Le Tour en Angleterre

For only the second time in its history the Tour paid a visit to the UK in 1994. Two stages in the south of England, the first from Dover to Brighton and the second, an out-and-back loop from Portsmouth, drew much bigger crowds than in 1974 when the race paid a low-key visit for a stage in Devon.

'In the Tour, everybody is watching you, everybody cares about how you're doing,' says Erik Breukink, the Dutch rider. 'The pressure is enormous but the victory is enormous too.'

'There's no race like the Tour,' the American rider Greg LeMond says. 'Everything is bigger, more important.'

'Enormous', 'bigger', 'more important', 'the summit' – the enthusiasm echoes the words *l'Auto* used in 1903 to announce its race.

The words apply also to the financial health of the race. If, only a decade ago, the Tour de France was barely in the black, that, as they say, was then: an era of limited television coverage and modest sponsorship and advertising fees. And this is now. The race has become so big a money machine that reporters joke about its very name. 'The Tour d'Argent,' one publication subtitled the race. 'The Tour de Franc,' punned another journalist.

Both acknowledged, of course, that

reporters and photographers, 264 team officials, mechanics and masseurs, 745 chauffeurs and technical assistants, 20 judges, 263 race officials and employees and 1360 sponsors' pitchmen.

The money also provides prizes twice as big as those of any other race. The national tours of both Italy and Spain are just as long as the Tour's three weeks and almost as demanding on the riders' ability to suffer and triumph in the mountains, but neither comes close to matching the Tour de France's prize list. The 1991 winner received a cheque for two million francs (about £210,000), just part of the nine million francs shared by the riders. In 1987 the prize money barely topped six million francs and in 1989 it totalled eight million.

Where does the money come from? The £45,000 or so that each of the twenty-two teams puts up as an entry fee does not cover much more than its hotels and meals. A significant part of the revenue is paid by the municipalities that welcome the arrival or departure of the Tour on each stage. The 1990 Tour began in the Futuroscope theme park, for example.

Not many people had previously heard of Futuroscope, which is why the high-tech park near Poitiers in western France was willing to pay some £590,000 to play host. For three days Futuroscope was the focus of newspaper stories and the background for live television cover-

The team time trial is held in the first few days of the modern race and often promotes a whole team into the top twenty overall.

vast sums of money are needed to power what is virtually a sovereign state, complete with its own motorcycle police force (members of the Garde Républicaine from Paris), its own travelling bank (the only one in France allowed to remain open on Bastille Day, 14 July) and more than 3500 subjects: the 198 riders who start each year are far outnumbered by the 660

age to dozens of countries. Eurovision was there and so was ABC from the USA, NHK from Japan and a handful of radio networks from Colombia. They were all back for the start in Lyons in 1991 and at San Sebastián, northern Spain, in 1992. In all, the municipalities furnished 15 per cent of the Tour's 1990 income of 100 million francs (£10.4 million), which represents an increase of

10 per cent on the figure for 1989.

A much bigger slice of income came from sponsors (65 – 70 per cent) including such corporate heavyweights as Fiat, Coca-Cola and the Crédit Lyonnais bank, all with three-year contracts costing between twelve and eighteen million francs each. Smaller fees were paid by secondary sponsors and by the twenty-two advertisers in 489 vehicles in the publicity caravan. The rest accrued from television rights (20 – 25 per cent), where fees had doubled in two years.

Of the 100 million francs income, ninety million was spent on the race, with nearly 90 per cent of that going on such fixed fees as teams' meals, hotels and police protection along all the roads plus salaries of the organizers' 46 permanent and 217 part-time employees. That left ten million francs for profit. Not a centime of income came from admission fees. Between ten and fifteen million fans watch the race live, but they do so free of charge. For that privilege, the fans pour their souls into their support for the race.

'The trouble here,' said the English rider Barry Hoban before the start of the 1978 Tour in the Netherlands, 'is that they don't know what to make of racers. But when we get to France, ah, there they know how to make a racer feel important.'

Take, for example, the climb to Alpe d'Huez along twenty-one hairpin bends that are packed every year by up to half a million spectators.

'It's a tremendous feeling, almost overwhelming,' says Greg LeMond, who has twice finished second by half a bicycle wheel after the 8.7-mile (14km) climb to the resort atop a 6100-ft (1860m) peak. 'There are so many people that it's like the Super Bowl stadium but they're within two feet of you for 10km. It's awesome.'

'That's a point where the spectators outdo all other spectators,' says fellow American Andy Hampsten of the Motorola team. 'The energy of the crowd, you can't help but absorb it. There's so much energy coming from the crowd that I don't think any rider can help but ride better.

'All those spectators are insane,' he continued. 'They've got heatstroke or something. They really go wild.'

That they do. Puffing and turning a

The most famous finishing straight in the sport – the Champs Elysees in Paris – has welcomed the weary survivors of the Tour since 1975.

The great climbers

For the climbing specialist the Tour de France is the greatest challenge of the year, and the famous red and white polka-dot jersey is the coveted prize. Top of the list of Tour climbers are two riders, Federico Bahamontes of Spain and Lucien Van Impe of Belgium. Both won the polka-dot jersey six times in their careers, and both also won the Tour once – Bahamontes in 1959 and Van Impe in 1976.

vivid shade of red, the fans run hundreds of yards uphill alongside the riders, screaming encouragement or pouring water over their heads. Many do both.

The water is almost always welcome, especially since riders are not permitted to get water from a team car within 20km (12½ miles) of the finish. To do so is to risk a time penalty.

Encouragement from a fan huffing and puffing alongside a rider is much less appreciated. Some riders say it demoralizes them to realize that an out-of-shape spectator is able to run at least as fast as they can pedal. Others, like LeMond, complain that the accompanying fans are a distraction. 'It breaks your concentration,' he said.

Another worry is that fans on a climb are close enough to the riders to cause mischief, as when a French fan punched the Belgian champion Eddy Merckx during a climb up the Puy de Dôme in the Tour some fifteen years ago.

'I'm always afraid that someone might be a little crazy, someone who doesn't like you just because he doesn't like you,' LeMond said. 'He might take a punch at you or knock you down.'

Just as bothersome is the illegal push some fans give riders who are lagging far behind, for which the riders can be penalized in time even if they did not request the help.

Many of the fans are Dutch, who flock to Alpe d'Huez in such numbers that a Tour joke has it that the resort is the southernmost town in the Netherlands. Most Dutch fans come in cars and camp out on the mountain for days beforehand to make sure that they have a front-row seat on the course. Others arrive in huge buses, having paid for a ticket that covers the long trip and a day at the Tour.

'It's something special for a Dutchman because there are four or five of us who've won this stage and they call it the Dutch mountain,' Raas explained. 'It's unbelievable, more than 200,000 Dutchmen there. It's a big party,' he added.

The attraction for foreign fans is a major distinction between the Tour de France and other big tours. The Tour of Italy rarely attracts more than Italians and Spain's equivalent more than Spaniards, but the Tour de France draws foreigners in large numbers. In the Pyrenees, both Spanish and French Basques always turn out in their tens of thousands in the hope of celebrating a local victor.

In the 1991 Tour, which he easily won, Miguel Induraín performed well, as he often has before in the Pyrenees, so close to his home outside Pamplona. With a magnificent ride over five mountain peaks under a searing sun, he captured for the first time the yellow jersey of the race's overall leader.

'Winning this jersey is my childhood dream,' he said on the victory podium. Induraín completed the last climb, a steep 3.7-mile (6km) ramp, with almost the same fluid stroke on his pedals that he exhibited at the start of the day. That said much about his condition since the stage lasted 144 miles (232km) and topped five peaks. Two of them, the Aubisque and the Tourmalet, are rated beyond category in height, difficulty, steepness and distance from the finish. Two others, the Pourtalet and the ascent to Val Louron, are rated as being in the first category and the last, the Aspin, is rated second-category. The lowest category is fourth.

From the moment that Induraín attacked and opened a 55-second lead on the descent from the Tourmalet, the nine riders nearest him knew they were in the battle that would probably decide the entire race. Groups split and

Italian Claudio Chiappucci gets some unwelcome attention from the crowd during a time-trial stage of the 1991 Tour de France.

rejoined as they rode up and up through lines of spectators who ran alongside and shouted encouragement or offered bottles of water.

The Basque flag seemed to be waved at every turn in support, first of Induraín, the leader, and then of those trying to catch him. The Basques' presence contrasted with the meagre attendance the day before in Jaca, in the Spanish Pyrenees, where the Tour stage finished before the smallest crowd in memory. That turnout plunged a knife into the heart of the race's organizers, who awarded the 1992 start to San Sebastián, in Basque country.

The organizers need not have feared. Jaca, after all, is in Aragon, far from the home of the Basques, who are a nation within the nations of France and Spain.

When the decisive stage started in Jaca, many fans were still staying away, but not for long. As the riders began climbing, the crowds mounted into the hundreds of thousands.

Inigo Ibarreche and Kepa Zarate, two students from Bilbao, were among them. With half a dozen friends they had driven in two cars from the industrial city. 'We drove all yesterday and got here early,' Inigo said. They spent the night in sleeping bags on a hill in Val Louron, a resort and the finish of the stage. Their enthusiasm for cycling was great, but even greater was their desire to see a Basque win – Miguel Induraín or Marino Lejarretta, say. If not either of these, they would be content to see a Spaniard win – perhaps Pedro Delgado or Melchior Mauri. Their priorities were reflected in Zarate's garb. As a cape, he wore the Basque flag. Indeed, few in the vast crowd lining the route waved the Spanish flag.

Still, there was no doubt that the stage started in Spain. For the first 26 miles (42km) the riders passed brown fields of stubble, sun-baked earth and dried-up streams. Here and there an eagle soared, ceaselessly searching for food. Ageless villages perched on the side of brown hills, flanked occasionally by stylish town houses.

During the first climb, up the 5886-ft (1794m) Pourtalet, the babble on the side of the road changed from Spanish to French. At the peak, the policemen posted at every side road were no longer wearing green uniforms but blue uniforms with stiff caps.

In a long line, the 183 remaining riders plunged into a sinuous descent and ended the Tour's first visit to Spain since 1974. The landscape turned greener and more populated, with foothills dotted by the tents and trailers of the French on their month-long annual holiday.

The country was France but at Val Louron the territory was Basque. In just that way, the Tour de France belongs to all the world.

After Merckx came Bernard Hinault, another all-rounder, who equalled the Belgian's record of five Tour victories. After his retirement in 1986 he became technical director of the Tour.

The Classics

Races which date back to the end of the last century form the backbone of the professional calendar. All are one-day events, mostly from place to place, and a victory in one of the great 'monuments' is highly prized. **Phil Liggett**

R ik Van Looy knew more about the world's great single-day races than anyone else, and from the best possible angle, as he won every one of them. To this day he remains the only rider to have done so.

Rik II, as he was known, followed in the next generation after Rik 'le Grand' Van Steenbergen, and The Emperor of Herentals – Van Looy's popular name linking him to his home town in the Belgian Ardennes – used a fiery sprint that few could ever master.

In a later era, the legendary Belgian Eddy Merckx, although the world's greatest rider, did not possess as instinctive and powerful a sprint as Rik II. In all, Merckx won twenty-six classic races, more than anyone else, but never Paris-Tours.

There is a third great name that must appear near the head of this look at the single-day classic races, and that is Freddy Maertens, another Belgian sprinter. He, like Merckx, won eight stages in a single Tour de France. He took just four days to win his first professional race in 1972, using his stunning sprint at Zwevezele in Belgium. The best riders in the world knew immediately that they had a problem with the young, aggressive Belgian.

When he won Paris-Brussels in 1975, Maertens' average speed of 28.652mph (46.110kph) was, and still is, the fastest ever recorded for a classic, winning him the Yellow Riband. As with the Tour de

Left: Paris-Roubaix is the quintessential Classic, combining a tradition of great winners with a route across northern France designed to provide the ultimate test in strength, skill and courage.
Right: At the other end of Europe from Paris-Roubaix, Milan-San Remo in Italy takes the bunch along the Mediterranean coast on a more picturesque opener to the Classics season.

Rik Van Looy is the only rider to have ever won all the great one-day classics. The strongly built Belgian was ideally suited to these gruelling tests and he was twice world road-race champion, in 1960 and 1961.

France leader's yellow jersey, the Yellow Riband is awarded to the greyhounds of the sport in the gruelling single-day races.

Maertens, however, was inconsistent and his career was a controversial one. After crashing in the Tour of Italy (Giro d'Italia) in 1977 he was as surprised as everyone when he won the world title in Prague in 1981, but he won only a few races afterwards and retired three seasons later a rather sorry figure.

Before taking a closer look at the classics, let us compare the careers of Van Looy and Merckx. There have been other great classic performers, but the records of these two riders make them premiers in this branch of the sport.

RIK VAN LOOY

Born:	20 December 1933
Professional:	18 years
World Championship	1960; 1961
Paris-Roubaix	1961; 1962; 1965
Paris-Tours	1959; 1967
Milan-San Remo	1958
Tour of Lombardy	1959
Liège-Bastogne-Liège	1961
Tour of Flanders	1959; 1962
Paris-Brussels	1956; 1958
Flèche-Wallonne	1968
Ghent-Wevelgem	1956; 1957; 1962

In all, Van Looy won 371 races.

EDDY MERCKX

Born:	17 June 1945
Professional:	14 years
World Championship	1967; 1971; 1974
Paris-Roubaix	1968; 1970; 1973
Milan-San Remo	1966; 1967; 1969; 1971; 1972; 1975; 1976
Tour of Lombardy	1971; 1972
Liège-Bastogne-Liège	1969; 1971; 1972; 1973; 1975
Tour of Flanders	1969; 1975
Paris-Brussels	1973
Flèche-Wallonne	1967; 1970; 1972
Ghent-Wevelgem	1967; 1969; 1972

In all, Merckx won 525 races from 1800 starts as both amateur and professional.

Many organizers of major races around the world call their events classics. While this may show respect for a sport with a great history, the title is more likely adopted as a strong selling point when it comes to attracting television coverage and sponsors.

A classic race cannot be created overnight and in a changing sport it is arguable whether such a race will ever be created again. Modern racing, with its slick action, colour and glamour, is far divorced from the bad roads, poor bikes and great distances of yesteryear. By contrast, those who have studied the sport from its beginning will remember only the great monuments on which racing worldwide has been built for well over a century.

Paris-Rouen is the oldest classic race, first held in 1869 and won in that year by an Englishman, James Moore, and it still takes place each year as an amateur event. Others more easily come to mind because their reputations grew with them, such as the longest, Paris-Brest-Paris, and the motorcycle-paced Bordeaux-Paris, both of which are, sadly, no longer held.

The current list of classics, to which top professional riders bring both glitter and style, is as follows:

Milan-San Remo (*Italy, March*);
Tour of Flanders (*Belgium, April*);
Ghent-Wevelgem (*Belgium, April*);
Paris-Roubaix (*France, April*);
Flèche-Wallonne (*Belgium, April*);
Liège-Bastogne-Liège
    (*Belgium, April*);
Paris-Brussels
    (*France-Belgium, September*);
Paris-Tours (*France, October*);
Tour of Lombardy (*Italy, October*).

In addition to these, two time trials have become representative of this branch of the sport: the Grand Prix Eddy Merckx in Belgium and the Grand Prix des Nations, both in September.

The growing interest in the World Cup series has also launched a number of newer races, so to the list should be added the following:
Amstel Gold Race (Holland, April),

San Sebastián-San Sebastián
    (Spain, August),
Leeds Classic
    (England, August),
Zurich Championship
    (Switzerland, August)
Grand Prix of the Americas
    (Canada, September)

The professional world championship must also be included, although this race is held in a different country each year and is never run place-to-place. Whether the rider who wins it would have preferred to add a Paris-Roubaix or Tour of Lombardy to his record instead is debatable. I think many would have.

MILAN-SAN REMO

By the time the first race from Milan to San Remo was proposed, the Tour of Lombardy was two years old and the French and Belgians had already established what are still seen as the two most wanted races in the professional rider's calendar: Paris-Roubaix and Liège-Bastogne-Liège.

In the early days it was the British riders who dominated the races, but the field soon broadened and now Britain relies on a handful of riders to produce an occasional result.

The 'Primavera' opens the classic season in March and although it is the

Plummeting descents

Although Milan-San Remo is the most southerly spring classic it is often plagued by heavy rain and filthy roads which blacken the riders' faces until they look like coal miners after a day-long shift. Slippery road conditions on the final climbs of the Poggio and the Cipressa also play into the hands of the most daring bike handlers and it is not unusual for the winning move to be made on the plummeting descents of these roads.

Fausto Coppi won Milan-San Remo three times — he is pictured winning the 1949 edition before a huge crowd in San Remo.

Cobbled roads figure in the Tour of Flanders and although the cobbles are not as treacherous as those found on the route of Paris-Roubaix, they still play a major part in thinning out the field, especially on the steep 'bergs'.

newspaper. In Italy the *Gazzetta dello Sport*, which arguably shares with the French newspaper *l'Équipe* a reputation as the finest sports paper in the world, opened the first race in 1905 to both amateur and professional riders.

After a 3.30am start, the organizers gave the riders a cut-off time of fifteen hours to reach the finish. No help, food or spare equipment was allowed, and riders had to provide for themselves – the same principle behind the evolution of triathlons and mountain-bike racing in recent times.

Unlike many of the early classics, no pacing by cars or motorcycles was allowed. The winner received 500 lire, but if he had been an amateur a non-cash prize would have been given instead. All the finishers received a medal, and some would say they deserved it!

Only thirty-three riders faced the first journey south, and the 1745-ft (532m) climb of the Turchino Pass hurt the leaders at the midway point, as it still does, leaving the great Frenchman Louis Petit-Breton to win in 11 hours 4 minutes, an average speed of 15.74mph (25.33kph).

When the top Italian rider, Giovanni Gerbi, finished only third this added to the problems that had arisen in organizing the race, and the *Gazzetta* took a long time to announce that the race would continue in 1908. However, it was held and has been every year ever since, apart from the breaks imposed by two world wars.

longest race and has the biggest field, the long haul down to San Remo is often wind-assisted and becomes a battle of the strong men when they face the last few climbs, the most famous of which are the Cipressa and the Poggio, just before the finish.

Gianni Bugno's lone win in 1990 at an average speed of 28.463mph (45.806kph) almost matched the record Yellow Riband ride of Freddy Maertens in Paris-Brussels in 1975, coming at the end of a remarkable escape by a number of riders who had caught the field napping early on. Bugno was not a lucky winner – but then the winners of classic races rarely are – and in 1991 he won the deserved world title, as all the greatest classic riders have done in the past.

The Milan-San Remo, like many of the formative races, is organized by a

TOUR OF FLANDERS

For many riders, especially the British and Americans, finding a base in the Flanders area of Belgium to learn the trade of professional cycling is a must.

At a glance, the flatlands, beaten by winds from the sea, are an uninteresting landscape torn by two world wars and many of the roads are unfit for the modern motor car. But the area is a magnet for those with the desire to say that they have climbed and conquered such *bergs* as the Kwaremont, Muur, Kemmelberg and Bosberg.

The Tour of Flanders, the second big

classic of the season, draws as many spectators as it did when first held in 1913. The Belgians, at least the Flemish-speakers, are tough, weather-beaten people who match their roads. Their love of the sport is second to none, not even to the Italians, whose excitable Latin temperament make them something special too.

There are sixteen *bergs* on the current route, which takes the race on a gentle meander around Flanders, where it begins innocently enough from the market-place beneath the cathedral in St Niklaas. The trap in the 165-mile (266km) race to nearby Meerbeke lies at the southern end of the course, where all sixteen climbs hit the riders in fast succession. The last, the Bosberg, is only 550 yards (500m) long, but its average gradient of 10 per cent has given Belgian Edwig Van Hooydonck his chance to ride home alone on two occasions.

The first Tour of Flanders was won by a Belgian – like most of them – and Paul Deman covered the long ride of 230 miles (370km) in just over twelve hours. Deman was twenty-four when he won, but the First World War interrupted an excellent career. After the war, which he was lucky to survive, having been sentenced to death by the

Germans for spying for Britain and France, who both decorated him, Deman won Paris-Roubaix in 1920 and Paris-Tours in 1923. He never again took the honours in Belgium's answer to Paris-Roubaix, but he did finish fourth in 1924.

GHENT-WEVELGEM

A race like Ghent-Wevelgem, coming early in the season and too near the other big races, is often called a Belgian classic or a semi-classic, but, sadly, never simply a classic.

The race, which began in 1934, has associations with all of the great names. Even Britain can claim a notable success: Barry Hoban produced a dazzling sprint finish to beat none other than Eddy Merckx in 1974. The Belgian had already won three times, and he looked surprised beyond belief when beaten by Hoban, who, as an eight-times stage winner in the Tour de France, was no mean finisher on his day.

Like the Tour of Flanders, this race also wanders around the Flemish hillsides, covering the cobbles and taking the full force of the winds before arriving in Wevelgem. It is a course that suits the Belgian style of racing and only two French riders have won, although both are famous names.

Eastern success

Soviet sprinter Djamolidine Adujaparov became the first eastern bloc rider to win a classic when he outsprinted the whole field at the end of the 1991 Ghent-Wevelgem. 'Abdu' won one of the flattest editions of the race, after the famous climb of the Kemmelberg was left out due to concern over damage to the cobbles.

Riders take to their feet on the Koppenberg, once the steepest climb in the Tour of Flanders but deleted from the route since 1987 due to its width and environmental conditions.

Jacques Anquetil and Bernard Hinault have each won five Tours de France and have followed classic careers in a similar vein, although their successes were rare. Hinault won Ghent-Wevelgem in 1977, when he broke clear from a leading group of eighteen with 10 miles (16km) to go. He won by almost two minutes, the first Frenchman to win for thirteen years.

PARIS-ROUBAIX

The Queen of the Classics richly deserves her title, and as the years go by one can only fear for the future of this marvellous race. In modern times it follows its first route as closely as possible, and uses the roads once trodden by Napoleon's armies and ravaged by the bombs of two world wars.

The 'Hell of the North' – the nickname refers to the stretches of cobbled road used all summer by walkers or farmers but rarely by anyone else – keeps 'La Pascale' at the head of the classic races table. Nowadays rarely more than 35 miles (56km) of cobbles are ridden, but on a good day (that means wet weather and plenty of mud) you will see re-enacted a marvellous race of yesteryear.

In 1896, when modern cycling was taking shape and the velocipede was fully accepted in the big towns (and twenty-seven years after the Englishman James Moore had won Paris-Rouen), the first race from Paris (Porte Maillot) to the velodrome in Roubaix was held. Unlike Milan-San Remo, the Paris-Roubaix followed the trend set in Bordeaux-Paris and Paris-Brest-Paris, and allowed the 118 riders to be paced by trainers on bicycles, who changed *en route*.

Welshman Arthur Linton was among the favourites, but in 1991 Britain is still awaiting a winner, although Yorkshireman Barry Hoban finished third in 1972 behind 'Mr Roubaix', Roger De Vlaeminck, who finished in the top three nine times. Jozef Fischer, a

Punctures, crashes, cobbles, mud, mayhem – all part of the Paris-Roubaix epic – a race which takes the riders back in time to the days when classics were not just races, but ordeals.

German, won the first race by 36 minutes, and Linton finished fourth. Third was the best-placed Frenchman Maurice Garin, who distinguished himself by winning the race for the next two years, adding in 1903 the first Tour de France.

Few riders ever reach Roubaix, even today, without a crash or at best a flat tyre. The first bad roads are found after 63 miles (101km) have been covered, at Troisvilles. Thereafter, with a few minor route changes each year, the race follows a tortuous path in search of the worst surfaces possible.

The Arenberg Forest near Valenciennes is the first black spot for most. It is long, more than 1½ mile (2.4km), and is all over cobblestones that usually only reverberate to the gentle pressure of walkers' feet. This sanctuary, where no cars are normally allowed, is opened once a year to the thousands of spectators and the 180 or so riders who, for a few short minutes, go back in time.

Moreno Argentin on his way to victory in the 1991 Flèche Wallonne. Four days later he did the double, winning Liège-Bastogne-Liège for the fourth time in his career.

FLÈCHE-WALLONNE

It is a shame that this race takes place so close to Liège-Bastogne-Liège, because it pays the price by being left out of the annual World Cup competition, whose policy is to favour races of varying character.

Even so, the Flèche is a great classic in the eyes of the riders, and even though it lacks World Cup status, they all want to ride it – if only as valuable preparation for the Liège-Bastogne-Liège a few days later (in 1994 Fleche Wallonne was held three days after Liege-Bastogne-Liege).

Many of the roads are the same in both races, but the Flèche starts in the gentle town of Spa and races across the Ardennes to finish at Huy, on top of its famous hill, the Mur de Huy. Shorter than Liège-Bastogne-Liège, the race is only 127 miles (204km), but the Mur is climbed four times, including the ride up to the finish, where the crowds wait in their thousands.

The race was first ridden in 1936 between Tournai and Liège, but has settled in Spa since 1986 after experiments with Spa and Huy since 1980.

No rider from the English-speaking nations has ever won the race, but Tom Simpson, who carried British hopes in most races throughout the 1960s until his untimely death on Mont Ventoux in the Tour de France on 13 July 1967, finished third in 1965.

At the top of the main-road climb of the Côte des Forges, which comes early on in the Flèche-Wallonne – it is the last crucial climb in Liège-Bastogne-Liège – stands a memorial to one of Belgium's great stars, Stan Ockers. Although not an outstanding talent, like a Merckx, Ockers was immensely popular and when he was seriously injured racing at the Palais des Sports in Antwerp in September 1956 the sporting world was stunned. At his funeral two days later emotions overflowed.

The memorial, a magnificent three-dimensional statue of Ockers on his bike racing out of a wall of stone, looks at the riders each time they pass over the summit of the Côte des Forges. The site was chosen in 1957 because the Flèche-Wallonne was the Belgian rider's first major success, in 1953.

There was no doubt as to who was the star of the Ardennes in 1991, when Moreno Argentin became the first rider since Merckx, in 1972, to win both races in the same year.

LIÈGE-BASTOGNE-LIÈGE

By winning this race five times, Eddy Merckx established himself as the all-time classic great. Even his record-

Double triumph

The Flèche-Wallonne and Liège-Bastogne-Liège used to be run as two races counting towards a combined overall classification. The 'Ardennais Weekend' as it was known was a prized 'double' and only the strongest riders, Merckx for example, and latterly Argentin, have won both races in the same year.

breaking seven wins in Milan-San Remo did not equal this feat. Liège-Bastogne-Liège is half of what used to be the Ardennais Weekend when the event was coupled with the Flèche-Wallonne. Both races are held in a wooded area of Belgium that abounds with red squirrels and deer. Its towns nestle, usually at the base of steep hills, and the populace is too small to muster a great following for any event.

In 1991 Claude Criquielion, a Walloon and one of the rare breed of top riders from the French-speaking sector of Belgium, retired from the sport with his second runner-up spot in Liège-Bastogne-Liège, the one race he had always wanted to win.

The race is organized by the Royal Cyclists' Pesant Club Liégeois with added finesse recently added by the Société du Tour de France. In the early Nineties when the race appeared to have become too dangerous because of a route that was both narrow and badly

surfaced, riders indicated they might not return if something was not done. Had the race been cancelled, it would have been a tragic blow to the sport, as this is the oldest race left on the professional classic calendar.

The first two races were held in 1892 and 1893 and both were won by the diminutive Léon Houa. At 5ft 5in (1.68m) and weighing only 10st 8lb (67.1kg), he was ideal for the many hills. After being banned by the Belgian Cycling Federation because he took money as an amateur, he returned in 1894 and won the professional race, which started and finished at Spa. Houa took an interest in car racing and retired in 1896. He was killed in an accident in 1918 at the age of fifty-one.

Sean Kelly, the great Irish champion, is the only English-speaker to win the doyen of classics, scoring in 1984 and 1989, and he should have been joined by Stephen Roche in 1987. Roche, leading with Criquielion and almost in sight

Frenchman Jean-François Bernard leads Soviet Dimitri Konyshev in the 1990 Liège-Bastogne-Liège – a race which favours strong climbers rather than specialist sprinters.

of the finish, began to argue about the pace-making, so allowing the great Ardennes champion Moreno Argentin to catch them and beat them for his third of four wins. He is the only rider who at present threatens the record of Merckx.

PARIS-BRUSSELS

Over the years the race between the two capital cities has lost much of its appeal, yet it is a classic that, since 1893, has been a backbone of the world sport. It is not included in the World Cup series, but the riders still want its name on their Palmares. In 1991 Brian Holm became the first Danish winner by leaving the field with 4.3 miles (7km) to ride. This was unusual, as, like Paris-Tours, Paris-Brussels can be more favourable to the sprint finishers.

The race started in 1893, a year after Bordeaux-Paris, and covered an enormous 253 miles (407km). It stayed strictly amateur for two years before allowing the professionals their place. Nowadays the race starts to the north of Paris, rather like Paris-Roubaix, and cuts a path through to Belgium, where it approaches Brussels from the direction of the Ardennes.

PARIS-TOURS

This race has always been one for the sprinters. The first Paris-Tours was in 1896 and organized by Paris-Vélo to coincide with the opening of the new velodrome in Tours. Since then the race has changed its route many times, to Blois-Chaville and Blois-Montlhéry; hence its more generic name these days of the Autumn Grand Prix.

The Italians, who have played their part in developing the history of most of the classics, have won this race only once, when Jules Rossi came home in 1938 a minute ahead of Belgium's

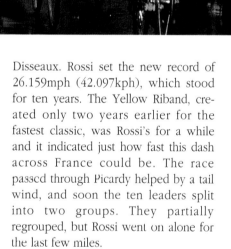

Disseaux. Rossi set the new record of 26.159mph (42.097kph), which stood for ten years. The Yellow Riband, created only two years earlier for the fastest classic, was Rossi's for a while and it indicated just how fast this dash across France could be. The race passed through Picardy helped by a tail wind, and soon the ten leaders split into two groups. They partially regrouped, but Rossi went on alone for the last few miles.

In 1965 the race returned to the 'good' old days when riders faced agonizing decisions on what gears to use, as the multi-gear derailleur was banned. The race was won that year by Dutch sprinter Gerben Karstens, whose average speed was a magnificent record of 27.98mph (45.029kph) which remains today the best by far.

Karstens may have won, but the hero of the day was Britain's Tom Simpson, who broke clear of the field to show what a master pedaller he was. Simpson chose a gear of 51 (front chainwheel) x 17 (rear sprocket). (Raymond Poulidor also chose 51 x 17, and Jacques Anquetil 49 x 13.) Simpson was clear away after 144 miles (232km), but he was facing a head wind when

With few hills to speak of and a long rolling route, Paris-Tours has become the sprinters' classic. In 1991 Belgian Johan Capiot won the bunch sprint in near darkness after the bunch, feeling the effects of a long season, had completed the 283km at a leisurely pace.

Variable route

Paris-Tours is a sprinter's race and a glance at the winners in recent years will confirm this. It has not always been called Paris-Tours either – the original route was discarded in 1974 when the organizers tried a number of different start and finish towns. Tours-Versailles, Blois-Montlhéry, Blois-Chaville, Créteil-Chaville – all have hosted the race until 1978, when the old route was reinstated.

The bunch tackle the Passo d'Intelvi en masse in the Tour of Lombardy. Below them is the shoreline of Lake Como.

1993, after Tony Rominger in 1992, the race was won for the second year running by a Swiss, Pascal Richard. The route brought the hills around Como to the end, since the race both started and finished here, as it did in 1961.

The great Italian champion Fausto Coppi – the Merckx of his era – stamped his complete authority on the Tour of Lombardy by winning it four successive times between 1946 and 1949, and again in 1954. The Master died six years later after contracting malaria during a trip to Africa with Jacques Anquetil, Roger Rivière, Rudi Altig, Raphael Geminiani and other great names of the era.

Coppi's other classic wins included Milan-San Remo (three times), Paris-Roubaix and the Flèche-Wallonne, but it was in the Tour of Lombardy that he was outstanding during his nineteen years as a professional. During his reign Coppi won every Lombardy alone, but it must be said that the top French and Belgian riders of the period did not ride, because they hated the roads, which were in a bad state of repair and very narrow. This seemed rather strange, especially as the roads in Belgium were known by all to have an equally poor reputation!

In 1947 Coppi took great pleasure in leaving his most bitter rival, Gino Bartali, over five minutes behind, and a year later he escaped during the last 52 miles (84km) to finish almost five minutes ahead of Adolfo Leoni. He was a rider of great class.

There was another rider around just ten years after Coppi's last victory, who may not have possessed such talent, but did have a similar fragile build and the heart of a lion. To this day Tommy Simpson remains Britain's most respected rider and only world professional road champion. He won the Lombardy in 1965 after having animated the race the previous year with a show of the typical Simpson aggression that often followed no pattern but always enlivened the race – the reason why everyone loved to see him ride.

That year Simpson was wearing the world champion's rainbow jersey after his great success in Spain a month ear-

he was joined by three or four others who, he claimed, had taken advantage of following cars and caught him only by riding in their shelter.

The twenty-three-year-old Karstens, in his first professional season, had taken advice from fellow Dutch professional Jo De Roo, the winner in 1962 and 1963, and started the race with 53 x 16. Later he changed gears and finished on 53 x 15.

TOUR OF LOMBARDY

Just as Milan-San Remo opens the classic season, so does Italy's Tour of Lombardy close it. In 1990 the 'race of the falling leaves', which was beginning to lose its appeal, altered its route. In

lier. These days few world champions manage to win races after donning the coveted jersey, but for Simpson this victory in Italy was to serve as confirmation of his world-beating status.

Simpson left behind, among others, Gianni Motta, who had won the previous year on the climb of San-Fermo, to finish ahead of Gerben Karstens by over three minutes. In less than two years Simpson would be dead and Britain would have lost its finest rider.

Success in the Lombardy proved elusive to Eddy Merckx, who did not win it until his sixth attempt in 1971, having in previous years finished second and third. This must have annoyed the proud Belgian, and in 1971 he beat Franco Bitossi, the man with the palpitating heart, who often stopped to listen to it, by 3 minutes 31 seconds.

Bitossi had also won the previous year.

Merckx attacked alone on the climb at Schignano during its early stages and no one followed. It was a typical move by the Belgian, then world champion. The Spaniard Luis Ocaña was the pre-race favourite, and although he chased later with an elite group of riders, he retired with 12.4 miles (20km) to go to Como, because the others would not work hard enough to catch the flying Belgian.

Today, the Tour of Lombardy is still one of the most sought after classics in an increasingly busy end of season calendar. After experimenting with world cup races after Lombardy, the organizers quickly realised that tradition dictated that the Tour of Lombardy and the Grand Prix de Nations time trial were rightfully placed at the end of the road season.

Maurizio Fondriest was the outstanding Classics rider of the 1993 season. The Italian former world champion won Milan-San Remo, Fléche Wallone and the Grand Prix of Zurich.

The National Tours

The Tour de France may be the biggest and best-known stage race in the world, but it is certainly not the only major national stage race. Virtually every cycling nation has its own tour and quite often it is the most prestigious race held all year, attracting professionals and sometimes amateurs from far afield. **Sam Abt**

Many countries have bicycling tours, among them Italy, Spain, the Netherlands, Switzerland, Britain, Colombia, Sweden, Morocco, Norway, Portugal, Ireland and often the United States and Belgium. Martinique has a tour and so does the Ivory Coast. Eastern Europe has the Peace Race, which amounts to a tour of Poland, Czechoslovakia and what was East Germany.

Some of these races, such as the Peace Race and those in Sweden and Morocco, attract mainly amateur teams and are thus unimportant to the professionals. Others, such as those in Martinique and the Ivory Coast, are unimportant because they are held after the European season and so become only a way of spending a vacation in the sun. Because of geography, some tours are short – none of the Benelux tours, for example, can be stretched into more than three or four days – and therefore minor.

Left: Tony Rominger leads Alex Zulle in the 1993 Tour of Spain. The Swiss pair dominated the race and although Zulle wears the leader's yellow jersey, Rominger was the final victor.
Right: The Tour of Spain takes place in May and often encounters wintry conditions in the north.

Others, such as the Tour of Switzerland, can last more than a week, and yet not be much more important because they are primarily used as tune-up races for a bigger tour.

The tours that matter are the three-week ones of Spain, Italy and France, which are held in that order in the spring and summer although the lords of bicycling, the International Cycling Union (UCI) and the International Federation of Professional Cycling (FICP), are considering moving either the Spanish or the Italian race to the autumn to balance a crowded calendar.

The Tour of Italy, the Giro d'Italia, is the only real if distant rival to the Tour de France in prestige. Its records are studded with the names of great winners since its start in 1909: Alfredo Binda, Gino Bartali, the immortal Fausto Coppi, Fiorenzo Magni, Felice Gimondi and Guiseppe Saronni among the Italians and Bernard Hinault (three times), Miguel Indurain, Laurent Fignon

and Andy Hampsten among the foreigners. The spirited Coppi-Bartali duels of 1947 and 1949 are just as legendary as those between Merckx and Poulidor in the Tour de France.

But in recent years the Tour of Italy has not always been as serious a race as it might be. In the 1980s, for example, the organizers consistently bowed to the wishes of the *tifosi*, the overheated Italian fans, who wanted Italian riders to win this Italian race. So, to assist Francesco Moser, who was certain to collapse in the highest Alps, the organizers eliminated the most demanding mountain stage in 1984, insisting that the pass was snowbound. When curious French team officials visited the pass, it was open and lined with no more snow than the Tour de France sees on any summer days in its own Alps.

In quest of his first Tour of Italy victory in eleven attempts, Moser was also allowed to benefit, without penalty,

Stephen Roche (shadowed by Roberto Visentini) faced the wrath of the Italian *tifosi* when he ignored team orders and went for overall victory in the 1987 Tour of Italy.

from a chain of pushers on lesser mountains. He did indeed finish first, aided also by the début of the now-standard aerodynamic bicycle, which he had used earlier that year to break the record for the hour's ride against the clock. Alone in using that bicycle in the final day's time trial, Moser won by nearly four minutes over Laurent Fignon and edged the Frenchman out by one minute three seconds in the overall standings.

The *tifosi* were thrilled but Italian cycling had suffered another setback: the country's best riders of the last decade – Moser, Giuseppe Saronni, Roberto Visentini and Moreno Argentin – were not good climbers and, to accommodate them and their fans, the race was made less demanding. This only made the fans more eager for an Italian victory. In 1985 Bernard Hinault, the French champion, was warned that the *tifosi* would spread nails along his route in the final time trial, and in 1987 Stephen Roche, the Irish champion, had to be escorted by policemen to keep them at bay.

Roche's problem was that he was battling with an Italian teammate, Roberto Visentini, who was seeking his second successive victory in the race. When the Irishman took the overall lead, Visentini indulged in tantrums that inflamed his fans against Roche, who went on national television to plead for understanding. After his victory Roche announced that he would quit the Carrera team and Italy. 'In Italy,' he said bitterly, 'riders are far too coddled. They're treated like princes and they don't know how to suffer.'

Finally, in a celebrated obituary in 1989, the *Gazzetta dello Sport* pronounced Italian cycling dead. All the vital signs were missing, said the Italian paper, pointing to the few and unim-

portant races that its country's professional riders had won in recent years. Finding no trace of breath, the *Gazzetta* removed the mirror from the corpse's lips, shrugged and walked away in sorrow.

The paper had got it wrong. Early in the 1990 season the body began stirring, the eyelids began flickering and colour returned to the cheeks. What was this talk of rigor mortis when Gianni Bugno opened the World Cup season with a victory in Milan-San Remo? When Claudio Chiappucci won the mountain-climbing jersey in Paris-Nice? When Moreno Argentin won the Tour of Flanders? When Argentin jumped to the top of the World Cup standings? When Marco Giovannetti won the Tour of Spain? The final accounting revealed victories in six classics and two major tours for riders from Italy.

In 1991 it got better: Chiappucci won Milan-San Remo and in the Tour of Italy finished second to Franco Chioccioli, another Italian. Mario Cipollini boasted openly and accurately that no other sprinter could beat him when he was right. Argentin won Liège-Bastogne-Liège and the Flèche-

Home favourite Gianni Bugno was unbeatable in the 1990 Tour of Italy, leading from start to finish for the first time since the legendary Eddy Merckx.

Tough climbs

The Tour de France has the Alps, the Tour of Italy has the Dolomites and occasionally the Alps too. Famous climbs in the Dolomites include Passo Pordoi, the Tre Cime de Lavaredo, Val Gardena and the Gavia. Inclement weather can make some passes extremely treacherous in June and occasionally, as on the Gavia stage in the 1989 Giro, the route is diverted due to snow on the mountain roads.

The bunch passes beneath the viaduct at Segovia in the 1991 Tour of Spain.

A Spanish classic

The Tour of Spain, the Vuelta de España, has rapidly grown in stature since Spain became a major cycling force in the late 1980s. A full international field contests the Vuelta every May over the Nevada, near Granada, the Picos mountains in the north, the peaks near Segovia and of course, the Pyrenees. In 1992 the race crossed into France for a classic Pyrenean stage which included climbs of the Tourmalet, the Peyresourde, the Aspin and Luz Ardiden.

Wallonne. Bugno and Chiappucci were second and third to Miguel Induraín of Spain in the 1991 Tour de France and Argentin's Ariostea team won three successive stages.

The days of Moser, Saronni and Visentini were over and the Italian Renaissance was in full sway. In the 1990 Tour of Italy, Bugno won the prologue and held the pink jersey for the rest of the race, becoming the second rider in modern times, after Eddy Merckx, to have led the race from wire to wire. He excelled in the mountains and in the time trials. For the first time in years the notorious *tifosi* heard their hearts sing.

The music was, of course, by Mozart. Somewhere between his 'Haffner' symphony and his 'Jupiter', Bugno learned, *allegro vivace*, how to become a champion. Given a month of musical therapy to cure vertigo, Bugno blossomed from a timid rider who seemed able to win only small races into the man who led the computerized rankings of the world's top 600 professionals.

One of his undetected problems was vertigo, or dizziness and fear of falling when he descended from a mountain peak at high speed. Bugno finally bared the secret after he was first over the top in the 1989 Milan-Turin classic but was easily caught by the pack on the

descent. 'A priest in a cassock could have made it down faster than I did,' Bugno admitted. 'I felt so dizzy that I slowed down almost to a stop.'

The trouble was traced to a bad crash in the 1988 Tour of Italy and to a congenital obstruction in the canals of his inner ear. As a cure, Bugno tried ultrasound treatments laced with music. 'I listened to Mozart at different speeds and degrees of loudness for a month,' he explained. 'After that, the vertigo was gone.'

Then he visited an allergist, who discovered that he could not tolerate wheat, milk and milk products. A combination of pills was prescribed and his diet was changed. Afterwards he was put into the hands of Claudio Corti, a veteran Italian rider, who taught Bugno how to take charge of his team. Finally he began seeing a psychologist, who helped resolve Bugno's timidity. This problem was traced back to his childhood, which he had spent with his grandparents in Italy while his parents were working in Switzerland. Bugno was born in Brugg, Switzerland, where his father was a carpenter.

All this took place in the 1989-90 off-season. The rider who had won only the minor Tour of Calabria in 1988, the Tour of the Apennines in 1986, 1987 and 1988 and the semi-classic Tour of Piedmont in 1986 suddenly was storming down the Poggio hill to win Milan-San Remo while other riders took the descent more prudently and slowly.

Chiappucci's rise was just as spectacular. After turning professional with Carrera in 1985, he toiled away as team leaders came and went – Visentini, Roche, Urs Zimmermann, Flavio Giupponi. Never did Chiappucci move into their ranks. 'I'm an attacker,' he likes to boast. 'That's my temperament. But I know what people said about me: I make a lot of noise but I don't win.' Not until 1989 did he record his first victories, in the Coppa Placci and the Tour of Piedmont.

Then, in 1990, at the age of twenty-seven, he exploded: in Paris-Nice, a stage victory and the jersey of the best climber; in the Tour of Italy, twelfth place and another best climber's jersey; in the Tour de France, second place behind Greg LeMond and eight days in the yellow jersey. Coming off the Tour de France, he finished third in the Championship of Zurich and fourth in two more World Cup races, the Wincanton Classic and the Grand Prix of the Americas. From the depths of the computerized standings of the world's top 600 professionals, Chiappucci vaulted to second place.

Revelling in their depth and new-found ambition, major Italian teams had ended years of isolation and begun competing seriously outside the home country. Italians are showing up in force at classics that formerly drew only one or two of their teams. The Tour de France, not the Tour of Italy, became Bugno's prime goal this year as he – and Chiappucci, of course – tried to become the first Italian to win it since Felice Gimondi in 1965. Both of them failed, but not by much in their two-three final rankings.

But every action has a reaction. In a return to the bad old times, Bugno began to complain that the Tour of Italy had become too tough. Now, he said, it sapped the strength of those hoping to use it as a springboard for glory in the Tour de France.

'I think if the Tour of Italy continues to be designed on such hard and selective routes the foreigners will end up not taking part any more,' Bugno complained. 'There can no longer be Tour of Italy-Tour [de France] doubles if our race continues to be so hard.'

He was answered quickly by, of all people, Moser, now a technical consultant to the Tour of Italy's organizers and the man who had toughened its routes in the last few seasons. 'It used to be that the Tour of Italy was just used as practice for the Tour de France,' he said. 'Now it stands for itself as a great race.'

To a slightly lesser extent, that evaluation is also increasingly true of the Tour of Spain, which was first run in

The Picos mountains in northern Spain provide a dramatic backdrop to the 1991 Vuelta de España.

Miguel Induraín, race leader Marco Giovannetti and Pedro Delgado pile on the pressure in the 1990 Tour of Spain.

US victory

The Colorado Classic was a major US stage race from 1975 on. Known as the Red Zinger Classic in its first five years, it steadily attracted bigger and better fields. It became known as the Coors Classic in 1980 and one year later a young professional with the Renault-Gitane team called Greg LeMond outrode the Soviets to score a momentous home victory.

1935, and Spain itself.

Long isolated from the rest of international cycling, Spanish teams broke out in the mid-1980s, a few years before the Italians. The reason was basically political: after the death of Franco and the inward-looking governmental policy he had fostered for decades, Spain became eager to join the rest of Europe. The spark was the emergence of Pedro Delgado as a probable winner of the Tour de France. No matter that he won the Tour of Spain in 1985 and 1989; once again, a country's professional cyclists measured themselves by the Tour of Tours. After his first Tour of Spain victory, Delgado moved to the PDM team in Holland for two years and got that extra polish, finishing second in the Tour de France in 1987, that allowed him to become a top favourite in the Tour when he rejoined the Reynolds team in 1988. He won handily.

If his victory was widely regarded as tainted because he failed a drug test before it was noted that the masking agent for steroids he used was not yet on the banned UCI list, at home there was no stain attached. Thousands of his countrymen flocked to Paris for the end of the Tour, waving the red and yellow Spanish flag on the Champs-Élysées. King Juan Carlos congratulated Delgado

and in his home town of Segovia the parties went on for days.

All of a sudden young Spaniards were as eager to become professional racing cyclists as their fathers had wanted to become bull-fighters. The country's number of teams rose to eleven in 1991, the most in Europe. Of those eleven, Banesto (the successor to Reynolds), ONCE, Clas, Seur and Amaya ranked among the top twenty-five computerized team standings, with Banesto, ONCE and Clas in the top dozen. With the victory of Induraín in the 1991 Tour de France, the sport undoubtedly received another great nudge forward. His was only the fourth Spanish victory in the Tour, after Delgado's, Luis Ocaña's in 1973 and Federico Bahamontes's in 1959.

Bahamontes – the 'Eagle of Toledo', the great climber whose yellow jersey still hangs in the rafters of the cathedral in his home town – was for decades the embodiment of the Spanish rider. He won the polka-dot jersey of the 'King of the Mountains' a record-setting six times in the Tour and was so strong a climber that legend says he once reached a peak in the Pyrenees so far ahead of the pack that he could afford to stop and eat an ice cream. Ocaña gave the sport a different dimension, that of the all-round Spanish rider, powerful in the time trials and on the plains as well as in the mountains.

But the mountains are where the Spanish still shine and the Tour of Spain is made for climbers. The 1991 race, for example, included thirty-four peaks, four of which were rated beyond category in length, steepness and difficulty. The surprise winner was the unproven Melchior Mauri of ONCE, with Induraín a distant second. Mauri handled with equal aplomb the climbing and the often stormy weather of Spain's mountains in May.

Induraín is by now an expert on the distinctions between the Tour of Spain, which he has never won, and the Tour de France, which he has now won three times. 'The pressure is lower away from Spain,' he says. 'And the weather is better. Coming from the north of Spain, I never like it better than when it's hot, like in the Tour. In the Tour of Spain, too often it's rainy or cold. And it isn't my type of race tactically. Too many attacks and surprises. What I really like is that the Tour [de France] is raced at a higher, faster rhythm than the Tour of Spain, faster and more continuous. That suits my style.'

Aside from the Tour de France, all other stage races rank far below the Tour of Spain and the Tour of Italy. Mainly they are used by most professionals as preparation races for a bigger race ahead. Thus the Tour of Switzerland is mountainous and challenging but mainly a springboard for the Tour de France, which follows it by a week to ten days. The Tour of Holland is similarly treated since it is scheduled in mid-August, conveniently ahead of the world championships.

In somewhat the same situation is the Kellogg's Tour of Britain, which celebrated its fifth anniversary in 1991 with a good field of British and European professionals. The five-day race included a flat opening stage and three days of climbs in the Peak District and the Pennines. Starting in Windsor and ending in Leeds, the race attracted such major teams as Panasonic, Tulip, Z, Motorola, Helvetia, Weinmann, Lotto and Clas – many of whose riders had competed two days earlier in Britain in the Wincanton Classic, part of the World Cup series of one-day races.

What lured such strong riders as Z's Robert Millar, a Scotsman, Motorola's Phil Anderson, an Australian, Sean Yates, an Englishman, and Tulip's Allan Peiper, another Australian, was not only the chance to compete before a British crowd but also the opportunity to snaffle the all-important points awarded by the International Federation of Professional Cycling, which is known as the FICP from its initials in French. The Kellogg's awards ninety FICP points to the overall winner, plus fifteen to each stage winner, the same as the Tours of Belgium and Holland although considerably below the 220 to the

Tour of Britain

British professional Joey McLoughlin won the first Kellogg's Tour of Britain in 1987, snatching the lead from Dutchman Steven Rooks after the penultimate stage into Cardiff. The final stage was held in the centre of London, where McLoughlin coolly defended a slender five-second lead over Rooks to win overall.

Lance Armstrong took second place in the Tour DuPont in 1993 to Mexican Raul Alcala. The Texan went on to win a stage in the Tour de France and the world road race championship.

winner and forty to the stage victors in the Tours of Italy and Spain.

In Ireland, the tour of Ireland (formerly the Nissan International Classic), which was not held in 1993 but returned to the calendar in 1994, draws a similar field to the Kellogg's Tour in late September. This time the stage race is often used as a tune-up to the final classics of the season, Italy's Tour of Piedmont and Tour of Lombardy. Crowds are vast and adoring, especially of the Irish stars Sean Kelly and the now retired Stephen Roche, and the organizers are convinced that the race will have value that is sufficiently enduring to outlast their careers.

Similar feelings would be debatable in the United States, where the Tour Du Pont (the successor to the two-year reign of the Tour de Trump) is closely linked to the participation of Lance Armstrong and Greg LeMond. Despite the popularity of cycling as an American recreational sport, road racing is a little-known and less-understood offshoot in the USA.

Perhaps because the 1991 race offered FICP points for the first time and a prize list of $300,000 in cash and merchandise, the Du Pont lured four amateur and eleven professional seven-man teams, including such name riders as Gilles Delion and Gérard Rue of Helvetia, Steve Bauer and Phil Anderson of Motorola, Ronan Pensec of Seur, Erik Breukink and Sean Kelly of PDM, Alexi Grewal and Davis Phinney of Coors Light and LeMond and Atle Kvalsvoll of Z.

'It shows the United States that cycling is truly one of the premier sports in the world,' said Tom Kaplan, the *directeur sportif* of the Spago team, based in America. 'To see these superb athletes in great form only makes our riders work harder to develop to the Europeans' level.'

After a third place in 1990, Breukink won the Du Pont in 1991. 'It's a nice victory because this race is getting tougher every year,' said the Dutchman. 'It's not the Tour de France, the Tour of Italy or Spain, but you can put it just after them.'

Westerdale ford gives the international field a fright in the 1990 Kellogg's Tour of Britain.

Breukink was being courteous. In fact, the Du Pont ranks with such well-organized races as Paris-Nice or the Dauphiné Libéré in France. Both have been run for five decades and include nearly all the great racers on their list of winners. Paris-Nice is nicknamed the 'Race to the Sun' and opens the serious spring season in March; the Dauphiné is usually the mountainous alternative for riders who skip the Tour of Italy.

The Dauphiné was also the setting for one of the great episodes in cycling history, as second-echelon stage races often are. In 1977 the young Bernard Hinault was in the leader's jersey when he opened a gap of more than a minute on his rivals in a descent from the Alps. But Hinault was rolling at such a speed that he was unable to negotiate a curve and, in full view of the television audience, the Frenchman plunged off the road and into a ravine.

'I gave it all I had,' he muttered when he climbed out and was helped back on his bicycle to finish the stage. The next day the weakened Hinault was still in the leader's jersey when he was attacked. He rode with such courage and determination that he preserved his lead, and held it until the

finish of the race. Eddy Merckx, who knew about such things, saluted the twenty-two-year-old Hinault, who was at that time still a year too young to participate in and win the first of his five Tours de France: 'Bernard Hinault has accomplished an exploit. No doubt, he's going to be a great.'

Five victories in the Tour de France, three in the Tour of Italy and one in the Tour of Spain confirmed the wisdom of Merckx's judgement.

The way forward for the national tours is to a large extent determined by the role of the media, particularly television. At present the lesser national tours, such as those of Britain, Ireland and the USA, depend heavily on television coverage. Their organizers need to secure this before they can attract backers and sponsorship. By contrast, the organizers of the Tour de France, and those of Italy and Spain, can choose among potential sponsors, because their greater popular appeal guarantees the keen interest of the television companies. Many cycling fans hope that the television exposure received by the lesser national tours will ensure greater interest and perhaps allow them to share some of the greater freedom enjoyed by the major tours.

Huge crowds turn out for the Nissan International Classic tour of Ireland – many of them hoping to catch a glimpse of their heroes Sean Kelly and Stephen Roche.

Nissan hero

Sean Kelly has won the Nissan Classic four times since the inaugural race in 1985. In that year he came to the race at the height of his powers. Starting in front of his hometown crowd in Carrick-on-Suir, he destroyed the field in the third stage time trial over 13 miles (21km). His time of 24 minutes and nine seconds, at an average speed of 32.42 mph (52.17kph), was the fastest ride ever in a road time trial longer than 20km. Kelly went on to win the race, and again in 1986, 1987 and 1991.

Track racing

The first superstars of cycle racing were track riders. Track racers in Europe and especially the United States were national heroes when the bicycle was an exciting new machine at the end of the nineteenth century. Today, track racing is not so popular, but it remains the most diverse discipline in the whole of cycle sport. **Peter Nye**

W hen bicycle racing was a young and growing sport, racing meant track events. Riders from the USA not only were among the best in the world but America also was where many of the top European and Australian riders for several generations came to compete. A vital venue for racing, known on both sides of the Atlantic as the 'Home of Cycling', was Newark, New Jersey.

New Jersey was home to Arthur Augustus Zimmerman, the first world cycling champion. He grew up in the coastal town of Asbury Park and came of age when bicycles started to capture the public imagination. Zimmerman was called the 'Jersey Skeeter' for his speed on high-ordinary bicycles in the late 1880s. These had no chain or sprocket, which meant the fastest pedaller won. Zimmerman developed exceptional leg speed that worked in his favour when he switched around 1890 to the modern safety bicycle with its chain transmission and wheels of the same size. At the inaugural world cycling championships in August 1893 on a ½-mile (0.8km) dirt track in Chicago, Zimmerman lined up against a dozen finalists. He beat the field in the 1-mile (1.6km)

Left: A paired team perform a hand-sling changeover during a madison chase in the 1993 Ghent Six.
Right: Fred Spencer – an early American racer inspired by track heroes like Zimmerman.

Herne Hill track in South London was the venue for the 1948 Olympics and a big crowd was always guaranteed when track meetings were held.

American challenge

Over the years a steady trickle of track riders from the USA have crossed the Atlantic to pit themselves against the best that Europe has to offer. Jack Heid, a New Yorker, went to London in 1948 for the Olympics and stayed on in Europe, riding for prize money in international track events. A year later he competed in the world championships in Copenhagen and took a fine third place in the amateur sprint. Heid later turned professional and continued to race in Europe until 1951, when he returned to the USA with his Belgian wife.

event, becoming the original world sprint champion.

Zimmerman was twenty-four and already a seasoned veteran. In 1892 he spent the summer competing in England, mostly on London's Herne Hill track. He won a handful of English national championships to go with his American national titles, which included the final US high-ordinary championship. Zimmerman also won dozens of races in France, Germany and Ireland before he returned home for the world championships.

Just like Greg LeMond today, Zimmerman needed considerable time to get into shape, but when he was fit he rose to performances that left the competition behind and held audiences in thrall. Rivals found him a shrewd competitor on the bike, yet relaxed and friendly off it. In the days before radio or television, Zimmerman became a favourite with newspaper and magazine writers. His photo was published regularly – something reserved for distinguished news makers. Zimmerman drew large crowds wherever he went around the USA and abroad, to become America's first superstar athlete.

Most of the action remained in amateur events. Merchandise prizes that he won, such as pianos and braces of horses complete with harness, fre-

quently made officials suspicious that he raced for more than glory. Zimmerman deflected trouble by competing for the influential New York Athletic Club, dedicated to amateur athletics, and he wore their winged-foot trademark on his jersey front to show he was an amateur of good standing.

In 1895 cycling's popularity exploded. Races held on horse-racing tracks across the country verged on making cycling a national pastime. Professional cycling burst wide open. Manufacturers hired pros to compete on their equipment. Promoters offered cash prizes. The money came from customers who lined up to pay so they could see their favourite riders. Zimmerman turned pro, becoming one of 600 American professional riders.

Frenchman Victor Breyer, a founding member of the Union Cycliste Internationale (UCI) and owner of the Buffalo Velodrome in Paris, signed up Zimmerman in 1895 to compete for the season. Zimmerman passed up the world championship in Cologne, which introduced the professional sprint category; R.T.C. Protin of Belgium won over American George Banker. At the end of the season, 'Le Grand Zim' accepted an offer he could not refuse to compete in Australia.

One of the Americans who followed Zimmerman abroad was Charles Murphy of Brooklyn. In 1899 Murphy paced on a carpet of boards laid between railroad tracks behind a New York locomotive to break the minute barrier for the mile (1.6km). That was the year Major Taylor of Indianapolis won the world professional sprint title in Montreal, becoming the first black athlete to cross the colour barrier in professional sports.

Riders from the USA dominated the 1904 world championship held near London. Iver Lawson of Salt Lake City dethroned the formidable Thorvald Ellegaard of Denmark for the world professional sprint championship. The amateur title was gained by Zimmerman's NYAC teammate Marcus Hurley, who edged out defending champion A.L. Reed of England.

In the year Americans did so well at the London world championship, Fred spencer was born in New Jersey. Spencer was eight when the 1912 worlds were held in Newark, near Plainfield where he grew up. This was the second world championship in two decades to be staged in the USA, which reflects the country's stature among cycling nations. Frank Kramer, a local professional and a veteran of European campaigns that included twice winning the prestigious Grand Prix de Paris, fulfilled expectations when he triumphed in the professional sprint championship. Donald MacDougall of Newark won the amateur title.

When the Newark world championship ended, 1904 world track champions Lawson and Hurley joined new world champions Kramer and MacDougall, all dressed in suits and ties, for a group photo taken on the Newark Velodrome's grassy infield. They remain the only US men to win world track championships this century.

Spencer was fifteen and riding a heavy delivery bicycle when two cyclists passed. He chased but could not catch them until they stopped about a mile later. One rider was Australian professional sprint champion Jackie Clark, who introduced himself and his partner, Walter Rutt of Germany, the 1913 world professional sprint champion. They had teamed up for victory in the 1909 six-day race in New York's Madison Square Garden. Teams of two riders alternated, racing for 144 continuous hours. (Madison Square Garden left cycling the legacy of the 'madison', meaning a two-rider team track race.) Teams regularly went more than 2500 miles – farther than the Tour de France, which takes three weeks. Clark and Rutt, with different partners in other years, won three other Garden sixes, which were immensely popular and lucrative. When the First World War broke out in 1914, Rutt was competing in Newark and promptly shipped out to return home. He enlisted in the Kaiser's Army and became a motorcycle messenger. Rutt was wounded in action against the US Allies and was perhaps the only

Black pioneer

Major Taylor was one of the first black athletes to achieve star status in the USA. He was world sprint champion in 1899, broke numerous world records and toured Europe in 1901 attracting much publicity and a wide following. After the boxer, George Dixon, Taylor was only the second black world champion in any sport.

Chris Boardman rocked the cycling world in 1993 when he set new figures for the hour record at the indoor velodrome in Bordeaux. After the world record the Englishman switched his attention to road racing and turned professional for a French team.

German whose hospital convalescence was reported in the US press. After the war he returned to the USA to resume his cycling career.

Cycling was no longer a new toy and its general popularity declined, although the sport thrived in the north-east. A circuit of outdoor wooden velodromes, linked by a network of trains, kept about 100 professional riders competing in eight programmes a week. Bicycle races were lively entertainment. Programmes had a variety of action-filled professional and amateur races, with twenty-four-piece bands playing popular music. During the winter, indoor six-day events kept the riders active and spectators continued to follow the sport.

Spencer was delighted to meet the

British world sprint champion Reg Harris **(left)** and Holland's Arie Van Vliet were regular opponents throughout the 1950s. Van Vliet won the world professional title three times, Harris, four.

famous cyclists. 'I told them I would like to be a bike rider,' recalls Spencer, now in his late eighties and living in New Jersey. 'I said "I would give anything to ride like you fellows".'

Rutt opened a leather tool pouch behind his saddle and pulled out a wrench. He adjusted the handlebars and saddle of Spencer's bicycle and spoke to Clark in French. 'When I asked what he said, Jackie Clark told me he thought I looked like a monkey on a stick.'

Spencer went away inspired. He also met Arthur Zimmerman when both were out riding bicycles. Zimmerman then ran a hotel in Point Pleasant, near Newark. He gave Spencer encouragement, which meant a lot coming from the oracle. Spencer bought a Tribune bicycle, the same make that Murphy rode in his epic mile-a-minute ride, and went to the Newark Velodrome to watch Clark race an evening programme. He stayed around and caught Clark as he left, telling him that he wanted to race.

Clark took Spencer out on training rides to practise sprinting, Clark's speciality. That led to Clark showing up to a Sunday morning 1-mile (1.6km) club race to watch Spencer.

'He knew I had speed and told me he would be standing down the road,' Spencer says. 'He told me, "When you see me, put your head down and go with everything you've got to the tape". I did just the opposite. When the five of us lined up for the start, I took off and kept going. I won and thought I would be congratulated by Jackie Clark. When I came back, he was gone.'

Spencer met up with Clark at the Newark Velodrome, but two weeks passed before Clark finally spoke to him. 'He told me that I rode like a plugger. He said, "Anybody can ride a bicycle, but you've got to get the speed out of it. I'll give you a tip, and I hope you listen. Go to a five-and-ten-cent store and buy a small red rubber ball and cut it in half. Put one half down on the edge of the road and put the centre of the front-wheel valve where the first half is. Then count seventy-seven pedal revolutions and put the other half of the ball down. Go up the road for a quarter mile [0.4km] or half mile [0.8km] and come back riding about five to ten miles an hour [8-16kph]. Talk to yourself. Say you're going to break the spokes, you're going to bend the pedals, you're going to squeeze the handlebars. Anything to get your mind off it. But when you get to that ball, put your head down and go!'"

Clark offered one more piece of advice: 'You must learn to pull the pedals up and push them down at the same time. That way, instead of having two legs, you'll have four.'

This was advice Spencer followed closely. He devoted hours to practising his spring: he pushed hard on the downstroke and pulled on the upstroke to pedal as though he had four legs.

As Spencer worked his way up in the sport, profound changes were taking place that were not readily apparent. Kramer had racked up sixteen consecutive national professional championships year after year, but he finally lost in 1917 to a stocky sprinter from Toronto, Arthur Spencer (unrelated to Fred Spencer). Kramer had been the country's best paid athlete, making more than $20,000 a year. This was when basketball was catching on as a college sport on north-east and Midwest campuses, and major league baseball players were averaging less than half of what Kramer was paid. Arthur Spencer expected that as the new national professional sprint champion he would automatically come into wealth. But the sport's promoter, John M. Chapman, was blunt and told him: 'Who are you? Kramer is the one the fans pay to see.'

Kramer was a resilient competitor and came back over the next five years to win two more national championships. But in 1922, aged forty-two, he announced in the middle of the season that he had had enough. Kramer retired as the reigning national champion.

For more than two decades spectators had turned out in large numbers – 12,500 filled the Newark Velodrome and 20,000 was the seating capacity of the New York City Velodrome – to watch Kramer take on the best in the sport. He competed mostly on wooden tracks, typically measuring six laps to the mile (1.6km), against world champions such as Ellegaard of Denmark, Émile Friol of France, and Bill Bailey of England. Kramer's retirement created a void that race promoter Chapman sought to fill with another American cycling hero.

Chapman was brusque. He ran cycling absolutely, in part to keep the riders in line and prevent race fixing. Chapman, a former professional in Zimmerman's glory days, had a network of European connections to give him the pick of top riders from all over the Continent. Foreign talent helped keep the standard of his races high, but he needed a fast and wily American rider to succeed Kramer and keep spectators coming. Sometimes Chapman's efforts looked desperate. He turned as many as two dozen promising amateurs into professionals – in a single evening's programme. In 1924 Fred Spencer was among the batch of amateurs that Chapman turned professional.

Spencer was adapting to professional cycling. Heeding Clark's advice, he pedalled as though he had four legs and got the speed out of his bicycle. He worked his way up the ranks, learning from European champions who came over to claim their share of the lucrative purses in American track races, a branch of the sport which was booming in the 1920s.

Professional cycling meant more than racing distances between ½ mile (0.8km) and 10 miles (16km), with

Britain has produced a number of world-class pursuiters and Hugh Porter has the best record of all of them, gaining four world titles between 1968 and 1973.

Speed above all

The individual pursuit, over 4000m (4374 yards) is a test of speed and concentration. Riding on opposite sides of the track, two riders set off, each with the aim of gaining an advantage over the other within the set distance. The kilometre (0.6 mile) time trial requires a shorter burst of speed and is held as an individual race against the clock.

Graeme Obree was the sensation of the 1993 track season. The Scot, who took years to perfect his revolutionary riding position, broke the world hour record (updated less than a week later by Chris Boardman) and then obliterated the opposition in the world pursuit championship.

York's sixes, held in Madison Square Garden in March and December, were the race of races, with purses of $50,000 and the best international riders competing in them. Close behind in importance were the Chicago sixes held in Chicago Stadium.

'Even the days before the start were exciting,' says Bill Brennan, whose father, Pop Brennan, was the chief mechanic for Chapman's six-day races. 'The riders would arrive and take their bikes out of the wooden trunks. These were handmade bikes from all over the world, made by the best frame builders. Every bike was always more beautiful than the last one.'

Spencer's trunk bore his name and the word 'Theatrical'. 'That was because the American Express workers who shipped trunks by rail knew that in theatre the show must go on,' Spencer explains. 'No matter what, they would send the trunk on to the next city.'

When the sixes came to town, newspaper reporters wrote about riders like Spencer. His scrapbooks document the voluminous coverage he and other riders attracted. Racers included Gérard Debaetes of Belgium, Charles Lacquehay, Alfred Letourner and Georges Wambast of France, and Gustav Killian and Heinz Vopel of Germany. Radio was a new medium and cyclists were invited to studios for interview broadcasts. Ticket sales were brisk. Spectators by the thousands went to watch cycle racing at its best. Sixes were glamorous.

They were also fiercely competitive. 'I hated them at first,' Spencer admits. 'I didn't want to ride them because if I could make $600 in two minutes riding a match race, why the hell should I ride twenty-four hours for $600? That couldn't sink in my head. These guys from Europe were powerful bike riders. Many a time, my tongue was hanging a foot out of my mouth, and corks were flying out of my rectum. Those European riders would go and go and go and try to wear you down, wear you out. My being a sprinter, it was hard. But I got so I caught on.'

In the March 1925 Madison Square

occasional races of 25 or 50 miles (40 or 80km), on outdoor velodromes from April to September. It also meant the grinding routine of the six-day circuit between November and March, on wooden saucers ten laps to the mile. Fifteen two-rider teams in the sixes were made up mostly of the best foreign riders. Fewer than ten US cyclists received contracts.

'I was very fortunate, out of all the Americans, to be picked,' Spencer says.

Six-day races enjoyed a phenomenal following. Chapman put on sixes in Montreal, Toronto, Cleveland, Pittsburgh, Milwaukee, Buffalo, Indianapolis, St Louis, Kansas City, Chicago and New York City. New

Garden six, Spencer paired with Bobby Walthour Jr, for an impressive victory. It showed Spencer had emerged as the rider Chapman sought. A cyclist Chapman had signed up for that six was the Dutchman Pete Moeskops, who reigned for four years as world sprint champion. Moeskops was lured over with an appearance fee of $10,000 – enough then to buy a three-bedroom home. Moeskops remained in the USA for the season in a attempt to add the American championship to his earlier accomplishments.

One of his first 1-mile (1.6km) match races was against Spencer, at the Newark Velodrome. Moeskops towered over Spencer, 5ft 8in (1.73m) and 145lb (65.8kg). But Spencer won in two straight races for the match. A second Spencer-Moeskops duel followed later, packing the Newark Velodrome. Spencer won again.

Spencer wound up the season as the new American champion. Moeskops went back to Holland impressed enough to prevail on promoters to engage Spencer to race in Europe. He sent Spencer a cable inviting him over.

In October Spencer teamed with Walthour for the Chicago six, their second victory of the year. That generated so much press attention that President Coolidge invited them to the White House in December for a private meeting. (Not until Greg LeMond won the 1986 Tour de France and was invited by President Reagan to Washington did another racing cyclist receive a personal invitation to the Oval Office.) Chapman heaped praise on Spencer for being such a wonderful rider and signed him up with a six-year contract that bound him to Chapman's races in the USA.

Spencer kept taking on the big names in the sport, and in Kramer's tradition kept winning. In the February 1926

Chicago six Spencer teamed with Italy's Franco Giorgetti for another victory. That summer came world sprint champion Ernest Kaufmann of Switzerland.

'Kaufmann rode a big gear,' Spencer recalls. 'I liked guys with a big gear. I would hop around to get in front, slow him down, then jump.' Records show that Spencer beat the Swiss world champion in two straight matches – in Hartford, and again in two straight rides in Newark.

Other riders who came over from Europe were Belgian national champion Alois De Graeve, Italian champions Avanti Moretti and Orlando Piani and Australian champions Harris Horder and Alex McBeath. Spencer accumulated a streak of match race victories that drew crowds to watch him compete against the best. His six-day riding remained consistent. Teamed with Charlie Winters of New York City, he won the December 1927 Garden six, and triumphed at the Garden a year later with Giorgetti.

'Giorgetti had made enough racing here to put $50,000 in the bank when he left to go back to Italy,' Spencer says. 'Later he came back and told me that when he went home his money was confiscated by Mussolini.'

In 1928 Spencer broke Kramer's world record for the ½ mile (0.8km), in 52.6 seconds, at Newark. He won his second national championship. At

The Hour

In 1993, nine years after Francesco Moser set figures of 51.151km for the hour record, two Britons shocked the cycling world by both attacking and bettering Moser's old record. Scot Graeme Obree was the first to update the figures, covering 51.596km at the indoor velodrome at Hamar, Norway. Six days later his great rival, England's Chris Boardman, went even further, recording 52.270km at Bordeaux Lac velodrome in France.

British pairing Spencer Wingrave and Tony Doyle during the 1993 Ghent Six. Doyle, twice the world pursuit champion during the Eighties, is the UK's most successful six-day racer.

Chapman's suggestion, Kramer went to Geneva to use his connections to persuade the Union Cycliste Internationale to award the 1929 world championship to Newark.

Moeskops returned to America, but for no apparent reason ignored Spencer. 'I couldn't figure it out,' Spencer says. 'So I asked Pete what was

Patrick Sercu (top) has the best record for a six-day racer, with eighty-eight wins to his name.

going on. He was mad that I never acknowledged his cable. I asked him, "What cable?" It turned out that he sent it to the National Cycling Association office, where Mr Chapman got it. Mr Chapman never told me about the cable. Instead, he signed me up for six years here in America. When I finally asked him about it, he said if I went to Europe it would be like taking Babe Ruth from the New York Yankees line-up. Pete and I got it straightened out between us and became friends again.'

Spencer's domestic tie was less an issue with the 1929 world championship set for Newark. But Chapman, an autocratic man who had put the 1912 championship together, had fallen behind cycling developments. UCI offi-

cials baulked when Chapman refused to acknowledge road events. The 1929 world championship went to Zurich.

Records show that Spencer set four world records that year, from 10 miles (16km) (19:24.4) to 25 miles (40km) (49:28.6). He also captured his third national title. By the following year Spencer had won sixty-five straight matches, taking on the best riders from North America, Europe and Australia. 'Mr Chapman decided there was nobody left for me to race against, so in the outdoor season he switched me to motor-paced racing.'

Chapman's confrontation with the UCI drastically undercut his stature in international cycling. At the same time the first effects of the Depression were being felt. Velodromes such as Newark's went out of business. American cycling went into a downward spiral. European tracks increased in importance.

Throughout the Depression six-day races kept cycling alive in North America. This was partly because, for the price of admission, a ticket holder could stay for the entire event and take shelter in the warmth of the venues where the sixes were held. In the December 1932 Madison Square Garden six, Spencer teamed with Canada's Torchy Peden to win his sixth six-day.

'My contracts stayed the same during the Depression, but I was getting paid in cash and IOUs,' Spencer recalls. 'People were staying home. As the Depression went on, my IOUs went up and my cash payments went down. I retired in 1938 when I got more IOUs than cash. I completed 99 of the 102 six-days I entered. Those six-days were too damned hard to ride for no money.'

Soon came the outbreak of the Second World War, which ended transatlantic commuting for athletes. Europe became the home of cycling.

A unique track star who kept his winning form to bridge the war years was Jef Scherens of Belgium. At the 1932 world championship in Rome, Scherens took the title from Lucien Michard of France, who had won four professional sprint championships. Scherens had such quick acceleration that he was called 'The Cat'. He was in high demand and often travelled to races by plane at a time when air travel was less common than today.

Scherens was a pure sprinter. He did not get involved in six-day racing. Year after year as he won world championships, the King of Belgium invited him to Brussels for ticker-tape parades. He was the toast of the nation.

The Dutchman Arie Van Vliet finally dethroned Scherens at the 1938 world championship in Amsterdam. Van Vliet, the 1936 Olympic gold medallist in the 1000-m time trial and silver medallist in the match sprints, was a brash young professional. Soon his career and everyone else's was caught in the vortex that led to the Second World War.

Not until 1946 was the world championship resumed, in Zurich. Van Vliet won a bronze medal while Jan Derksen of the Netherlands took the gold from Georges Senfftleben of France. Scherens came back in 1947 at the Paris world championship to defeat Louis Gérardin of France and win his seventh professional sprint title. That eclipsed the six that Ellegaard won between 1901 and 1911. It is open to speculation how many titles Scherens may have garnered if the war had not interrupted his career.

The same question applies also to Van Vliet, sometimes called 'Professor' because he was unusual in wearing spectacles. Van Vliet won world championships again in 1948 in Amsterdam and in 1953 in Zurich.

The post-war years also marked a major transition in cycling, with road races overtaking track races in importance. Road and track overlapped when the Tour de France resumed in 1947 after an eight-year hiatus and finished at Paris's Parc des Princes. The velodrome was packed with 35,000 spectators; they were there more because they wanted to see the road race conclude than to watch the track events earlier in the day.

Track stars such as England's Reg Harris enjoyed the twilight of track racing. Harris won the world professional championship from 1949 to 1951 and triumphed again in 1954. In England, he was a national hero. His likeness was duplicated in a wax statue, complete with the world champion's rainbow jersey, in Madame Tussaud's museum in London.

Italy's Antonio Maspes remains one of the last major-league sprinters in Europe, winning seven world professional championships between 1955 in Milan and 1964 in Paris. This magnificent tally matched the record of the legendary Scherens.

By the mid 1970s, however, racing on the roads eclipsed the tracks. Velodromes that had routinely packed the stands for decades were vacant and torn down, including the venerable Parc des Princes. In 1975 the Tour de France broke its long-standing tradition and left the track altogether to finish on the Champs-Élysées. Now more than 500,000 spectators line the boulevard to watch the event conclude.

Road races took over from the track everywhere but Japan, where Keirin racing thrives on cement velodromes. Japan emerged as the world power in 1977 when Koichi Nakano decisively won the world professional sprint championship in San Cristobal, Venezuela. He took an all comers at the championship. In 1986 the USA finally hosted another world championship, in Colorado Springs. There Nakano won his tenth title.

The renewed popularity of cycling, especially in the USA and throughout Europe, is helping to revive the reputations of track racers of the past, from Maspes and Scherens all the way back to Arthur Zimmerman. They laid the foundation of the sport and led the way for today's competitive cyclists.

Women's events

Female racers compete in three disciplines at the world track championships: the sprint, points race and pursuit. The points race is the newest event of the three – it was introduced in 1988 at the world championship in Ghent, Belgium, where Welsh rider Sally Hodge became the first British world champion since Mandy Jones took the road title in 1982.

Francesco Moser was a great all-round track rider. The former world pursuit champion and ex-hour record holder made a one-off comeback in 1994, on the same track on which he broke the hour record in 1984.

Mountain -bike racing

From innocent beginnings involving a group of friends who wanted to try the cycling equivalent of downhill skiing, mountain biking has grown into a sport with its own world championship and top-class competitors. Mike Kloser

M ountain biking started in Marin County, California, with riders such as Gary Fisher, Jow Breeze, Charlie Kelly, Tom Ritchey and many more of their cronies. These founder members of mountain biking began racing down Mount Tam, just north of San Francisco and across from the Golden Gate. They would race from the top, right down into the valley – a descent of about 2000ft (610m). This required bicycles that could handle off-road terrain and the only bikes around at the time suited to such riding were the 'clunker' type, made by Schwinn and other large manufacturers. These bikes had fat 'balloon' tyres, which were adequate at the time, and pedal brakes in the hubs, with an extra BMX brake bolted on for additional stopping power.

What the pioneers of mountain biking discovered at this early stage was that this type of riding was a lot of fun but the bikes they were using did not last for long over rough terrain. One of the biggest problems was the brakes, which soon wore

Left: Ruthie Matthes of the USA is a top-class road racer as well as the 1991 women's world champion.
Right: John Tomac wears the rainbow jersey of world champion at the 1991 venue of Il Ciocco, Italy.

heavier. As the mountain bike evolved, the founders decided it would be fun to ride the bikes to the top of the mountains instead of loading them into a car for the trip. This was when the demand for gearing arose and there were soon modified three-speed, ten-speed and twelve-speed machines on the off-road tracks. As the bikes became more and more specialized it was decided to go one step further and build frames to match all the new components and accessories. At the same time the sport started to gain in popularity as more and more people saw the trail-riding pioneers. Magazines started to write about the phenomenon and within a couple of years mountain bikes were being mass-produced by companies such as Specialized, one of the first mass producers of the off-road bike.

Competition began to grow quickly and events were on a larger scale than the original Mount Tam races on 'clunker' bikes. It was the early 1980s when mountain biking really began to take off in the USA. Some of the early and more popular races

World champion in 1990, Julie Furtado of the USA became the first-ever woman to hold an officially sanctioned world mountain-bike title.

out when used constantly on steep descents. One of the famous descents in those days was called 'Repack Downhill' because after each downhill race the riders would have to repack the wheel bearings, owing to overheating caused by the hub brakes.

In time the bikes were modified with motorcycle parts, becoming heavier and

were the Whiskey Town and the Rock Hopper. Both were held in northern California.

More mountain bike manufacturers sprang up. Companies could see the potential of the mountain bike and formerly road-oriented manufacturers such as Schwinn and Trek became interested in the mountain bike. NORBA (National

Off-Road Bike Association) and similar bodies began organizing and promoting racing events throughout the country, mainly in California and Colorado. Europe did not catch on until around 1983, when Peugeot and a few others saw the possibilities and began building bikes resembling those from the USA.

As for mountain-bike racing in Europe, not much existed during the early development of the US racing scene. The USA held its first national championship in 1983, but once mountain biking was introduced to Europe it met with an enthusiastic response and on both continents it is now immensely popular. Racing has continued to grow in the USA and American riders are a force to be reckoned with internationally.

Mountain-bike races originally consisted of long cross-country courses over which the racers had to be totally self-sufficient, and apart from a few food and drink stations no outside help was allowed. Team managers and support crews were virtually non-existent. Each racer depended solely on himself and his equipment; that was the spirit of the sport and what separated it from other branches of traditional cycling.

As the sport has grown in stature, some of the bigger sponsors have highlighted the need for television coverage. Television producers have in turn put pressure on race organizers to design shorter circuits where the competitors do more laps, spectators have better access to all parts of the course and cameras can take in more of the action. This is fine for television and the sponsor, but the purist mountain-bike racers seem to prefer long, point-to-point cross-country races.

Once mountain-bike racing began to escalate in Europe many countries started their own national, world cup and world championship series. The USA held its first world championship at Mammoth, California in 1987 and for the next three years Mammoth hosted it unofficially. Also in 1987, France held Europe's first unofficial world championship. In 1988 it was held in Switzerland and in 1989 in Belgium.

John Tomac has the essential qualities of a great mountain biker – he is strong, fearless and extremely skilful.

Author Mike Kloser pushes his bike up a steep incline. Mountain bikes are difficult to carry and riders will often push, rather than carry them up hills.

Then, in 1990, UCI (Union Cycliste Internationale), FIAC (Fédération Internationale Amateur de Cyclisme) and USCF (United States Cycling Federation) came together to form the first unified official world championship in Durango, Colorado. The following year the world championship was held in Il Ciocco, Italy.

The World Cup started in 1988 and was sponsored by Grundig Electronics of Germany, which still sponsors the series today. For three years it was the unofficial world cup, then in 1991 UCI and FIAC recognized it as an unofficial world cup complying with the international rules for mountain-bike racing. In 1991 the World Cup comprised nine events in Europe and North America.

Mountain-bike racing has picked up a lot of cyclists from different areas of cycling. In the USA, for example, some of the early converts were from BMX racing. Cyclo-cross has also been a popular recruiting ground for mountain-bike racing in the summer. In Europe mountain biking has attracted many cyclo-cross racers. Riders who come from the road find mountain-bike racing very different and seem to do quite well once they pick up the bike-handling skills that are needed for off-road racing.

So competitive is mountain-bike racing that new challengers are emerging at a frightening rate. No longer do one or two riders dominate most of the races. Indeed, to finish in the top ten or fifteen in a major race is an achievement. In a World Cup race in Europe all the top cyclists show up and there is a dog fight to get a good position after the starting flag has dropped. Starts are so critical now, and unless a rider has a good start he has to make a huge effort to get near to the front before the leaders disappear. If the course is narrow just after the start then positioning is even more crucial. In order to preserve the spirit of a mountain-bike course, with some single-track and technical sections, fields should be limited to 100 riders or even fewer.

In the USA I prefer racing in

Colorado or on mountainous terrain to anywhere else. I also like racing on the east coast, because there is usually a lot of mud and technical sections. With the dryness typical of the west, especially California, you rarely get a good muddy race. Racing in the mud brings a whole new element into the strategy of a race – it requires skills that are not called for in many races. I enjoy racing in Europe, especially the races that lend themselves to true mountain-bike courses. Some European courses are so extreme that it is hard to compare them to any course in the USA. But at the other end of the scale there are some that are like a small circuit, criterium or cyclo-cross-style course laid out around a city park.

The Swiss and French tend to lay out and organize extreme, difficult and technically challenging courses. In many cases, there is a lot of running and carrying of the bike. In general, those nations plan the courses very well. Italian courses vary considerably, but there have been some great races in Italy. As for my favourite courses in Europe, I liked best the World Cup

World Junior champion in 1991, John Mutolo battles up a climb on Italy's dusty Il Ciocco course.

races of the last two years that were held in Switzerland, specifically the Château d'Oex course (once the cattle gates were opened) and the Lenzerheide course. There is another race in the Swiss Alps called the Verbier-Gremenze, a place-to-place

The first VCI-recognized world mountain-bike champion, US evergreen Ned Overend, who was thirty-five when he took the title in Durango, USA.

Championship events are often held in ski resorts where the riders use whatever means are available to reach the start!

extremely technical and at times very exposed and dangerous. There is also about 6-9 miles (10-15km) of steep climbing and lots of running with the bike. I only raced it once and failed to finish, because my bike broke. The race took five and a half to six hours for the winner, who averaged about 9mph (15kph) – not exactly a record-breaking speed.

It would be good to have a big stage race in Europe, along the lines of the Tour of the Rockies, which was held in Vail, Colorado, in 1988. It should be seven or nine stages, run along similar lines to a road stage race but all off-road. In Europe, the Trans Maurienne rally is perhaps closest to this ideal. Held over four to five days, across the Maurienne mountains in the south of France, it had, however, too many stages per day and the stages were too short. Eventually there should be more stage races but it could take some time because at the moment much importance is placed on national championship series, the World Cup and the world championships.

Prize money in mountain-bike racing has steadily increased over the years and continues to do so at an encouraging rate, although it is not as high as in tennis or golf. Big money races in the USA, such as the Ride of Your Life, the O'Neil Race and the 1990 Mammoth race, have offered $10,000 for the winner and reasonable money for the top ten riders. The 1992 World Cup had a $15,000 purse per event, split between the men and the women.

My most memorable race was the unofficial world championship in Switzerland in 1988. It was one of those days when my preparation was right and my form was good. As usual I started from the back of the pack on the Crans Montana course. At that time I don't think there was a better field of racers. A few of the top American riders were missing but the two best were there: John Tomac and Ned Overend. I came out on top. I believe I was the true world champion that day and I hope I have a few more days like that before I stop racing.

event between the two towns that takes about seven hours to complete. It covers several mountain passes and is an extremely tough challenge. The women's race takes about five hours.

The race in Aviemore, Scotland, is a real classic: a total of 40 miles (65km) over three large loops taking approximately one hour a lap to complete. Aviemore is unique, and may in some ways be compared to the Paris-Roubaix classic road race. At Aviemore you are out there battling with the elements and dealing with the extremes of mud, heat, very deep cold-water crossings and a very difficult climb each loop.

Another extreme race is held at the Transvésubienne course in the south of France. It is about 37 miles (60km) long with probably 19-25 miles (30-40km) of downhill racing. The descents are

Some people say that mountain-bike racing is a fad, like BMX racing. But the numbers of people riding and of bikes sold continue to grow, as does interest in this kind of racing, and there is no reason why it should not last as long as road racing has done. In the USA mountain-bike racing is already overtaking road racing as the most popular form of bicycle sport. The mountain bike has also boosted the bike industry in general and contributed greatly to the advance of bicycle technology. In particular, innovations pioneered by the mountain bike have had a knock-on effect on the road world and now virtually every professional racer uses a 'click' shift gear-changing system. Also, a mountain bike with front and rear suspension weighing less than 20lb (9kg) has already been developed – who knows where that might lead?

Every year, the calibre of riders at the world championships goes up a notch, especially in Europe where more and more cyclo-cross racers and road racers are turning to mountain-bike racing. At the 1991 world champ-

German cyclo-cross and mountain-bike star Mike Kluge negotiates the river crossing in the Scottish round of the Grundig series.

ionships in Il Ciocco, Italy, Motorola professional John Tomac, who had raced a full season on the road till then, won the cross-country event and another US all-rounder, Ruthie Matthes, won the women's cross-country title. A year before, Matthes had finished second in the world championship road race in Japan. Winner of the veteran women's title was Maria Canins, 1985 and 1986 Tour de France Féminin winner and 1988 gold medallist in the world championship team time trial. At

Fierce competition and beautiful settings have attracted increasing numbers to mountain-bike racing in recent years.

forty-two she was competing in only her eighth mountain-bike race and was delighted to have won an individual gold medal at world championship level.

Other top road racers who competed at the 1991 women's world championship included Eva Orvosova, Czechoslovakia's number one rider, who became the first eastern bloc rider to win a medal (silver) in the world championship, and Canadian Alison Sydor, bronze medallist in the world road championships in Stuttgart just over a month before Il Ciocco. No one at Il Ciocco could have failed to be impressed by the level of competition

and organization that went into the championship series. Even Gino Bartali and Felice Gimondi, two of Italy's greatest champions sanctioned the events, proof, if it was ever needed, that the cycling establishment of Italy approved of this exciting new sport.

The main results for the 1990, 1991, 1992 and 1993 world mountain bike championships are given below.

1990

MEN'S CROSS-COUNTRY
Ned Overend (USA)
2:28:31

WOMEN'S CROSS-COUNTRY
Julie Furtado (USA)
2:9:27

MEN'S DOWNHILL
Greg Herbold (USA)
6:37.7

WOMEN'S DOWNHILL
Cindy Devine (Canada)
7:34.3

JUNIOR MEN'S CROSS-COUNTRY
Jimi Killen (USA)
1:59:10

JUNIOR WOMEN'S CROSS-COUNTRY
Jersey not awarded owing to insufficient entrants.

1991

MEN'S CROSS-COUNTRY
John Tomac (USA)
2:38:56

WOMEN'S CROSS-COUNTRY
Ruthie Matthes (USA)
2:20:2

MEN'S DOWNHILL
Albert Itten (Switzerland)
7:11.3

WOMEN'S DOWNHILL
Giovanna Bonazzi (Italy)
8:4.3

JUNIOR MEN'S CROSS-COUNTRY
John Mutolo (USA)
1:23:9

JUNIOR WOMEN'S CROSS-COUNTRY
Karin Romer (Germany)
1:52:29

1992

MEN'S CROSS-COUNTRY
Henrik Djernis (Denmark)
2:41:06

WOMEN'S CROSS-COUNTRY
Silvia Furst (Switzerland)
2:00:25

MEN'S DOWNHILL
Dave Cullinan (USA)
4:28

WOMEN'S DOWNHILL
Julie Furtado (USA)
5:09

JUNIOR MEN'S CROSS-COUNTRY
Jeff Osguthorp (USA)
2:30:38

JUNIOR WOMEN'S CROSS-COUNTRY
Rita Burgi (Switzerland)
1:42:04

1993

MEN'S CROSS-COUNTRY
Henrik Djernis (Denmark)
2:56:53

WOMEN'S CROSS-COUNTRY
Paolo Pezzo (Italy)
2:43:4

MEN'S DOWNHILL
Mike King (USA)
4:44.05

WOMEN'S DOWNHILL
Giovanna Bonazzi (Italy)
5:34.09

JUNIOR MEN'S CROSS-COUNTRY
Dario Acquaroli (Italy)
1:35:26

JUNIOR WOMEN'S CROSS-COUNTRY
Karin Romer (Germany) 57:53

Tim Gould is one of Britain's best mountain bikers. He is pictured in the 1991 world championship in Italy, in which he finished a disappointed sixth.

Since 1990 when the world championship was officially recognized, mountain bikers from all around the world have gathered for the title race weekend, hoping to achieve fame and fortune, and the opportunity to wear the coveted rainbow jersey for a year.

In 1992, at the start of the season, Greg LeMond announced that the world championship cross-country race was on his provisional programme for the year. Other road stars have also expressed an interest and this can only be good for mountain biking, which becomes ever more organized.

Cyclo-cross

From its origins as a diverting way to pass the time and keep fit in leafy surroundings, cyclo-cross has grown to become cycling's most popular winter discipline. It combines a wide range of skills and a level of fitness that many road-racing cyclists find invaluable. **Noel Truyers**

Winter creates big problems for the cyclist who wants to go out for a daily ride but finds that is not always possible. When the roads are covered with snow and it is slippery, going out on a bike is dangerous. Finding an alternative form of winter cycling that provides exercise and prevents weight gain is not easy, and it is a shame that more cyclists do not consider the great sport of cyclo-cross. All you need is a park, a forest or a grassy area.

Basically cyclo-cross is a kind of cross-country race on bicycles. Seven-times world champion Eric de Vlaeminck of Belgium describes his favourite sport this way: 'First there is nature. I still love riding through the fields and the forests and enjoy the silence around me. Then there is the mud, the sand, the short and steep climbs. They keep up your strength. There is the riding and running on small, narrow and winding forest or meadow roads – perfect for endurance, skill and suppleness.'

For decades racing cyclists all over Europe used cyclo-cross as the perfect way to get into shape for the road season. The sport was tolerated because of this; if it had not been for the training element, cyclo-cross could not have justified its existence. But the origins of cyclo-cross have nothing to do with road racing at all. The sport has its origins in France at the beginning of the century. In 1900 a private in the French army, Daniel

Cyclo-cross courses include sections where the riders must shoulder their bikes. A nimble and sure-footed style is essential, especially in slippery conditions as experienced by competitors in the 1985 world championship in Munich. On the far left is Adri Van Der Poel, five times a world silver medallist.

Roadman and cyclo-cross racer Jean Robic of France was the winner of the first cyclo-cross world championship in 1950. Three years before, he had won the Tour de France.

Gousseau, was a member of the cyclists' division on manoeuvres with his company, led by General Bonal. Bonal and Gousseau had one thing in common: they both loved nature. Bonal rode through the fields and forests on horseback and Gousseau did the same on his bike. Gousseau was able to keep up with the general and was so excited by this that he asked his friends to join him on short rides.

'Riding a bike in the forest is even more interesting than riding on the road,' said Gousseau. He was a member of the French Cycling Federation, so the instinct to race was there and those short rides soon became real races. Gousseau's enthusiasm affected his colleagues at the federation so much that he was given the

opportunity to organize the first French cyclo-cross championship on 16 March 1902. But Gousseau did not win; that privilege went to Ferdinand de Baeder.

The new sport was not very popular with the many riders who, then as today, were put off by the muddy image. It was a struggle to survive in those early days but that changed in 1907 when Octave Lapize won the French championship. Three years later Lapize won the Tour de France and said: 'My cyclo-cross activities during the winter helped me a lot.' From that day on his example was followed. He had shown cyclists a new way to get into shape. One interesting development was that Lapize was the first cyclo-cross rider to put his bike on his shoulder when he had to climb a hill or run for a considerable distance.

In 1908 cyclo-cross began to spread slowly throughout Europe. Belgium was the second country to organize an annual national championship and Philippe Thijs was the first winner, in 1910. Thijs was another great roadman and his three wins in the Tour de France in 1913, 1914 and 1920 gave cyclo-cross another boost. Other countries followed with their own national championships: Switzerland in 1912; Luxemburg 1923; Poland 1928; Spain 1929; Italy 1930; Czechoslovakia 1952; East Germany 1953; Great Britain and West Germany 1955; Austria 1962; Holland 1963; Denmark 1970; Portugal 1980. However, these dates reveal how slow the international growth of the sport has been.

In the USA cyclo-cross made a similarly cautious debut in 1975, when the first senior national championship was won by Lawrence Malone. The popularity of the sport varied widely across the country, and although sizeable fields have contested the national championships since 1975, most of the riders come from California, Colorado, Oregon, Washington State and Massachusetts. Clark Natwick won in 1976 and again in 1981, 1982 and 1986. Natwick, later a team manager for the Ritchey mountain-bike team and the national cyclo-cross squad, has witnessed the slow development of the sport in the USA: 'There are still only a handful of cyclo-cross specialists. The States are so broad that interest varies from region to region. Mountain biking has its own identity – there is very little cross-over between the two, although cyclo-cross riders have always done well in mountain-bike races. In the early 1980s Steve Tilford was first in the American mountain-bike championships and cyclo-cross champion at the same time.'

A lack of funding from the national body, because cyclo-cross is not an Olympic sport, has also handicapped the USA's fortunes in Europe. Joe Ryan put up the best performance to date, when he finished in the top twenty at the amateur world championships in Saccolongo in 1979. Italian Vito di Tano, a master in the mud, had a field day on a course turned into a quagmire after heavy rain. But there is one facet of cyclo-cross where America leads the world. Every year since 1975 women have competed for their own national championship. Early stars were Mary Allan and Elizabeth Chapman. Lisa Muhich in the senior women and Don Myrah are currently the top performers on the US cyclo-cross scene.

Germany's Rolf Wolfshohl was another useful roadman who was able to perform at the top level in cyclo-cross. He won the world championships three times, in 1960-61 and 1963.

Eric de Vlaeminck won the world cyclo-cross championships a record seven times. He won his first title in 1966, and in the years that followed few could match the Belgian's acrobatic style and superb fitness.

Lawrence Malone, several times a national champion, with international class, ranks as the doyen of US cyclo-cross, according to Natwick: 'He lives in Albuquerque, New Mexico, nowadays. He has his own catering business but he still likes to race, more at a recreational level. In 1990, in his late thirties, he rode the veterans' championship and dominated it. Then he rode the senior race and took the bronze medal.'

The first international cyclo-cross race was held in 1924. For twenty-five years this 'Critérium International de Cyclo-Cross' was held in the Malmaison Forest, west of Paris. Because it took place in March, on the eve of the new road season, it became the first event of

the year in which many of the top roadmen came together. The Critérium International became so important that in 1950 it became the first venue for the inaugural cyclo-cross world championship. Professionals and amateurs rode together and victory went to Frenchman Jean Robic, a tough little professional who three years earlier had won the Tour de France. It was not until 1967 that the two categories were awarded separate world titles. In Zurich Italy's Renato Longo became the first professional world champion and Frenchman Michel Pelchat the amateur title holder. From 1976 junior riders were given the opportunity to ride internationally and in the same year the

first European championship was held, followed a year later by the first junior world championship. Both races were won by the German Ralf Wincke.

Despite a steady increase in international racing the sport had to wait until the 1980s before gaining full support and recognition. To a large extent this was thanks to the launch, in the winter of 1982-3, of the season-long Super Prestige Series of races. At that time there were so many cyclo-cross events all over Europe that spectators rarely got the chance to see all the big names racing together. In response to this situation, the organizers of the four big Belgian events started a classification system, attracted some big prizes and offered contracts to entice the best riders. It was an instant success and nine years later the series included four races in Belgium, two in Holland and Switzerland and one in Spain, Italy and France. The Super Prestige Series has become so important that it is the thread that runs right through the winter cyclo-cross season.

More than forty years of world championships have created a long list of great champions and the rider with the greatest haul of medals is the German Rolf Wolfshohl. As well as fourteen national titles he collected three gold medals (1960, 1961 and 1963), five silver and four bronze. Although Wolfshohl was only twenty-one when he pulled on his first rainbow jersey in cyclo-cross, he decided to follow another career path after 1963. 'I had no choice,' he said in those days. 'I loved the sport, but I couldn't make a living out of it. I was well paid but there weren't enough races. So I had to ride on the road more and more. The reality is that you cannot reach the top in both disciplines – you have got to make a choice – so I changed direction.'

Wolfshohl was a fighter and that mentality paid off for him. In 1965 he won the Tour of Spain, in 1968 he wore the yellow jersey in the Tour de France, eventually finishing sixth overall. He won Tour stages in 1967 and 1970 and although he retired from

racing in 1975 he is still involved in the sport as the German cyclo-cross coach. He owns a bike shop, has his own bike company and a son, Rolf-Dieter, whose promising amateur career was cut short by a terrible accident that left him in a wheelchair.

The Frenchman André Dufraisse is another big name in cyclo-cross. He won eleven world championship medals, taking the world title five times (1954-8) and being runner-up twice and bronze medallist four times. Italy had Renato Longo, who won the world championship five times between 1959 and 1967, the silver twice (1961 and 1963) and the bronze in 1969. After twelve national titles he finished his career at the end of 1972, aged thirty-five. Tall, an excellent runner and very acrobatic, Longo was nevertheless rather frail.

Although cyclo-cross started in

Albert Zweifel was the first cyclo-cross superstar from Switzerland. He won five world titles in all, taking his first at Chazay d'Azergues in 1976.

with his long list of victories but with his spectacular way of racing. He was an explosive rider, who jumped over obstacles, loved the smaller gears and adored the faster circuits, although his numerous successes proved he could tackle any course. Despite a brilliant career De Vlaeminck did not make a fortune. In fact his life went to pieces, for he was involved in a drug scandal and then cured in an institution, before getting divorced and remarrying. When his career ended in 1980 he found himself a job as a construction worker until the Belgian Cycling Federation made him its national cyclo-cross coach. De Vlaeminck's son Geert also turned professional as a cyclo-cross rider but he lacked the qualities of his father.

Belgium did not have to wait long after the demise of Eric de Vlaeminck for along came another superstar, Roland Liboton, possibly the greatest rider cyclo-cross has ever had. Unfortunately much of this talent was wasted, as Liboton did not have the

Artificial wooden hurdles are placed on a course to make the riders dismount and jump over them. Some riders have other ideas, however, and one of them, Belgian Danny de Bie, successfully 'bunny hopped' his way to a world title in 1989.

France, Belgian riders have often led the field internationally. Foremost among them is Eric de Vlaeminck, who was world champion seven times between 1966 and 1973. He started to ride cyclo-cross on the same day that the track in nearby Ghent was destroyed by a fire. His brother Roger, known as a very good road racer, was also a useful off-road man who won the amateur title in 1968 and the professional title in 1975. But it was Eric who captured the fans' hearts, not just

right mentality to live for his sport the way he should have done. Even so, he won eleven national titles and the amateur world title in 1978, and was four times world professional champion between 1980 and 1984. Liboton was strong, less spectacular than Eric de Vlaeminck, but he had a winner's spirit that also brought him three Super Prestige Series wins. After his last major victory, in 1988, Liboton's career went downhill and at thirty-one he stopped taking care of himself. He had made a lot of money but could not handle the luxury. Having prepared badly during the summer road season, he failed in the winter.

The first cyclo-cross racer to earn large amounts of money was Albert Zweifel, a tall, red-haired Swiss rider who won eight national titles and was the world champion in the four years 1976-9. He also won three silver medals and two bronzes. Zweifel was more strong than acrobatic and he was a better runner than pedaller. He loved the mud and the sand.

Cyclo-cross has its own rules, laid down in 1988 by FIAC and the International Amateur Cycling Federation. The basic rules are as follows. A professional cyclo-cross race should last about one hour, and 40 minutes for juniors. One lap of the circuit should not be longer than 3km (1.9 miles) with a maximum difference in height of 30m (98ft) to ensure safe descents. The riders should get off their bikes between four and six times during a lap but they should not be running for more than ten per cent of the total distance. Hard-riding sections and man-made obstacles such as low hurdles may be permitted. Ploughed fields may not be included.

Cyclo-cross is a very fair sport. The strongest rider wins, and the tactics are therefore simple. Team tactics hardly ever play a part – individual fitness is paramount. Eric de Vlaeminck explains: 'The basis of a good winter season is the work you put in during the summer. A good road rider prepares his season

in the winter. The opposite is true for a rider who wishes to concentrate exclusively on cyclo-cross. The season finishes in February and I advise riders to take three weeks off. At the beginning of March the time has come to start work on your general fitness by doing some running or gymnastics. From early May, training on the road is essential, first to build endurance, then strength and then resistance. In June it is time to do some road racing and in August specific cyclo-cross training must begin. You should run twice a week, a maximum of two hours, train

Mike Kluge of Germany is a top performer in both mountain bike racing and cyclo-cross. He is one of a growing number of professionals who race all year round in off-road competition.

Two competitors cross paths in the arduous Three Peaks cyclo-cross in the north of England.

Cyclo-cross marathon

The Three Peaks cyclo-cross is always the first major event of the British cyclo-cross season and it is one of the toughest challenges the brave competitors will face all season. Started in 1960, the race takes the riders over three small mountains in the Yorkshire Dales: Ingleborough, Whernside and Pen-y-Ghent. In 1991 the winner Nicky Craig covered the 35- mile (56km) course in 3 hours, 13 minutes – more than 6 minutes ahead of the second-placed rider.

with the bike off-road, and concentrate on improving your speed. The worst thing for a cyclo-cross rider is to lose his speed.'

But it is not just fitness that decides the outcome of a race. Technical competence and skill also determine who will win and who will lose. Because a cyclo-cross race is short, the consequences of a mistake can be severe. De Vlaeminck explains: 'The climbs on a circuit are the most important part and that is where you can gain quite an advantage. It is important to know some time before the climb which gear you are going to use – changing gear on the hill is dangerous and you lose too much speed doing it. It can only be done when your approach speed is too high to use a smaller gear at the bottom. On the hill never push your weight to the front; sit towards the back of the saddle and put your hands on the tops of the bars to stop the front wheel digging into the sand or mud. If the speed keeps going down you have to decide when to get off and run with the bike over your shoulder. Experience will teach you the best

moment. On the descent do not put your weight over the front wheel, nor over the back, but in the centre. Descending is a matter of guts and nerve – only use the brakes when absolutely necessary and then only the back brake. Hesitation kills your chances, and wrong decisions invariably destroy winning chances.

'A very important part of cyclo-cross is getting on and off your bike, but do not forget that you always go faster on than off the bike. Choose the right moment, put the bike into the gear you are going to use after the obstacle and push the pedals a few times to make sure everything is okay, put your hand on the brakes and your right leg over the saddle, while at the same time grabbing the top or down tube with your right hand. As the obstacle approaches jump off, take a few steps over it, lifting the bike with your right hand, and jump back on again in one movement.'

To carry the bike you must dismount in the same way and lift the machine onto your shoulder, with the top tube resting along the top of your shoulder and the seat tube down your back. To keep the bike steady, and take some of the weight, the right arm can go through the triangle of the frame and hold the end of the handlebar, or stay inside the bike and hold the left-hand end of the bar.

Cyclo-cross specialists who have crossed over into the world of mountain-bike racing have injected new vigour into cyclo-cross. They have also raised the standard, coming into the cyclo-cross season stronger and fitter after a summer racing mountain bikes.

Mountain biking gives the cyclo-cross racer extra strength when pedalling and also more stamina – as mountain-bike races tend to be longer in duration as well as favouring riding over running.

Established stars of the cyclo-cross world are still the top performers at world championship level, but the mountain bikers among them are proving to be the strongest riders.

That was certainly the case at the 1992 world's in Leeds where German Mike Kluge, a cyclo-crosser turned mountain-bike racer, ran away with the professional title with a crushing display of all-round riding.

Held on a technically demanding course in a parkland setting, the Leeds title races heralded a return to the traditional cyclo-cross format with taxing run-ups and hazardous descents. This provided a sharp contrast to previous years, when fast courses had failed to split the leading riders and titles were decided by tactical breakaways and bunch sprints.

In the same way that mountain-bike racing has capitalized on its attraction as a glamour sport for risk takers, cyclo-cross must also build on its appeal as one of cycling's toughest, most technically challenging disciplines. Courses can reflect this, but above all, riders must continue to take up the sport which for nearly 100 years has been the supreme off-season challenge.

Mud can turn a rideable course into a nightmarish quagmire, where only the most resolute survive.

Time trials

'The race of truth' is the ultimate challenge for many road racers, combining as it does a test of speed, concentration and confidence. Time trialling has for nearly a century captured the imagination of competitive cyclists, and none more so than the British. **Dennis Donovan**

Alone and unpaced: three words that sum up the philosophy of time trialling British-style as it has existed since the turn of the century. You either love time trials or loathe them, but ever since F. T. Bidlake came up with the idea of riding alone and unpaced to combat police objections to road racing, the idea has appealed to the British mentality, with its attachment to honesty and fair play.

No tactics, no 'wheel-suckers', just the lone competitor versus the old enemy of time. The time achieved is through individual effort and not in any way influenced by the actions of others. At least that was the theory put up when cycle racing was being forced off the roads – a victim of its own popularity – with the police laying traps to catch speeding cyclists, who were regarded as a danger to horse-drawn traffic.

Such was the emphasis on keeping a low profile that at one time even the starting time and the location of the time trial were kept a close secret, dates being given a 'weekend number' and courses identified by a code reference. Competitors were required to dress inconspicuously – no multi-coloured jerseys as now, but an all-black costume from neck to toe. It was not until after the Second World War that shorts were allowed.

There were attempts to bring back road racing, but they were frowned upon by the Road Time Trials Council, who ruled out home racing on the roads, and when Percy Stallard

Left: Switzerland's Tony Rominger races against the clock during a stage of the 1993 Criterium International.
Right: Advances in aerodynamic equipment have steadily improved average speeds in recent years.

Popular distances

British time trialists race over a number of set-distance courses, of which there are many around the country. The most popular distances are 10, 25, 50 and 100 miles (16, 40, 80 and 160km), with 12- and 24-hour events strictly for the long-distance experts.

Mutli-title champion Beryl Burton is one of the few British time trialists to make her mark on the world stage.

and his British League of Racing Cyclists ran a road race from Llangollen in Wales to Wolverhampton in 1942, fears that the authorities would ban all competition on the road were as strong as they had been at the turn of the century. Stallard and his fellow visionaries were subject to all sorts of harassment in the struggle to get Britain back into the twentieth century and in line with the rest of the world.

There is a huge difference, however, between British time trials and those held in other countries. The 'race of truth' is still respected as such, but other nations see no reason for veiling it in secrecy. Following cars, noisy air horns and equally noisy team directors will accompany each of the riders as they wend their way through a varied course with hills, bends and other obstacles, watched by big crowds.

The British time-trial programme runs from February to November, with top riders competing two or three times a week. This practice is unheard of on the Continent, where there are a few specialist time trials at the end of the road-racing season but time trials are used as a prologue or included in a stage race either as an individual time trial or as a team time trial at some point in the race.

Over the years the British code has been tarnished. The use of dual carriageways has increased speeds to produce some amazing times, with many riders believing themselves to be superior to their Continental counterparts, only to find when they have ventured abroad that they finish nowhere.

The Grand Prix des Nations time trial in France is one race where top British time trialists have often come unstuck. Former Best All-Rounder champion Ken Joy rode it as a Hercules professional, Alf Engers, once the king of 25-miling (40km), also fared badly, but seven-times world champion Beryl Burton did a ride of merit as an accepted British

time trialist. She was allowed to ride the 1968 version as a guest rider, whereas only professionals and men are normally allowed to ride.

The race started at Auffargis to the south-west of Paris, turning south-east for a third of the 45.7 miles (73.5km) then north-west before entering Paris to finish at the Vélodrome Municipal at Charenton, on the edge of the Bois de Vincennes. Burton rode 12 minutes ahead of the professionals – and her pre-race publicity said that she would be covering the course at over 25mph (40kph) – to finish in 1-50-0. She actually covered the course in 1-45-22, at an average speed of 26mph (41.853kph), but found afterwards that she had a ½-in nail embedded in her rear tyre.

The winner of the time trial was the great Italian rider Felice Gimondi, who covered the course at a speed of 29.5mph (47.518kph). Burton was only 12½ minutes down on the 1965 Tour de France winner. To give full details of her domestic time-trial achievements would require several books. Suffice it to say that she won the women's Best All-Rounder title for twenty-five successive years, and during that time was the 100-miles (160km) champion on eighteen occasions, the 50 miles (80km) twenty-three times, the 25 miles (40km) twenty-five times and the 10 miles (16km) four times. In 1967 she became the only woman to beat a men's competition record, when she rode 277.25 miles (446.19km) in 12 hours.

Perhaps of all Burton's achievements, this latter ride must rate as her best time trial as she not only beat the men's record but beat the best man on the day, Mike McNamara, who was seeking a big distance to win the Best All-Rounder championship. The event was the Otley CC 12-hour held on 17 September 1967. Ahead of her were ninety-nine men, with McNamara two minutes in front of her, but Burton's target was her own record of 250.37 miles (402.93km). She had already won the women's Best All-Rounder title, and she could devote all her energies to updating yet another of her records. The first indication that she was 'on a

ride' came after she had covered 200 miles (321.87km) in 8-33-37. She was told that she was 'up' on McNamara, and as she entered the 15.87-mile (25.54km) finishing circuit after 206 miles (331.52km), she had caught ninety-eight of the men who had started in front of her. There was just one male left: McNamara.

After the first circuit she was 46 seconds up on McNamara. It was the challenge she needed – not that Burton normally needed much encouragement. After 11 hours on the road she saw McNamara ahead of her. He needed a distance of 270 miles (434.52km) to take the men's Best All-Rounder title, and it looked a certainty, but Burton was about to make history.

She caught him, froze momentarily,

Time-trial star of the 1950s Ray Booty was the first man in Britain to break the four-hour barrier for 100 miles (160km).

then drew level. Incredibly, she offered him a sweet. He took it, and Burton went past to record 277.25 miles (446.19km). She had caught all ninety-nine of the male competitors and beaten her own record by 27 miles (43.45km), leaving McNamara with 276.52 miles (445.01km), a British record, but one that was eclipsed by a

Games, and he represented Britain at world championships with distinction, yet he will be best remembered for two rides against the watch that made the fans gasp.

For years cyclists had dreamed of someone beating four hours for 100 miles (160km) at an average 25mph (40kph), something that most riders were unable to keep up for 25 miles (40km), let alone four times the distance. They had their wish in 1956, when Booty, affectionately known as 'The Boot', did just that with 3-58-28 on the famous Bath Road. He had been near the record on several occasions, making it a distinct possibility earlier in the year with 4-1-52, which bettered his own record of 4-4-30 set a year earlier.

A young Jacques Anquetil on the way to his first victory in the 1953 Grand Prix des Nations, in France.

Italian course

In 1991, for the first time in its fifty-nine-year history, the Grand Prix des Nations moved out of France to Italy, where it also served as the final round of the year-long World Cup series. A relatively flat 64-km (40 miles) route was used centring on the town of Bergamo and the winner was Tony Rominger of Switzerland. The course was criticized for being too easy and too late in the season to attract the big stars.

record established by a woman. Two years later Burton's record was broken, by John Watson with 281.87 miles (453.62km), but in a brilliant half day of racing she had done the impossible again. Her performance received scant attention in the national papers. What would have been the effect had a female athlete or a swimmer beaten a men's national record?

One of the few aspects of cycling that Burton never really got into was road record-breaking – that is, place-to-place records – for surely they would have been put on the shelf for all time.

If Beryl Burton was the greatest woman time trialist in the 1960s and 1970s, then Ray Booty was the best among the men in the 1950s. Before the war Frank Southall had won time trials by huge margins, and in the 1950s Booty did the same. He was a lanky, bespectacled rider from Nottingham, and one of the most laid-back competitive cyclists ever seen. He won the Empire Games road-race title in Cardiff, before it became the Commonwealth

Booty did the seemingly impossible again in 1956 when he broke the Road Records Association straight-out 100-mile (160km) record, taking 16-32 off Ken Joy's 1953 figures, for a new time of 3-28-40. His record stood until 1991 when Raleigh professional Ian Cammish reduced it to 3-16-56, riding a titanium machine with disc wheels.

Unlike conventional time trialling, there are no competitors to catch in a road record attempt – just a lonely ride with a multitude of rules to ensure that there is no assistance from helpers, who are forced to make big detours to avoid passing the rider. Even so, he or she may get unwitting help from normal road traffic.

There are numerous records on the books, but the one that catches the public's imagination most is Land's End to John o'Groats, the 'End-to-End', 870 miles (1400km) from the tip of Cornwall to the north of Scotland. G. P. Mills was the greatest record-breaker before the turn of the century, first riding the End-to-End in 1885 on a high ordinary shod with solid tyres, albeit paced by a variety of other machines. He also set unpaced records for the End-to-End on a bicycle, on a tandem with T. A. Edge and on a tricycle using the new-fangled pneumatic tyres.

When John Woodburn knocked 1-36-33 off Mick Coupe's Land's End to John o'Groats record in 1982, establishing new figures of 1-21-3-16, that seemed to be unbeatable. Woodburn was at his peak as far as long-distance time trialling was concerned, having won the 24-hour championship in 1980 and 1981, but in 1990 a surprise performance by Andy Wilkinson took just 57 seconds off the record.

The greatest Continental rider against the watch was undoubtedly Jacques Anquetil, and it was in the Grand Prix des Nations in 1953 that the young rider from Normandy first came to prominence. Anquetil was just nineteen, but already the French amateur road champion and a bronze medallist in the Olympic Games team time trial at Helsinki. His potential had been spotted by two influential names, André Boucher and Francis Pellisier, and young 'Maître' Jacques was entered for this great end-of-season time trial.

Among the entrants was Jean Bobet, brother of the famous Louison, and two Englishmen: Ken Joy and Bob Maitland. Joy carried credentials as the former British Best All-Rounder and was riding for Hercules, while Maitland (BSA) was an excellent roadman with special climbing abilities. Much was expected of them both.

The race started from Versailles, following a westerly direction for the first 25 miles (40km), then at Houdan turned south to Ablis (50 miles/80km), then north-east through the Valley of the Chevreuse, with two steep climbs back to Versailles, and into Paris to finish on the Parc des Princes track.

Anquetil was soon into his stride, despite the south-south-westerly wind for the first two legs of the individual time trial, and he covered the first 12.5 miles (20km) in 32-31, with his nearest challenger, Coletto of Italy, at 56 seconds and Joy at 1-1. Maitland was out

of it, 2-49 down already. At the next check at 25 miles (40 km), covered in 58-20 (the British competition record was held by Stan Higginson with 56-29), Anquetil had increased his lead over Coletto to 1-59, while Joy had slipped to fifth place at 2-19 and Maitland was struggling a long way behind at 6-40.

The Frenchman's progress continued: 37.5 miles (60km), 1-31-20, 3-40 on Coletto, 5-52 on Joy, 9-20 on Maitland; 50 miles (80km), 2-8-42, 4-28 on Coletto, 9-41 on Joy, 12-24 on Maitland; 62 miles (100km), 2-33-5, 4-25 on his fellow Norman, Roger Creton, 4-51 on Coletto, 11-11 on Joy, 13-57 on Maitland; 78 miles (125km), 2-33-5, 5-14 on Creton, 6-44 on Coletto, 16-17 on Joy, 17-48 on Maitland; finish, 88 miles (142km) in 3-32-25, 6-41 on Creton, 7-35

Time trialling can affect the outcome of the Tour de France, a fact that was demonstrated to stunning effect by Greg LeMond on the final stage of the 1989 Tour.

Anquetil used his time-trial skills to win numerous stage races, including five editions of the Tour de France.

Record ride

British time-trialling history was made in 1991 when the thirty-five-year-old all-round rider Glenn Longland rode the first-ever 25-mph (40kmh) 12-hour race. In a sport where many riders are happy to average 25mph (40kph) for 100 miles (160km), Longland kept that speed up for an astonishing 300 miles (480km).

on Coletto, Maitland was fourteenth at 19-33, and Joy fifteenth at 20-23.

Anquetil had used gears of 52 x 14, 15, 16, 17, 18, the same as Joy, who was using Cyclo Benelux gears, while Maitland had a double chainring of 47 and 50, with 13, 15, 16 and 18-tooth sprockets. Anquetil had arrived in terms of cycling achievement, with 15,000 spectators at the Parc des Princes to witness his triumph, and he was to go on to win the Prix des Nations eight more times. That day British time trialling received a blow that it took a long time to recover from.

Anquetil's tally of time-trial wins included the GP de Lugano seven times, the GP Martini-Geneva five times, the GP Forli-Castrocaro twice, Mont Faron once, eleven time-trial stages in the Tour de France, six in the Tour of Italy and one in the Tour of Spain. In addition he had time-trial wins in Paris-Nice, the Critérium National (international from 1979), Four-Days of Dunkirk, Critérium du Dauphiné, Vuelta a Cataluña, Tour of Romandie, and team time trials such as the Baracchi Trophy.

Fausto Coppi, 'Il Campionissimo', the champion of champions, was perhaps a better all-round rider than Anquetil – devastating in the mountains, a brilliant pursuiter and time trialist, whereas most of Anquetil's Tour de France wins were because the races had been designed with many time trials, his obvious speciality. Coppi won the Tour twice, first in 1949 and then in 1952, the year before he won the world title at Lugano in Switzerland. On that day he simply rode away from his opposition to win by 6-16, in a manner that is held in esteem to this day.

He had already won the Tour of Italy before he started the Tour de France, beating Gino Bartali by 23-47, a massive margin, but then that was Coppi's hallmark. After five stages Coppi was lying thirty-sixth, 30 seconds down – a crash and a long wait for a replacement bike had seen to that – but on the seventh stage he fought back in the individual time trial, chopping 8½ minutes off his deficit. On the eleventh stage, through the Pyrenees, Coppi was at his best, finishing third after two punctures, to Jean Robic and Lucien Lazarides, but more importantly he was 'only' 14-46 in arrears.

After sixteen stages, Coppi's great rival Bartali was in the lead after beating him the day before in the sprint from Cannes to Briançon. Coppi was not too bothered, for next day on the road from Briançon to Aoste he won by 4 minutes after Bartali had suffered a puncture and the yellow jersey passed to Coppi's shoulders.

The twentieth stage was an individual time trial from Colmar to Nancy, a distance of 85 miles (137km). It was on this stage that Coppi confirmed his superiority, winning in 3-38-50, with an average speed of 23.5mph (37.8kph) over winding, difficult roads. When he finished his final lap on the Nancy track he was 7-3 faster than runner-up Bartali, who overall was now 4-55 down, and his overall victory was virtually assured. A few days later, when Coppi rode into Paris as the race winner, finishing seventh in the sprint, it was the first time that the double of the Tour of Italy and the Tour de France had been accomplished. His margin of victory over Bartali was 7-55.

It is easy to forget that all-rounders like Sean Kelly and Bernard Hinault were also great time trialists. Kelly was known as a great sprint finisher before the 1982 Paris-Nice, while Hinault won five Grands Prix des Nations. When Kelly lined up for the start of the 1982 Paris-Nice it was with a reputation as a sprinter – one of the fastest, with stage wins in the Tour de France, Tour of Spain, Tour of Belgium and Tour of Holland to his credit, definitely not a man to win this leg-looser before the start of the spring classics. Frenchman Gilbert Duclos-Lassalle was the favourite. He had won Paris-Nice before, and knew every inch of the route. He was as talkative as Kelly was not, but a surprise was in store.

The first upset came in the prologue time trial, which, inexplicably, finished in Mouscron, Belgium. Kelly was third to Bert Oosterbosch of Holland and Alain Bondue of France, two world-class pursuiters. Kelly won the St Étienne stage from Belgium's Roger de Vlaeminck – not so unexpectedly – then followed this up by winning at La Seyne from Duclos-Lassalle and René Bittinger – almost a foregone conclusion. As a result Kelly was leading overall by one second with two days to go. The stage from La Seyne to Mandelieu was 112 miles (180km), with the climb of the Col du Tanneron the major obstacle, followed by a swoop down into Mandelieu.

Kelly crashed on the descent, as did Duclos-Lassalle soon after, but the Frenchman was up quicker and finished five seconds in front of Kelly to take the leader's jersey by four seconds.

The final stage was split: a morning road-race stage, to be followed by the afternoon time trial of 6.8 miles (11km) up the Col d'Eze. Journalists were already congratulating Duclos-Lassalle on his victory before he had even ridden. Meanwhile Kelly was warming up. After the first kilometre (0.6 mile) Duclos-Lassalle was a second faster

Big Mig

Miguel Indurain based his three consecutive wins in the Tour de France (1991, 1992 and 1993) on his all-conquering power in the time trials. The tall Spaniard has undergone physiological tests which show that he can develop 550 watts of power – twice as much as an amateur racer. His lungs are so big (7.8 litres) that they can displace his stomach when racing.

Fausto Coppi, the great Italian road racer, was also a superb time trialist and lone breakaway specialist.

than the Irishman. At the 3-km (1.9 miles) point Kelly was nine seconds better, and then at the summit he was 44 seconds faster. He not only won the final stage by 14 seconds from Spain's Alberto Fernández, with Duclos-Lassalle fifth, but he had at the same time won his first major stage race.

Kelly's achievement had largely been forgotten when the first Nissan International Classic took place in Ireland in 1985. He had been given a rapturous reception by the general public in his first professional race in Ireland since establishing his reputation in Europe, and although everyone was hoping that he would win overall, no one was prepared for a 'Kelly special' on the third day.

The morning started with a 13-mile (21km) time trial from Kelly's home

town of Carrick-on-Suir to Clonmel. That other great Irish rider, Stephen Roche, had set the target of 24-58, with Holland's Teun Van Vliet and Adri Van Der Poel, and Kelly still to come. Van Der Poel caught Van Vliet, then Kelly caught Van Der Poel, to power to the finish in 24-9, beating Roche by 49 seconds. In the afternoon Roche beat Kelly into Cork, but Kelly had laid the foundations for his overall victory when the race reached Dublin.

Bernard Hinault, the other great all-rounder, was always someone to reckon with in a sprint finish, had the ability to read a race well, and could time-trial too. As an amateur he had been the French pursuit champion – something he never followed up as a professional, but he surely would have had a medal of sorts from the world championship.

He won the 1977 Grand Prix des Nations by beating Holland's Joop Zoetemelk, a fact largely forgotten by the time he made his Tour debut in 1978. Hinault was twenty-three and it was the Tour's sixty-fifth anniversary, but little was heard of him for seven days. On the eighth he won the individual time-trial stage at Ste-Foy-la-Grande and was in a commanding position to take the lead once the race reached the mountains.

Hinault's first Tour de France stage win was not without controversy. Belgium's Freddy Maertens was leading him by 19 seconds at 22km (13.7 miles), then increased it to 27 seconds at 25km (15.5 miles), yet mysteriously lost that 26-second advantage and a further 30 seconds on the last 25km.

'All I could see was the road ahead,' said Maertens, the former world champion. 'All Hinault could see were the cars ahead of him!'

The Frenchman won the road stage to St Étienne on stage fifteen, then five stages later won his second time trial, the 76km (47.2 miles) from Metz to Nancy, to take the *Maillot Jaune*, the yellow jersey, from Joop Zoetemelk, the eternal second. There were two stages to go and France prepared to greet its latest sporting hero. Hinault

Laurent Fignon lost the 1989 Tour de France by eight seconds. Had he used tri-bars, as the American winner Greg LeMond did in the final stage, the result may have been different.

finally rode into Paris with a 3-56 winning margin over Zoetemelk.

The following year the race included four individual time trials, and Hinault won the first on the second stage from Luchon to Superbagnères in the Pyrenees, then outsprinted his opposition next day on the stage to Pau.

Zoetemelk was leading the Tour by stage five, as he had the previous year, and Hinault was in second place at 2-8.

He took back half that deficit by winning the time trial at Brussels, then added his killer blow on the fifteenth stage, from Evian to Morzine-Avoriaz, a distance of 55km (34.2 miles). It was another individual time trial and Hinault was merciless, beating Zoetemelk by 2-37 and taking the yellow jersey.

Hinault added the final, master touches on stage twenty-one, when he beat Zoetemelk by 1-9 in the Dijon time

Five-times Tour de France winner Bernard Hinault was a formidable time trialist as well as an early pioneer of the aerodynamic bike.

trial, and then the most coveted stage win of all, the final one into Paris.

More Tour victories were to follow for Hinault in 1981, 1982 and 1985, and more time-trial stage wins too, plus five stage wins in the Grand Prix des Nations – a formidable record. When Hinault was asked by the great Jacques Anquetil why he had never gone for the world hour record, Hinault was quite honest. 'My times as a pursuiter were never good enough,' he said. 'You were wise,' said Anquetil.

In more recent times the best time trial ever witnessed came at the end of the 1989 Tour de France. With one day to go, Laurent Fignon of France was in the lead and about to enter his native Paris. His nearest challenger, the American Greg LeMond, was at 50 seconds, and it all rested on that final stage, a 25-km (15.5 miles) time trial from Versailles to Paris.

LeMond was off last-but-one, two minutes before Fignon. He was 21 seconds faster than Fignon at 11.5km (7.1 miles) on the slight downhill run into Paris. He was pulling back precious seconds on the Place de la Concorde and the Champs-Élysées, and finished

in a time of 26:57.

It was now down to the agonizing wait to see what Fignon would do. With a kilometre (0.6 mile) to go, it looked as if Fignon was down, but by how much? He finished in 27-38, 41 seconds down on LeMond, and the Tour had been won and lost by eight seconds. It was a great time trial by two great time triallists – the 'race of truth' had once again found out the best.

Any history of time trialling, however brief, raises the question of comparative standards of achievement over the years. While speeds are clearly improving all the time, it would be wrong to conclude that the slower times of yester-year indicate less commitment. Better training methods, improved roads and ever-developing technology have together undeniably produced a steady improvement in time-trial results, but we can be sure that every rider, from the earliest days of the sport, has felt bound to give of his best in this most individual of disciplines. For the time trial is still essentially what it has been from the start – the lone rider's gruelling battle against the clock.

Chris Boardman won his first race as a professional – the Grand Prix Eddy Merckx time trial – in Brussels in 1993. Later that year the Briton was fourth in the Grand Prix des Nations.

CHAPTER THREE

CYCLING FOR REAL

the adventure

Choosing a bike

Buying a bike requires careful consideration of the amount of cycling you want to do and how much money you wish to spend. Your new bike must then be set up properly. **Luke Evans**

Custom or off the peg?

This is the first decision to make and it will largely depend on how much money you have to spend and how specific your cycling needs are.

The Zipp 2001 is not to everyone's taste perhaps but a keen time trialist might be interested.

Many of the bikes featured in the first chapter are one-off creations, custom-built to a design brief specified by either an individual or a racing team. They are not the kind of machines that you can buy complete from a bicycle dealer, although it would be possible to have one built to your requirements, with the same components. However, while the fundamental design of a bicycle, based on the angles of the frame and the physical dimensions of the rider, should correspond to that of the professional equivalent, it is not necessary to duplicate every nut and bolt. Having made a decision to buy a bike, whether for off-road riding, road, time trial or track, you are faced with a choice of either buying a fully equipped machine, or just the frame, which is then fitted with a variety of parts. The second option is not as complicated as it sounds and many riders derive great pleasure from buying and building a new bike.

A bicycle frame can be made to measure by a custom frame builder, or alternatively, bought ready-made in the correct size. As most frames are measured in centimetres nowadays it is not difficult to find one that fits perfectly, made from materials ranging from carbon fibre or aluminium, to more traditional steel. Those wishing to take

advantage of lightweight tubes of carbon fibre or titanium must settle for a ready-made frame as small custom builders lack the tools and the money to offer custom-built frames in such exotic materials, working almost exclusively in steel. An off-the-peg frame will also come in standard road, track or off-road angles and there is nothing wrong with that. Indeed, the Italians, most notably, have perfected the design of the road frame to the point where it is hardly worth checking the angles when buying from a reputable name and all that really matters is the weight and type of tubing, the quality of finish and the colour scheme.

Prices can be high – not much less than the price of a custom-built frame – and, for many riders, if one aspect is not satisfactory, that is enough to justify paying a little extra for a frame assembled to their exact requirements. There are several areas where a custom-built frame scores over a mass-produced one and the most important is the conditions under which the frame is to be used. For instance, a light rider who pedals very smoothly can ride a lighter frame than a heavy cyclist of the same size who intends to race over rough

surfaces. Both might consider the same mass-produced frame, but a custom builder would advise building two that were quite different.

Women can benefit from custom-built frames, as in general they are poorly served by standard frame designs. A hand-built frame can take into account the shorter female torso and overall height, in some cases allowing smaller wheels to be used. Frames in small sizes are available ready-made, but they are often too long for women riders and heavier than necessary.

Allowing for one or two basic modifications, however, buying a complete cycle from a shop is both cheaper and quicker than embarking on a custom-built project. When the frame has been chosen, attention should turn to the cycle parts. Most off-the-peg machines come with a complete

This off-the-peg lightweight bonded carbon-fibre bike with combined gear and brake levers from US maker Trek is a high-specification bike at a reasonable price.

Legendary Italian frame maker Colnago produces factory-built frames to a high standard.

groupset – a full set of components including chainset, hubs, gears and brakes – made by one manufacturer. Shimano of Japan are by far the biggest producer of a range of quality groupsets, but other companies, such as Campagnolo (Italy), SunTour (Japan), Mavic (France) and Sachs-Huret (Germany), also produce alloy component sets to high standards of finish and operation.

The groupset should reflect the quality of the frame and overall price of the bike. There are very few rogue components nowadays, especially in the medium to upper price ranges, and often it is the quality of finish that sets one groupset apart from another. This can be a short-lived veneer where mountain bikes are concerned, as alloy really suffers in off-road conditions. Accelerated wear of chains, chainrings and sprockets will quickly take the edge off a new machine and it is worth bearing in mind the replacement cost of some of the most exotic groupsets available today.

After the frame, the wheels are the most important part of the bike. Again, if you are paying good money for a complete bike they should be in keeping with the overall standard. Narrow-section 700c rims, anodized silver or grey, with thirty-two stainless steel spokes and smooth-running quick-release hubs are the mark of a good wheel. High-pressure, wired-on tyres have come a long way in the last decade and it is now possible to race at the highest level on a Michelin slick or equivalent. Mountain-bike wheels should also be constructed with good-quality, preferably anodized, rims, sealed hubs to keep out the muck and stainless-steel spokes.

Bikes come in a number of sizes, all measured from the centre of the bottom bracket to the top of the seat cluster. To find the correct size for a road bike, standing barefoot, measure your inside leg from crotch to floor and subtract 10in (25cm). If it is a matter of deciding between ½in (1.25cm) either way, go for the smaller frame. Current practice

is to have the seat pin extended 5in (13cm) or so and it is always better to have a lighter, stiffer, smaller frame than one that is too big. Mountain bikes come in far fewer frame sizes, and again it is best to choose one that, when set up correctly, has around 5in (13cm) of seat pin showing.

With an off-the-peg bike or frame the seat-tube length is the only measurement on offer. If the top tube is the incorrect length you will have to compensate with a long or short stem. Many women, for instance, will want to fit a short stem as even on small frames the top tube is often too long for them.

Setting the saddle at the correct height is the most important task once you get the bike home. The idea is that at the bottom of the pedal stroke your leg should be neither overextended nor cramped. Stand up, lift one leg off the ground and, relaxed, let it hang naturally. There should be a slight bend in it and you should be aiming for a position like that or slightly more bent. One simple way to arrive at the correct seat

height is to sit on the bike with one leg fully extended, parallel to the seat tube. If the saddle is at the correct height your heel with your socks on, should be just touching the pedal.

There are scientific formulas for calculating saddle height but they do not take into account foot size or, more importantly, personal preference and riding conditions. For every rider there is a marginal range of vertical adjustment within which he or she can experiment. Winter riding, small gears and off-road riding are often better with a slightly lower saddle height. Fixed-position time trialling can be done with the seat marginally higher. Whatever the conditions, saddle height should always be adjusted by small increments.

This American made bicycle has a titanium frame and the latest Campagnolo Ergopower gear shifting system. Titanium is ideal for bike frames and components as it is very light, strong and corrosion-free.

Toe clips and straps, or clipless pedals, are essential and most quality machines these days come equipped with them as standard.

bracket, and then measure the distance from the weight to the centre of the bottom-bracket spindle. This measurement should be between 2in (5cm) and 4in (10cm), depending on the frame angles and saddle type. Once again, personal preference may lead you to make a slight variation on these measurements.

Stem length is another measurement for which there are few hard-and-fast rules. For years the technique was to measure the correct distance from saddle to handlebars by putting your elbow on the end of the saddle nose and, with your fingers extended, find them 2-3in (5-7.5cm) short of the bars. Tourists expect to touch the bars with their fingers but racers, more concerned than ever with a low, aerodynamic position, favour stems of 4-4¾in (10-12cm), giving them a more stretched out position. If you are starting out, keep the bars within 3in (7.5cm) of your outstretched fingers.

Drop handlebars should be as wide as a rider's shoulders, giving good control over steering and a comfortable, open-chested position. Complete bikes, especially from the major manufacturers, often come with narrow bars and short stems. The shop may change these for you, or you may have to buy new ones; they do not cost very much and it is well worth it. The bars should be positioned with the leading edge of the bend pointing straight ahead. This should leave the ends of the bars pointing down slightly. With new bars you will have to put the brake levers in the correct position. Find the point, just above that leading edge, where you can ride comfortably on the rubber hoods, or on the drops. In either

Used in conjunction with Shimano's SPD double-sided clipless pedal system, cross-country shoes can be used for training, cyclo-cross, mountain biking and walking.

Campagnolo's clipless system is similar to the original Look design from France which has inspired many alternative models.

The saddle should be set level, with a spirit level if necessary. A good saddle is designed for use when set flat and only the smallest of adjustments, moving the nose up or down, should be made. Many women prefer to use a saddle with a shorter nose and wider padded section. The position of the saddle on the rails is related to its position over the bottom bracket. It also affects weight distribution on the bike. Allow a weight on the end of a piece of string held against the end of the saddle, to hang level with the bottom

The shape of things to come? Mavic's Zap electronic gears have been tested by professionals and are now available to all.

position the brake levers should be within three fingers' reach.

Your new bike should be fitted with toe clips and straps or quick-release pedals. No bike is complete without these; they add another dimension to pedalling, allowing you to pull back at the bottom of the pedal stroke and then push your knee towards the bars. With practice, getting in and out of both types of pedal becomes second nature. Shoe plates, which either lock into the pedal or slot on to the back plate, should be carefully positioned with the foot at a comfortable angle. Normally this is with the toes pointing slightly outwards and the heel not more than in ½in (1cm) from the crank. Take a spanner or screwdriver with you for the first few rides and make minor adjustments if necessary.

Very few bikes sold in shops come with tubular tyres and 'sprint' rims, even though these are the choice of most professional riders. The advantages offered by tubulars are that they roll and handle better than most wired-on tyres, they are lighter and less susceptible to impact and the box-section rims onto which they are glued are extremely robust.

The disadvantage of 'sprints and tubs' is that good tubulars are expensive and have to be painstakingly glued onto the rims. Also, they are difficult to repair. Even so, if you are seriously interested in road racing and time trialling they definitely offer performance advantages.

This high performance wheel from Campagnolo has a rim suitable for wired-on tyres.

Basic maintenance

With a few tools and regular attention you can keep a bike in good working order for years. Neglect your machine, however, and it will soon complain. **Luke Evans**

Bare minimum

The very least you should do is keep the tyres pumped up and the chain oiled. You would be surprised how many cyclists who should know better, ignore routine maintenance.

Professional riders are lucky, as they have a mechanic who follows them around in a car, adjusting and fine-tuning the bikes whenever necessary.

Compared with many other machines, bicycles are remarkably simple and, unlike most modern devices, relatively easy to adjust and maintain. Every working part is on show – bikes are not covered in sheets of moulded plastic, metal or sound-proofing material, nor do they have 'Warning. Do not touch' stickers all over them. The mysteries of a gearbox are right there before you, and closer examination, armed with the simplest of tools, will reveal that the workings of a bike are not nearly as complicated as you might have thought.

Bicycles do not have service intervals, but they do require more attention than just a periodical opening up of a bonnet. As a result most component parts are designed to be easily adjusted and maintained. Certain tasks need specialist tools, and you must either buy those tools or take the bike to a shop to have

a more complicated job, for example the replacement of a bottom bracket or the construction of a pair of wheels, carried out by a mechanic. A carefully chosen basic tool kit, handled with a bit of understanding and sympathy, can ensure a sweetly running machine.

Regular riding and washing should be enough to pinpoint actual or potential problems. As you become more experienced as a cyclist, an appreciation of how the bike works, and the noises it makes when running correctly, will help you to diagnose problem areas. Washing is the best way to check for damage, but more importantly it prevents a build-up of dirt causing premature wear of the transmission and other moving parts.

Other maintenance jobs, such as oiling the chain, adjusting various components and checking the tyres, should all be done on a ride-to-ride

KEEPING YOUR BIKE CLEAN

1 *Run the chain through a rag soaked in degreaser, making sure that all the links are saturated. This is best done with a chain stop in the rear dropout, or with the chain hooked onto a braze-on above the dropout.*

2 *Squirt or brush degreaser, preferably water soluble, on the block and any other parts of the bike which attract oil. Try to avoid getting degreaser into the bearings by angling the wheel slightly.*

3 *Allow the degreaser a few minutes to dissolve the oil and then brush it away with warm, soapy water. Give the block a good scrub, working the bristles into the gaps where old oil and grit tends to collect.*

4 *Brake bridges and inaccessible areas of the bike can be reached with a narrow bottle brush. Scrub the brake blocks, with a toothbrush if necessary, and inspect them for any damage.*

basis. It is not worth neglecting these simple tasks, no matter how cheap or expensive the bike, as the resulting squeaks and sloppy ride will soon become unbearable.

Washing

Tools for the job: *Water-soluble degreaser, plastic container, selection of brushes, bucket, sponge, car shampoo, chain stop.*

With practice this is a 15-minute job and

should be carried out after every race or long ride, especially if it has been raining. It is also much easier to work on a bike that has just been cleaned.

First take the wheels off and either put the bike in a work stand or prop it up so that the pedals can turn freely with a plastic or metal chain stop screwed into the derailleur dropout. If neither is possible, stand the bike against a wall with the wheels in.

Using an old piece of rag soaked in degreaser and a thin brush, run the chain through the rag and the brush

CHECKING TYRES AND WHEELS

1 *You can see if the wheel is out of true by turning it on the bike and watching for any deflections away from the brake block or a screwdriver held close to the rim. Gently go round the wheel, feeling for loose spokes.*

2 *Adjust the cones until the hub spindle turns freely without any lateral movement. The cone spanner on the left holds the adjusting cone in place while the spanner on the right tightens the lock nut against it.*

3 *Only minor adjustments should be made with a spoke key and great care should be taken not to overtighten spokes. Anything more than the simplest jobs is best tackled by an experienced wheelbuilder.*

4 *Carefully check the tyres for cuts and bulges. Pick any small objects out of the tyre with a small screwdriver. Holes can be filled with a dab of rubber cement but a damaged sidewall requires a new tyre.*

over the derailleurs, front chainrings and rear sprockets on the back wheel. Some pedals and chainsets have threads that push water out, so make sure to turn them clockwise. Then, using a bucket of hot water and car shampoo, start washing the bike from the saddle down.

Wash away the dissolved oil and grit from the transmission, working a thick brush into the chain and block.

Use a kitchen or bottle brush to scrub off brake dust and road dirt from inaccessible places under the brakes and around the bottom bracket. Go easy with the water around the bottom bracket and never direct a pressure hose where bearings are located.

Clean the wheels with soapy water, using the sponge and a soft brush. Again, try to prevent too much water going into the block by holding the wheel face down. Scrub the tyres and check for cuts or foreign bodies at the same time.

Leave the bike to drip dry before oiling the chain, adding a few drops into the block.

TACKLING THE TRANSMISSION

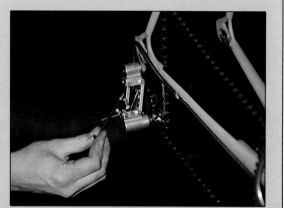

1 *Mountain-bike chains are particularly susceptible to rust and premature wear if regularly used off-road. The chain should be oiled and cleaned after every excursion and changed once a year.*

2 *Lateral movement of the rear derailleur is determined by two screws or Allen bolts. On 'click' shift systems it is important to maintain the correct cable tension as well as use compatible chains and blocks.*

Tyres and wheels

Tools for the job: *Cone spanners, tyre levers, track pump, spoke key.*

Periodically check the wheels for loose spokes, or a rim running out of true. Leave the wheel in the bike and check that it runs straight by looking at the deviation between the rim and the brake blocks. It is possible to make very minor adjustments, with the spoke key, that will pull the rim back into place, but great care should be taken not to exacerbate the problem. The spokes are attached to the rim by a threaded nipple, which screws on to the end of the spoke. Turning the key clockwise on the nipple (looking at it from above the tyre) pulls the spoke further up the hollow nipple, increasing tension between the hub and rim. Depending on which side of the hub the spoke is attached, the rim will be pulled either to the left or the right, and down a fraction too.

Only the smallest of jobs should be attempted, either to pull the rim back by a few millimetres, or to tighten up a loose spoke. A rim that has gone out of true, or has a number of loose spokes, is probably a poorly built wheel anyway, and the only remedy is a rebuild by an experienced wheel-builder. A buckled rim or a rim with a dent should be replaced.

Sealed hubs require very little maintenance but if you have standard hubs they should occasionally be checked for play and smooth running. With the wheel out of the bike the spindle should turn freely, without binding or any lateral slackness. Cones on both sides of the hub hold the bearings in place and any adjustment involves slackening off the locking nut and screwing one of the cones up or down the spindle until it fits snugly on the bearings. Using a spanner, free off the locking nut and then, using the narrow cone spanner, adjust the cones onto the bearings. Holding the cone in place with the narrow spanner, tighten the locking nut and check that the spindle moves freely.

Once a year, especially if the wheels have been used throughout the winter, the hubs should be stripped out and regreased. Sealed hubs can go on for longer without maintenance and they are now in common use on mountain bikes and many road bikes.

Check tyres for cuts and bulges in the sidewall. Small stones may also be embedded in the tread and they should be carefully picked out and the holes filled with rubber cement. Good-quality

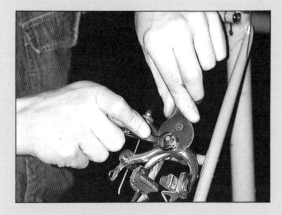 

1 Centre the brakes with cone spanners, checking that they operate correctly when the wheel is back in. Cantilever brakes on mountain bikes should be virtually self-centring but check for bent or damaged cables.

2 Do not overtighten the lock-nut – it just needs to be snugged onto the brake stirrup. Cables should always be greased before fitting and routing should not be too circuitous.

Brake systems

Hydraulic brakes, disc brakes and drum brakes have all been used on mountain bikes and tandems and although they are powerful alternatives to a conventional system, they are not widely adopted

inner tubes and tyres will give greater performance and resistance to punctures so it is worth spending a little extra on these items. A track pump is also a worthwhile investment, with a gauge that ensures correct tyre pressures every time.

Transmission

Tools for the job: *Screwdrivers (crosshead and standard), light oil (often in a pressurized can), pedal spanner, chain link extractor.*

Maintaining the chain is the most important factor contributing to the smooth running and long life of the transmission. A dirty, dry chain will wear down the sprockets, jump through the gears and squeak. It is vital to regularly clean and lightly oil the chain, making sure the oil penetrates between the plates before wiping off any excess on the outside.

Mountain-bike chains wear out very quickly if used off-road and should be replaced whenever necessary. If a chain is left on for too long it meshes with the block, which must then be changed when the chain eventually wears out. A few drops of light oil put into the block will keep it spinning sweetly. Amateurs

or professionals competing in races every weekend will replace chains on a monthly basis.

Gears are simple to adjust, with two screws on both the front and rear derailleurs determining the limits of lateral travel. Once done they rarely go out of adjustment, but it is a job well worth doing as anyone who has ever jammed the chain between the block and the back wheel will testify.

Click systems with a stepped rate of derailleur travel rely on a correctly tensioned cable and after some initial stretch they should provide years of trouble-free changes. Most systems come with detailed instructions on how to fine-tune the gear when the shifting goes out of adjustment. With click shifters be sure to buy compatible blocks and chains when swopping over wheels and equipment. Special clickshift cables, which resist stretching, should also be used.

Pedals are generally trouble-free but they can be bent in a crash, leading to long-term knee problems for the rider if left on the bike. To check for a bent spindle, remove the pedal, place it on a table and slowly rotate the exposed end of the spindle. If there are any deviations in the rotation, the spindle is bent and should be replaced.

Brakes

Tools for the job: *Allen keys, spanner, grease, light oil.*

Do not neglect your brakes – well-adjusted, smoothly working brakes are an aid to performance as well as the only thing between you and the back of a bus. A good criterium rider can gain metres on his rivals by braking late into a corner and a good pair of progressive brakes can take the stress out of many daredevil braking manoeuvres.

Emergency stops on a bicycle also require skill and a cool head. Bicycle brakes are nowhere near as powerful as their car or motorcycle equivalents and, apart from the extra stopping distance, you must allow for this. Much care must be taken to avoid locking the wheels. It goes without saying that bike brakes must therefore be in perfect working order.

There are two main components of a braking system that require regular checking and maintenance: brake blocks and cables. In normal, dry conditions brake blocks last for a long time. Training and racing in the wet, and mountain biking, will greatly accelerate wear and brake blocks should be replaced as soon as they are worn beyond the halfway point.

Brake blocks should also be regularly checked for sharp little stones embedded in their surface. Stones can score alloy rims and should be picked out with a sharp point. Mountain biking

The right stuff

Thanks largely to mountain biking there is now a wide choice of specialist oils and greases for both off- and on-road use. Many greases are water-repellent but make sure you buy the correct grade for mountain-bike or road use.

On a busy day a team mechanic might have to attend to damaged machines while on the move. Professional team cars have custom-built roof racks for holding spare bikes and wheels.

DEALING WITH THE BEARINGS

1 *Holding the cranks at both ends and moving them from side to side will indicate whether there is any slack in the bottom bracket. Even the slightest amount of movement will be felt along the cranks.*

2 *You need special tools to remove and adjust the bottom bracket and the first is a spanner to remove the crank retaining bolt. A socket wrench might be suitable if the socket body is not too wide.*

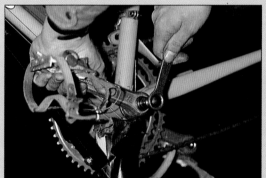

3 *The tool to remove the crank from the tapered bottom-bracket spindle screws onto the crank using the threads which normally hold the dust cap. Check before buying this tool that it fits your particular chainset.*

4 *Using the spanner for removing the crank bolts, the crank removing tool is screwed through the crank where it presses on the end of the spindle and eases the crank off the tapered end.*

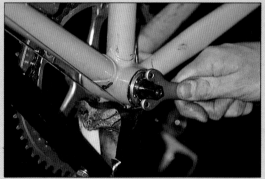

5 *The lock ring is removed with a semicircular toothed spanner. It is not necessary to have it done up too tightly, especially if the cup is made from alloy. Check that you have the correct tool before buying.*

6 *With the adjustable cup now exposed (the chainset side has a fixed cup) a peg spanner can be used to turn the cup until the spindle turns freely and smoothly, with just a hint of resistance.*

is really heavy on brake blocks and rims – mud and sand act like liquid sandpaper so it is vital that before every off-road excursion the brakes are checked and in good working order.

The brakes should be centred on the rim and not touching either side. You can do this with a flat cone spanner on the central pivot, moving the calipers to one side until the brake blocks are an equal distance from the rim. If necessary, the retaining nut on the end of the pivot can be backed off while the adjustment is made and then lightly tightened up again.

Cable failures are rare but potentially lethal, especially if the front brake is affected. Cables tend to deteriorate most at the brake-lever end and the most common failure point is where the cable enters the brake-lever housing. Check for frayed cables by pulling on the brakes and looking at the cable where it meets the lever.

Check along the length of the cable for damage to the outer casing. Stiffness in the lever action will indi-

cate a kinked or dry cable. Any evidence of fraying, kinks or stiffness justifies fitting a new cable. They do not cost very much and it certainly does no harm to replace cables every year as a matter of course.

Always grease the cable, even if the outer is Teflon-lined, before sliding it into the plastic housing. Care should be taken when routing a concealed cable along the bars. Ensure the cable is snug by taping it with insulating tape against the front of the bars. Try to route the cable cleanly, avoiding tight turns and extravagant loops. Cut the cable at the caliper end with wire-cutters or pliers and solder or cap the end with an alloy nipple.

Bearings

Tools for the job: *Grease, bottom bracket and headset tools, chainset remover.*

Apart from the hubs and the pedals, there are two main bearings on any

Team mechanics maintain bikes on a daily basis, often working into the early hours to have ten or more bikes ready for a race later that day.

Robert Millar receives some on-the-bike maintenance during a quiet moment in the 1992 Paris-Nice.

goes for the headset – there should be no slackness or clicking when the front brake is applied and the bike pushed back and forth. With the front wheel lifted off the ground you can also check for pitting and smoothness of the bearings by turning the bars slowly from side to side.

Special tools are required to remove the chainset and adjust or remove the bottom bracket. It is a relatively easy job with them, but nearly impossible without. After the cranks have been removed, adjustment of the bottom bracket is a simple matter of undoing the locking ring and either tightening or loosening the bearing cup on the opposite side of the chainset. The spindle should turn freely with just a hint of resistance.

The headset also comes in for abuse from shocks transmitted through the forks, as well as braking forces centred on the steering head. It does not have the same load on it as the bottom bracket but it still requires periodic attention.

bicycle: the bottom bracket and the headset. The bottom bracket is at the heart of the main load-bearing area of the bike. It is directly in line with water and dirt thrown up from the front wheel and should be carefully fitted and maintained.

Check for free play in the bottom bracket by holding both arms of the cranks and lightly moving them from side to side. Any slackness will be amplified along the cranks. If there is some sideways movement the bottom bracket requires adjustment. The same

A large spanner is all that is needed to loosen off the locking ring on the headset and usually the bearing cup underneath can be screwed in or out by hand. A flat spanner, however, is needed to hold the cup in place when the locking ring is tightened again. Fitting a new headset is a more complicated affair and best left to a trusted mechanic or frame builder. New bottom brackets are easier to fit, but you will still need the correct flat spanner to tighten the fixed cup on the chainset side. If the frame has been resprayed check that the bottom bracket shell has been faced off, leaving bare metal on both sides.

Many mountain bikes and a growing number of road bikes are now fitted with sealed bottom brackets which are virtually 'fit and forget items'.

Lightweight sealed bearing races are pressed into the cups and fitting is a simple matter of screwing in the cups, bearing races and spindle, making sure that there is no lateral movement, before securing the cups with a locking ring.

The bearings used in these bottom brackets are maintenance free and when they eventually wear out, they can be replaced with another set.

One thing to ensure when fitting a bottom bracket is that, when fitted, the chainset aligns correctly with the block. Viewed from the rear of the bike the centre of the chainset should line up with the centre of the block and if it does not you either have the wrong length spindle, or your sealed unit with adjustable cups is too far to one side.

Headsets come in a number of shapes and sizes and some mountain bikes come with oversize headsets, primarily to cope with the extra pounding taken off-road. Again, special tools are necessary to adjust and dismantle these headsets and care should also be taken not to damage their often lightweight alloy locking rings and cups.

A new headset should be fitted with great care, as any misalignment between the upper and lower cups will cause premature wear and could possibly affect the machine's handling.

A common problem is self-centring steering – caused by tiny pits in the cups which are the result of shocks transmitted up the forks from potholes and bumps in the road. You can feel for this by lifting the front wheel off the ground and turning the handlebars very slowly from side to side. If the handlebars centre themselves when the wheel points straight ahead, the cups are damaged and should be replaced.

Riders are allowed to hold onto the team car while adjustments are made, but after that they must make their own way back to the bunch.

Into shape

Cycling is a great way to get fit – the injury problems which bedevil many other sports are seldom experienced and the pleasure to be gained from riding is immediate. **Pat Liggett**

It's got to be worth it

Fitness does not just enable you to ride your bike for longer. It also improves blood circulation, increases lung capacity, strengthens muscles and gives a feeling of well-being.

Getting into shape in a group allows you to monitor your progress more effectively.

Cycling can be as challenging as you want to make it. Most people, whatever their level of fitness, could cycle and enjoy it provided they are not too ambitious at the outset. The secret of success is to know how to progress steadily, without causing too much discomfort, or overdoing it to the point where the body aches badly for days or you feel exhausted after a ride. The aim is enjoyment and a steady increase in fitness, hence also in speed and distance covered on the bicycle without undue fatigue. It may take a long time to reach peak racing fitness, but it should be surprisingly easy to reach a good average level of fitness in a relatively short space of time, say three or four months of regular riding, three or four times a week, for 30-90 minutes each time.

Serious cycling, as anyone who has tried it will surely know, is a hard sport. It is, however, a great way to become aerobically fit. Test the heart and lungs of any top amateur or professional rider and it may be quite a surprise to find that his resting heart rate – to find this the pulse is checked first thing in the morning, before any active movement – is as low as forty beats per minute. The heart rate of an average person is usually about seventy to seventy-five beats per minute. The pulse indicates the number of beats per minute that the heart needs to make in order to pump sufficient blood (containing nutrients) around the body to cope with the energy demand at that precise moment. The less effort made the less hard the heart needs to work. However, constantly working at

a low level will cause the heart, circulation and muscles to deteriorate, so that a sudden demand of a high level of energy may prove too much. Occasionally the consequences have proved devastatingly final! The heart, being a muscle, will also deteriorate in strength, or pumping power, in a less fit person. In this case the resting heart rate is likely to be higher, since less blood will be pumped out with each heart beat, whereas a certain amount must be pumped with each beat to allow general body functions to continue normally.

With each breath a top-class rider could inhale in excess of 80ml of air per minute (20 per cent of which is oxygen), by comparison with a less well-trained person who may only be able to inhale 30-45ml. (This is known as Maximal Oxygen Uptake, or VO2 Max.) The oxygen contained in this inhaled air is transported around the body via the blood circulation and then efficiently converted into muscular energy at the site of demand. Waste products from muscular metabolism are transported away in capillaries, venules and veins back to the heart and lungs for expiration. Competitive cyclists, whether amateur or professional, are often so efficiently trained that they can use their lungs to almost 100 per cent capacity. Average, less fit men and women would find it difficult to use their full lung capacity (referred to as vital lung capacity and measured as the maximal volume of gas that can be expelled from the lungs following a maximal inspiration, or intake of air). Thus the trained person has a much greater aerobic energy production potential than the less fit person, whose transportation of the vital oxygen may also be a little sluggish for a variety of reasons, including blockages within the circulatory passages, a paucity of capillaries ready to accept and transport blood, or because the demand has been reduced over years of inactivity. The energy potential of the less than perfect specimen will already have been limited dramatically.

Is the professional rider necessarily

a superman? No! He may be lucky enough to have been born of good, healthy stock (about 75 per cent of what we are is inherited, and about 25 per cent we can change), but he must also have worked hard, over many years, to develop his body to withstand the rigours of an astonishingly demanding sport. Tour de France riders, for example, will have been taking part in competitive cycling for years before they would be considered ready for this three-and-a-half week, 3000-mile (4830km) marathon.

How do they do it? They train hard,

Even a short ride, preferably on a regular basis, will have a beneficial effect on overall health.

Superman or mere mortal? The professional cyclist is the product of years of hard work and a disciplined lifestyle.

a regular supply of high-octane fuel – food that converts into energy quickly and efficiently – and the results may be very surprising indeed.

In the human machine oxygen, the prime ingredient necessary to produce energy aerobically, is transported via the blood, attaching to the haemoglobin (the red blood cell) to become oxy-haemoglobin more quickly in the competitive cyclist than in the average or occasional rider. It is then more efficiently converted (along with other substances) in the muscle 'factory' – the mitochondria, which are found within the blood vessels (capillaries) surrounding the muscle fibres – into a form of usable energy.

In order to make a muscular contraction, which itself takes energy, that energy, and all potential energy – whether it is stored in the muscle as glycogen (the breakdown of sugars and starches) or as the emergency supply, creating phosphate, which is created within the muscle cell – must first be converted into a form that the muscle can use. A complex chain of events takes place instantly a message is received via the brain within the muscle that energy (movement) has been demanded. This end product is muscular energy in the form of ATP (Adenosine Tri-Phosphate) and instantly the muscle contracts, producing movement. The demand placed on the muscle (the amount of effort involved), and the efficiency of the muscle itself, will together determine which source of energy the muscle prefers to use.

Long-distance, steady-paced riding

at least six days out of seven, and they eat well-balanced, nutritious foods. They ride for several hours at a time and often at a pace that demands just a little more than their body feels able to give. In other words, they make enough effort to stimulate the organs and body systems (primarily heart, lungs, circulation and muscle contraction) to work just a little more than feels comfortable, gradually increasing the demand for energy and improving the energy exchange at muscular level. This is rather like finely tuning a car engine to give maximum performance; more vulnerable to breaking down perhaps, but performing spectacularly when firing on all cylinders. Add to this will use as its energy source oxygen and other substances that are being transported in the blood at the time. Climbing an incline, thus demanding that the muscle work a bit harder, may bring about a little pain. If the pain increases, then the prime source of energy being used will switch from oxygen to the glycogen that has been stored in readiness in the muscle fibres. The final sprint for the line, perhaps the last 50 yards (50m) with a rival hot on your heels, will require even more effort and this last gasp of energy may well be obtained from our emergency supply of creatine phosphate, which again is stored within the muscle, ready to be used.

The first source of energy, aerobic, uses a high percentage of oxygen, small amounts of blood glucose and free fatty acids, and has little or no fatiguing by-products – just water, heat and carbon dioxide. Therefore, provided the level of work is within that person's aerobic capacity, and he has sufficient fluid and glucose replacement as he rides, he could carry on for many hours without much trouble.

But this is not the case with hill climbing, which uses a high proportion of stored glycogen as the prime source of energy. The pain felt as the hill steepens and effort increases is caused by the waste product of glycogen energy production – lactic acid. Less oxygen is used during this increased activity. It could be so hard that no oxygen is used at all. This is commonly known as anaerobic energy production. Lactic acid can eventually impair muscle movement to the point where a muscle seizes up and ceases to function. Cramp could also be the end product of a highly intense activity with less than efficient muscles. There is no alternative now but to stop cycling or slow down dramatically to allow the oxygen system to take over again and keep the muscles working. In fact, this is highly recommended, as aerobic work will help disperse lactic

Hill climbing is among the best tests of fitness. The ideal approach is to remain within your aerobic capacity – that is, to retain a core of reserve energy for use later in the race.

acid and speed up recovery from a hard effort. No muscle, fit or unfit, is likely to be able to contract anaerobically for more than two or so minutes at maximum effort.

And so to the final sprint, with a win in prospect. A 100 per cent effort is called for, and for the muscle this means drawing on every ounce of creatine phosphate it can muster, and using as many muscle fibres as possible. Interestingly, it is believed that not even the most highly trained athletes would be able to use all available muscle fibres with any contraction. Between 10 and 30 seconds or so of maximum effort is possible before the muscle seizes up owing to the excessive level of lactic acid. Again there is no alternative but to slow down and get into aerobic mode, so that all this hard muscular metabolism can be recycled via the circulation and by means of the conversion of glucose molecules to their compound storage form – glycogen. Glycogen can be stored within a muscle or in the liver, and unfortunately any excess will automatically be converted into fat and stored around the organs and directly under the skin.

What would happen if the ordinary rider were to try to match the hardened racer, pedal revolution for pedal revolution? As we have already seen, the former's oxygen transportation system is likely to be less efficient and may be out of practice at moving things around quickly, and so will soon find it impossible to cope with the demand. Not only is it not possible to take in as much air with each breath, but also the tubes that carry blood around the body (arteries, arterioles and capillaries, venules and veins) may have some restrictions or blockages. Thickened arteriole walls or fatty deposits, or possibly a poor or inadequate diet over many years, may be factors; the blood itself may be thicker in consistency, so that it circulates more slowly; veins may be weakened or damaged; and there may be fewer red blood cells available to pick up the oxygen from the lungs. As a result, the less fit rider will have nothing like as much oxygen

available as the professional for each muscular contraction or pedal revolution. To match the speed of the professional, he has to try much harder – harder than his aerobic system is able to cope with. More energy is needed, but where from? The glycogen stored in the muscle will have to play its part now, and there is not as much of that available either. Remember that if glycogen takes over, the waste product will soon make the muscle hurt and our average rider will have no option but to slow down. By now the professional is way ahead, working away very efficiently just using his aerobic system. No aching legs for him yet. The best thing the less fit rider can do is to

Above: Mountain biking is a great way to build strength and stamina.

Far left: Anaerobic activity such as hill climbing releases lactic acid, which causes pain, and before long forces the rider to slow down.

Anaerobic fitness

If it hurts then the chances are you are riding anaerobically – using glycogen stored in muscle which releases lactic acid. It is the lactic acid which hurts and prevents the pain from continuing for too long. Less oxygen is used up when you are riding anaerobically.

Irish rider Sean Kelly does battle with St Patrick's Hill, Cork.

turn around and pedal steadily, aerobically, home, replenishing his muscle glycogen stores in the process.

At the bottom of a climb, our professional catches up the ordinary rider's friend, who incidentally left a good half hour ahead, so has taken on his anaerobic (glycogen) energy source to keep him going. Can he perhaps match the professional up a climb? The effort for both of them is likely to be mostly anaerobic, but the highly trained rider has a plentiful supply of muscle glycogen (his diet has been well planned, and contains lots of carbohydrate foods such as wholemeal bread, pasta, rice and potatoes, all of which convert quickly and efficiently into muscle glycogen) and he has far more highly tuned muscle fibres, just waiting to be

called on to help when the going gets tough. It will not be very long before our second less fit rider is puffing harder and hurting sooner, unable to continue at the same pace. He is likely to end up walking to the top, while the professional has practised using his glycogen energy system over several years. Climbing the hill for him will be both aerobic and anaerobic. He has judged his pace perfectly and tried just hard enough to arrive at the top, having avoided any 100 per cent effort, which would also make him have to slow down. He knows that when he reaches the top he can take a well-earned breather and aerobically replenish the stores, ready to tackle the next hill, or mountain.

So what is the secret of success?

The 'Training Zone' Chart

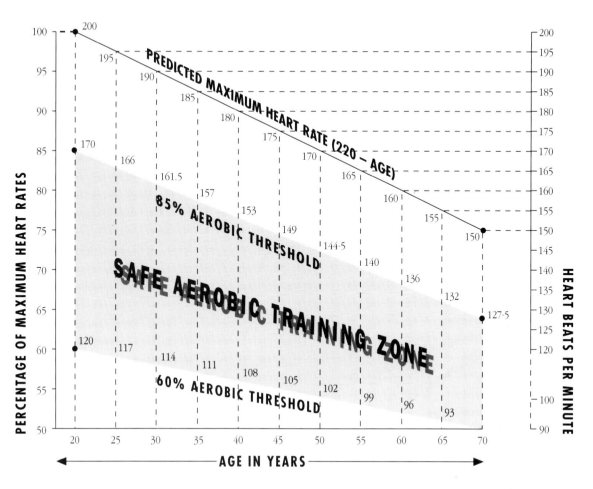

PERCENTAGE OF MAXIMUM HEART RATES

HEART BEATS PER MINUTE

PREDICTED MAXIMUM HEART RATE (220 – AGE)

85% AEROBIC THRESHOLD

SAFE AEROBIC TRAINING ZONE

60% AEROBIC THRESHOLD

AGE IN YEARS

Monitoring your own progress by linking what is happening in your body to how you feel. Knowing when energy is being produced aerobically, appreciating when the work rate is enough to stimulate the cardio-respiratory system to take in more air, to efficiently pump it around the circulation and to teach the muscles to quickly convert circulating energy into efficient contraction.

The breathing and work rate must be increased to a point where the body temperature and circulation are increased. This will mean breathing more deeply, feeling much warmer and sweating a bit. There are many sophisticated methods of measuring increased breathing, or pulse rate, but if a heart monitor is not available (it is not an essential item of equipment initially), then the BORG Scale of Perceived Exertion may be the answer. It has

been proved that checking your own pulse rate during, or immediately after, exercise is not a particularly efficient method of monitoring, since many people find it difficult to locate the pulse quickly. (It is found on the thumb side of the inside wrist about an inch (2.5cm) from the junction of hand and wrist; in the carotid artery within the thick muscles at the side and slightly forward of the neck; or on the heart itself, slightly to the left of centre of the breast bone.)

To assess the pulse rate over one minute, it is usual to check it for 6 or 10 seconds and multiply by 10 or 6. Checks over 15 or 30 seconds or one minute are deemed inaccurate during exercise. The chart above shows you how to assess when your body is working within its aerobic training zone. This chart is age-related and per-

Aerobic fitness

This is work done with oxygen as the main energy source. Blood carries the oxygen and if the level of work is steady the rider can continue for hours without undue fatigue.

tains to healthy individuals without any medical history that might render the chart, or such a level of aerobic work, unsuitable. You will notice that a healthy individual will be aiming to work at between 60 and 80 per cent of his maximum recommended heart rate.

BORG SCALE OF PERCEIVED EXERTION (RÉSUMÉ)

Ask yourself 'How do I feel at this moment?' when exerting yourself. Establish your rating by using the 1-10 scale below.

I FEEL . . .

1   *I am doing nothing to increase my breathing rate. I am freewheeling along the road.*

2   *I am moving gently along the flat, not having to do anything except turn the pedals.*

3   *I am still riding along the flat, but putting slightly more effort in now.*

However, there is a slight increase in breathing rate.

4   *The terrain is becoming undulating, and an occasional effort is needed to maintain the same pace. My breathing has further increased and I am feeling warmer. I am now warmed up and have been riding for at least 10 minutes.*

5   *I am aiming to maintain the same pedal revolutions even though the terrain is becoming tougher. My breathing fluctuates from quite easy to a fair degree of effort. I feel much warmer and am beginning to sweat a little.*

6   *I am now making a conscious effort to speed up a little and am noticing that my breathing is deeper, and I am sweating (or feel an inner warmth) but my legs are feeling quite comfortable at the moment. I can still talk relatively easily to my companion.*

7   *I am beginning to feel good, my body is stimulated to continue the*

Professionals and top amateurs use laboratory testing to help them draw up detailed training programmes.

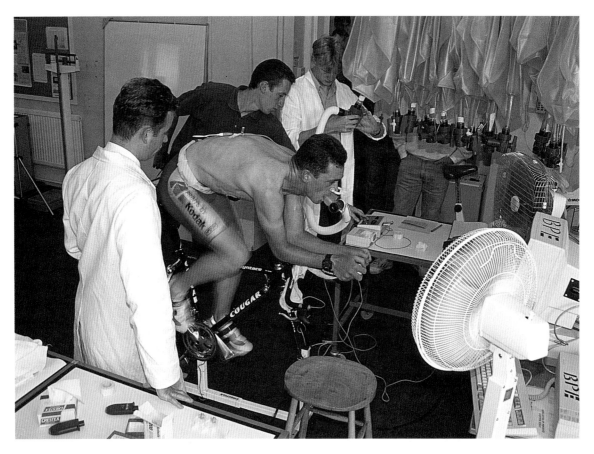

effort, and I feel strong, but my muscles are definitely telling me that they are doing some work.

8   The pace is increasing, but I try to match it. It is an effort now and the thighs and gluteals are beginning to feel very worked. My breathing is still OK but it is much more of an effort to hold this conversation. I begin to wish the pace would ease off a bit. Seven words without taking a breath is just about the maximum I can manage.

9   On reaching a hill, I aim to maintain the pace, but I find that there is a slight burning sensation in the throat and lungs. The leg and buttock muscles are definitely hurting and I can't hold a conversation at all. I know I can't keep this pace up for long.

10   I'm going to give up and take a welcome break. I definitely don't like the burning sensation within the muscles, and I am sure I'm going to cramp up any second now. Speech is impossible now!

The BORG Scale of Perceived Exertion has been in existence for many years, and relies on an individual assessing how he or she feels on a scale. The scale is 1-10 or 1-100, depending on who is advising. It is intended to relate to the pulse rate, and in making assessments for yourself it is important to relate it very much to the question: How do I feel at this moment? If we take a rating of '1' as meaning that there is very little or no physical effort involved, then the breathing rate will not have increased from that of a sedentary state. Our energy will be produced aerobically, but we will certainly be doing nothing to improve aerobic energy efficiency. As exercise increases, so does the perceived exertion rate. If the top of the scale – 10 or 100 – is likened to the effort involved in the final few yards of the two-up sprint for the line, then we have a maximal effort, which could be continued for only a few seconds. We would definitely have been working anaerobi-

cally. We aim to find a level that is between 6 (or 60) and 8-9 (or 80-90) on the scale. At 6 or 60 we would definitely be breathing harder, feeling very warm and sweating a bit, but not actually feeling individual muscles hurting to any great degree. We should feel able to continue for many minutes at this level; we would be able to hold a conversation, albeit slightly breathlessly, with a companion. At 8-9 or 80-90, when the breathing rate would have increased quite significantly, the muscles would also be letting us know they were beginning to hurt a fair amount, but we would not feel the necessity to slow down yet; a conver-

Exhaustion – Dutch professional rider Teun Van Vliet recovers after a gruelling mountain stage of the Tour de France.

The final sprint – this is the time when every last ounce of anaerobic energy can be exploited.

Fat

Fat is contained in many foods, especially highly processed ones, and although a little fat in the diet is beneficial, most cyclists should aim to keep their fat intake at below 30 per cent of the daily intake. To lose weight you should be riding at a steady pace for two or more hours.

sation would be quite difficult – a maximum of seven words could be uttered between breaths. We would know now that we were at the top end of the aerobic training zone, and certainly bordering on anaerobic work. We may feel that to maintain this pace for long would be quite difficult.

It is important to realize that a good basic aerobic fitness level is an essential part of every athlete's road to success, so if you are just beginning, or have not cycled for many months or years, I urge you to work at about 6-7 or 60-70 on the BORG scale, for several weeks, working at least three or four times a week for in excess of 30 minutes at a time, before moving up to the next level.

Working at or around the anaerobic threshold (7-9 or 70-90) will quickly increase aerobic capacity, but it could place too high a demand on a sluggish or inefficient cardio-respiratory system, as well as on joints and muscles, which may well need a bit more gentle lubrication before they feel ready to be stressed thus.

Set yourself long-term fitness goals; weeks, months and years rather than

days and weeks. Give the body a chance to adapt both physically and mentally before making too much effort. Do not be too hard on yourself. Cycling is supposed to be pleasurable as well as occasionally hard work. Trying to ride above your current level of fitness or ability will lead to aches, pains, possible injury and a lack of enthusiasm. Even worse, you may decide that the quest for fitness and enjoyment from this superb sport is not for you after all.

Monitor your progress carefully by assessing how you feel during and after rides, including even the next and subsequent days. Do not ride six days out of seven until you have been riding regularly for several months. Initially three or four rides per week will be plenty. Later on, never ride hard seven days out of seven. One day off a week is a good rule of thumb.

The incentive to carry on will come from the way you should begin to feel. You will have more energy during the day, as well as an inner glow of satisfaction at actually doing something positive about improving your personal life-support machine – the heart.

Physically you should have begun to look better. You will perhaps have lost a little fat from the subcutaneous level of the skin, rediscovered muscles and improved in shape. It may be that on the scales you see little or no difference to your former body weight. But don't forget: muscles weigh more than fat!

Eating your way to fitness

Above I have talked at length about energy, primarily aerobic energy, explaining that aerobic energy is produced in the presence of oxygen. But I have made little mention of the other factors that must be present to enable this energy conversion to take place. To a muscle fibre, energy production means ATP (Adenosine Tri-Phosphate), and before a muscle can contract, the energy must have been converted into this source of usable currency.

Circulating in the blood, to be used in this process, are two important nutrients: the first is the result of the breakdown of carbohydrate foods. This, in its simplest form, is known as glucose. Only single molecules of glucose are able to circulate in the blood. When glucose is stored, either in the muscles (to be used when anaerobic activity is undertaken) or in the liver as an overflow store, it is known as glycogen. Glycogen is quite simply several molecules of glucose joined together in a chain. The same glucose will be stored in the long-term deposit – as fat, generally under the subcutaneous skin tissue (also known as adipose tissue) when the stores within the muscles and the liver are full. The muscles are only able to store a relatively small amount of glycogen, although training anaerobically will increase their storage potential and improve the convertibility of glycogen into ATP. This food source is, however, recognized as being very rapidly converted, when necessary, into ATP.

Good dietary sources of carbohydrate:
Vegetables – primarily root vegetables
Fruit – apples, oranges, pears and particularly bananas

It is vital to eat during a long race – a professional will take on food handed up and prepared by team personnel at least twice during a long event.

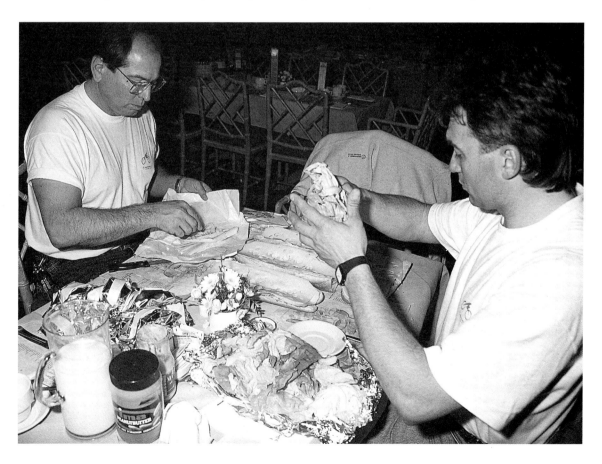

Eating for riding

The following snacks are recommended:
Muesli or fruit bars with minimal or no added sugar
Dried fruit such as raisins, figs and apricots
Bananas, sliced apples and other fruits
Carbohydrate-based foods of own preference

Pulses – peas, and beans such as haricot, kidney, soya
Nuts – unsalted
Wholemeal bread
Pasta
Rice
Cereal
Potatoes

It is recommended that at least 65 per cent of the daily diet should be based on the above foodstuffs, but many athletes increase this proportion to as much as 85 per cent.

Simple sugars (sucrose, fructose, maltose, or anything ending in 'ose') are not recommended as a good food source. Their breakdown requires very little digestion since they are generally so highly processed that they are also of very little nutritional value. Only during extreme exercise, for example in a long-distance event, when there is no time for the body to digest a more complex carbohydrate, can a simple sugar be recommended. Even then, there are many more nutritious products available in liquid form that would be preferable. Simple sugars are contained in jam, pastries, cakes, sweets, chocolate and drinks such as lemonade, colas and fruit squashes.

The second nutrient that is vital to aerobic metabolism is fat. This, having been digested, is broken down into free fatty acids and glycerol, and is transported either in the blood or in the lymphatic system, depending on its type, to sites where it is needed. Excess fat is stored as adipose tissue under the skin. Fat is a vital constituent in the diet, although it is generally agreed that we eat too much of it. It is recommended that no more than 30 per cent of our daily intake of food should be in the form of fat, the majority of which should be unsaturated. Quite a lot less than 30 per cent would be sufficient for the majority. Fat hides in many foods, particularly highly processed foods, and is often eaten unwittingly. A good tip is to read food labels carefully. Recent legislation on product labelling is making it easier to identify fat content.

When you are working aerobically

fat is broken down with glucose, in the presence of oxygen, to form ATP (muscular energy). Good news for people who want to lose weight? Yes, provided that the exercise is of the right type, aerobic, such as steady-paced cycling; at the right level for the person – 6-7.5 on the BORG Scale of Perceived Exertion – and for the right length of time – in excess of 30 minutes continuous cycling, but preferably at least two hours. The level and duration of work determines how the body reacts to the reabsorption of fat from adipose tissue. If the work level is too high and the duration too short, then the stores of glycogen within the muscle are more likely to be converted instead. Fat takes time to metabolize.

Recommended fat sources are unsat-

urated, and are characteristically in liquid form at room temperature. Beware of hidden fats in cheeses, meats, nuts, cakes, chips, crisps, mayonnaise etc.

Protein also forms an essential part of the diet, and appears in meats, cheeses, eggs and fish. It is also found in legumes, lentils and peas. Beans are a prime source, as are nuts and seeds. Protein is also found in breads, pastas and other carbohydrate foodstuffs.

Protein breaks down in the body into amino acids, which are vital for building and repair of tissues. Of the twenty-one amino acids there are eight that cannot be made by the body itself and so must be consumed. The others are interchangeable and can be combined within the body to produce pep-

tides and protein when needed. The amount of protein an individual needs is surprisingly small, even for an athlete undergoing a heavy training programme. One gram of protein per kilogram (2.2lb) of body weight per day should be enough. This means an average 70-kg (154lb) male should eat about 70-100g (2½-4oz) and a female a little less, say 70g (2½oz) on average per day. Approximately 15 per cent of a balanced diet would be derived from protein sources.

Protein powders and high-protein diets are a thing of the past in the eyes of the athlete. For it is now understood that increasing muscle strength and endurance come from hard work and the continued improvement of carbohydrate metabolism. Instead of seeing a

Eating on the move is tricky but essential during lengthy races. Stephen Roche of Ireland (right) shows the professional's solution to the problem.

Drinking

Water
Diluted fruit juice
Carbohydrate-based drinks
(there are plenty on the
market)

139

plate of steak and eggs facing a rider before a hard stage of, say, the Tour de France, you are more likely to see enormous plates of spaghetti with a light sauce, or bowls of cereal with additional fruit.

Other vital nutrients are vitamins, minerals, and trace elements. Much has been written about vitamin intake and it is easy to be trapped into spending large amounts of money on vitamin tablets in the hope that they will improve performance. Generally speaking, if the diet is well balanced and nutritious, then additional vitamins should not be necessary. Indeed, many are toxic if taken in large quantities. Beware in particular of taking excessive amounts of vitamins A, D, E and K, all of which can easily be stored within the body.

Minerals and trace elements (electrolytes) are essential, but in minute amounts. They often appear in the fluid-replacement drinks that are recommended for athletes. During exercise it is much more likely that concentrations of these electrolytes within the body will become stronger since water is lost in large amounts through sweating. Much more beneficial will be replacing the water without taking in any additional electrolytes. However, it could be sensible to dilute commercial drinks by many times more than the manufacturers recommend, thereby ensuring the speediest possible absorption of fluid.

A balanced diet, combined with regular rides, can allow an amateur rider to compete well into middle age.

Nutrition in a nutshell

1   *If calorific (food) intake exceeds calorific output (energy used), then all excess, whether it is derived from carbohydrates, protein or fat sources, will be stored as adipose tissue (fat) under the skin.*

2   *Carbohydrate metabolism will stimulate and increase basal metabolic rate or BSM (this refers to the basic body functions that take place throughout life, and does not refer to muscular metabolism). Carbohydrate high diets, provided the intake is controlled, are recommended to anyone wishing to lose weight. Cutting out carbohydrate or reducing it dramatically and disproportionately, will lead to failure in long-term maintenance of weight loss.*

3   *Complex carbohydrates are converted into energy more readily than any other foodstuff.*

4   *Eating little and often maintains energy levels throughout the day more efficiently than eating one large meal a day. Eating and drinking are also*

Luis Herrera is a superb hill climber, thanks to his light build and, in some part, to having trained at the high altitudes typical of his native Colombia.

important during races, and again little and often is the key.

5 A carbohydrate-based breakfast is the most important meal of the day for anyone, but particularly for an active cyclist or exerciser.

6 Drink during long-distance rides. It is essential to drink before you feel thirsty. Begin drinking little and often within 15 minutes of starting the ride, especially if the day is hot, and then drink regularly at a minimum interval of every 15-30 minutes, to prevent dehydration and imbalances. Water is highly recommended.

7 Avoid sugary foods and drinks. Energy levels will fluctuate violently as a result of too sudden an increase of blood-sugar levels. If in doubt, drink plain water.

8 In calorific (energy) terms, fat contains twice as many calories per gram – in comparison to carbohydrate and protein, which contain 3.75 and 4 respectively. Alcohol contains 7.

9 Always allow at least a two-hour gap after eating a large meal before riding vigorously.

Get fit

Scientific preparation and a meticulous approach to training, diet and lifestyle are the key to race fitness. Being fit not only improves your chances of success – it also makes you feel better. **Allan Peiper**

Fitness and health

Both should go hand-in-hand says Allan Peiper, who knows that when he feels well he can ride well and perhaps even win.

Author Allan Peiper is one of the most experienced professionals riding in Europe today.

The last ten years as a professional cyclist have made me realize that no two people are alike. This holds true for everyone, not just competitive cyclists, and I hope this chapter will act as a guide to the two most important factors involved in cycling – training and diet. You can integrate these ideas into your life, but remember: your needs are always different from those of others.

Ever since I began cycling there has always been a driving force inside me aiming to be the best. When I reached professional level I had to fight hard against the top riders in the world. I made great progress in my first three or four years as a professional but then I reached a peak and could go no further. I felt that if I could change various aspects of my life maybe I could improve again, enough to give me that elusive big win. This quest has led me to new ideas about training and diet.

Feeling good in everyday life depends on the energy level of our bodies. This level can be greatly improved by careful exercise and a well-planned diet. A professional cyclist will endeavour to do better in order to gain results and eventually make more money. The recreational rider should strive for the same excellence, and a bonus of feeling more alive and healthy is that these improvements will radiate through other areas of your life.

The beginner

The most important thing about cycling is the enjoyment it gives. When you enjoy something you do it better. We all begin cycling for fun in the first place and the emphasis should always be on having a good time. That way you won't get bored and overfatigued.

Beginners should wear a helmet and pick roads that are not too busy, for traffic is the cyclist's biggest curse. Use a reasonably low gear and pedal quickly instead of pushing high gears. You probably won't have the basic fitness to do really heavy work to start with. Using high gears only causes a high heart rate and possibly injury

such strain. Overweight people should put the emphasis on long and easy training. I see a lot of overweight people riding hard to lose weight. This type of high-pulse-rate training only causes muscle energy to be burnt. Professionals train for long hours by doing long, slow rides that teach the body to burn fat before muscle energy. Overweight people should also remember that their hearts are untrained, for this condition goes hand in hand with being overweight. Faced with the strain of excess body weight and hard physical effort, an untrained heart can be dangerously overloaded. Easy is best.

Training for the beginner should last from 30 minutes to two hours, depending on the amount of free time you have. By enjoying each ride you will build for the future and will long for the next outing. But if each ride becomes a slog and you do it only to lose weight, your interest in cycling will be short-lived. Top physical condition is built over a long period of time. It is better to ride for one hour a day for six months than to do two hours four times a week and stop after two

Training can be fun even in winter, as long as you wear warm clothing that does not restrict movement, and steer clear of busy roads.

Crash helmets should be carefully selected for a good fit and comfortable strap system. Most are made from expanded polystyrene and are very light. Racers should ensure that there is enough ventilation for summer riding.

months because you are sick of it. I cannot advise you on how much you should ride and how often, except to say that training every day is better than training every few days, even if the time allotted is smaller. Try not to ride in traffic, as the fumes are worse for you than bad food. Sunset or sunrise are beautiful times to ride. The more often you ride the better you will learn to handle your bike and the more aware you will be of traffic and your own physical fitness.

To summarize, use low gears, do not ride too hard and stop when you start to get tired. Remember to take a pump, a spare tyre, money, drink and

possibly some food.

The theory of training

In the last few years training methods have changed dramatically. When Francesco Moser set a new world hour record in 1984 cyclists began to take a more scientific view of training. Old ideas were put to death, such as the notion that there is no substitute for racing. Not long after his record rides Moser won one of the biggest one-day races, Milan-San Remo, with no racing beforehand. The old method of training basically revolved around long-distance riding, which was done with a relatively low pulse rate. This trained the muscles for the distance but also taught the body to burn fat so that the muscle energy would be saved for the final phase of the race, when really hard, power riding would be called for.

Long-distance training is still relevant today but what Moser and his doctors did was to find a way to increase muscle energy so that more power could be produced, giving bigger efforts and greater results. To explain what muscle energy is, all you have to do is remember the last time you made an intense physical effort and how your muscles felt the next day. Tired muscles need rest to recover lost energy.

I have done many lactic acid tests to determine my training levels and doing so has improved certain aspects of my cycling. To do a lactic acid test you sit on a bike, usually in a laboratory, and ride for three-minute periods while the load is gradually increased, making ped-

A group of amateurs, well wrapped up against the cold, take part in a training ride. Group riding in winter can provide some of the most enjoyable cycling of the year.

alling more difficult. At the end of each three-minute period a sample of blood is taken from the end of your finger. This continues until you can pedal no more: usually after between 20 and 27 minutes. After the ride the blood samples are tested to determine the lactic acid levels. A crude comparison can be made between lactic acid and the ash from a fire. Energy is burnt in the muscles, leaving lactic acid, as a fire leaves ash. As the level of effort increases, the lactic acid builds up and becomes more concentrated until the muscles are saturated. This occurs because the blood cannot get rid of it quickly enough to let the muscles work freely. By determining the levels of lactic acid the aerobic and anaerobic thresholds can be measured. These two terms mean your endurance level, which is about 70 per cent of maximum effort, and your resistance level, which is about 90 per cent of maximum effort.

Having found these two levels, you can use a pulse meter and ride just below them, thus training the body to get used to working at one intensity. The body then moves up to higher pulse-rate levels that allow for the same pulse rate but with a lower lactic acid level. The difference may be minute but at the end of a 280-km (174 miles) race, when only the best survive, it can mean the difference between winning and losing. This type of training helped me improve my power during climbing. It did not make me a climber but when the good guys rode away I was always a bit slow to go with them. After a small amount of pulse-rate training I could take more of a pounding.

This type of training has its advantages and also its problems. After a period of hard racing and training using intervals, fatigue sets in like never before. There are two theories to explain this. One is that during strenuous effort lactic acid is built up and, since it is an acid, it must be counterbalanced to keep the blood in equilibrium. This is done with stores of alkaline buffers or deposits. These alkalines

eventually run out, so that the muscles are not serviced as they would be in normal circumstances and chronic fatigue sets in. The only cure is rest. Making maximum efforts only in races and breaking these up with long, easy rides or recovery days gives the body time to build up its alkaline levels again.

The second theory is that the muscle energy has been used to depletion so many times that the muscles do not have the reserves (vitamins, minerals, trace elements) at hand to recover completely and so the total muscle-energy level gets lower each time, leading to a loss of form. This type of laboratory-tested, body-breaking training should only be undertaken by mature adults at least twenty-four years old. Under that age the body is not completely developed and deep usage of body reserves could impede total beneficial growth. In the last couple of years I have been using a mixture of three types of training: recovery, before and after racing; long-distance training, for endurance and fat burning; and also high-intensity interval work to increase the volume of muscle energy. There is a fine line between peak con-

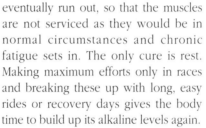

Many riders, both amateur and professional, now use pulse meters for training and sometimes racing.

Strict rules

Training and racing should be fun in the fifteen to seventeen age group but serious riders of eighteen or more must learn to follow a strict physical and mental programme if they are to achieve success.

dition and going over the top, which is why I have a trainer who designs my programme each week, discusses with me how I am feeling and makes adjustments when necessary.

Riders of 15-17

When I was this age I had a drive to win that kept me training all the time. I used to drag my friends out riding in the rain and over mountains, and I used to love it. My parents did not involve themselves in what I did and so I only had myself to blame if I did not train. I used to train for 40-100km (25-62 miles) a day and on Sundays I would do a long ride of up to 160km (100 miles) with all my friends of the same age. We raced some of the time, stopped for picnics and had the occasional mountain or sprint race. It was great fun to train and race without a care in the world.

Since then I have seen many riders in this age group being pestered and trained by their parents. It is great to have parents who are involved, but not to the extent that they demand that the rider goes training or that they are angry if he does not race well. This can turn the young cyclist away from the sport. Sadly, in many cases it is due to the parents' frustration at not having had the same opportunities as a youth. If a young rider yearns to be a champion he will train hard and live for what he wants. No parent can give this to a child because in the end the courage to race comes from within.

At this age the body is still growing and needs one complete day off the bike every week. Train lightly before or after a race, spinning the legs to get the lactic acid out. On the other days do 40-100km (25-62 miles) per day, remembering to have fun while you do so. Find some hills and do a couple of sprints each day. If you ever get a period when you are physically drained or mentally tired do not be afraid to have a week or two off – you will benefit from it in the long run. Always use your gears when you are out training. The more you practise with them the better you will know

how to use them in a race. Remember, the aim is to have fun!

Riders of 18-20

At this age the serious work begins. Maybe you do not have the ambition to become a top pro but you may want to be a good club or national rider. I never really thought about being a professional until I was nineteen. I received an offer to ride with Roger De Vlaeminck in the DAF Trucks team, and I would have loved to have done so, but I had just caught hepatitis and I knew I would not make the grade.

Learning to set some strict rules for yourself may be hard in the beginning but when the results start coming the incentive will be greater. Mental application is not a button that you just press; it is an ongoing process of training yourself. Start by paying attention to resting, because your training will be no good if you are not getting enough rest to allow your body to recover. Setting a strict time for bed and not deviating from it is one of the first things to do. When I was seventeen I was in bed every night at 9pm and up at 7.30am. I trained the next morning from 8.30 until 11.30.

At that time I was living with the famous Planckaert family in Belgium, and I trained with the three brothers, Willy, Walter and Eddy. We had a 100-km (62 miles) circuit and we rode Indian file all the way round, each taking 1km (0.6 mile) at the front. My highest gear was 52 x 15 and I used it most of the way. After training we washed out of a bucket because they had no bathroom and then slept for half an hour before lunch. Between 1pm and 6pm I mowed grass, and by 9pm I was back in bed again. This routine was only broken by race days.

I have always needed rest and this has been the case throughout my racing career. Even now, in my thirties, I hit the sack at 9.30pm and sleep for an hour in the afternoon to offset tiredness after training, and this schedule is only broken if I am very busy or travelling. I have had to sacrifice television, parties, concerts and movies all my life.

But I do not think I am a martyr, although at times it has taken a major effort to stick to my routine.

Maintaining your equipment in good order and being careful about what you eat and drink are important factors in your daily routine. Try catching a fly with your hand; normally he gets away. But if you use all your concentration, slowly moving your hand and then making a powerful thrust, you will get him. The same focus is required for cycling, and paying close attention to your equipment, rest, diet and training produces results.

Carry on training as in the previous age group, but extend your rides by 50 per cent. Remember to take a day off and easy days before and after competition. Once a week do a long ride of four to five hours and look for hills – don't avoid them. Spend the first and last 30 minutes of each ride warming up and down on a low gear like 42 x 16. Do two sprints in the last 30 minutes to increase the heart rate and dis-

perse the lactic acid more quickly.

Riders of 20-24

The possibility of Olympic Games or international selection is the goal for this age group. Even if you lack the ability to be a star, there is no reason why you cannot improve, even if it is just to win your own club race.

By the age of twenty the body is beginning to mature and muscles are well developed. The time has come where you can really train hard and aim for big results. Between the ages of twenty and twenty-three I trained over long distances – and not ones that were too easy, for I have always preferred to train hard. I find my body responds best when alternating days of tiredness and rest. Doing two rides a week of six to seven hours, plus a few others, really built up my endurance. The days in between I did 30-70km (19-43 miles) to work and back.

If possible, riding behind a motorbike is fantastic for the day after a race

International selection and racing abroad should be the aim for an ambitious rider in his or her early twenties. Races in France and Belgium have traditionally attracted amateur teams from other countries and the competition is always tough when national pride is at stake.

or between long rides. This gets the legs spinning at 40-45kph (25-28mph) in 52 x 16. When you are really tired it is hard to get the body going, but when paced by a motorbike you just follow. An hour to an hour and a half is enough to loosen up your muscles and get the blood moving so as to clear out the waste. This will also help to get some speed into the muscles after long endurance work.

Planning your season is a great way to build toward success in competition. If you plan to hit peak condition two or three times every season, with each peak lasting about three weeks, you will do much better in the long run because you have a focus that you can build towards – instead of just racing from week to week without a goal. Without a goal your attitude is 'I'll see how it goes', but this lack of focus has no direction. Remember the fly!

After a peak period you can take a week of rest, which will be well deserved if you have trained and raced to your maximum. Do things you enjoy

Thermal clothing like this winter jacket has revolutionized training in cold and wet weather.

other than cycling, but remember you are a cyclist with a goal. Don't end up in a night club drinking beer until 3am. Keep your build-up plan at the back of your mind so you know what lies ahead and can breeze through it. This type of attitude will be an advantage to you if you wish to become a professional. You would not believe how many professionals are totally confused because they have no planning. If you were to ask what goals they have for next year, 90 per cent would say nothing and look baffled.

If you work hard there is no reason why you cannot be fit and share the same objectives as other full-time riders. The accent must be on quality, not quantity. Try to put in a three or four-hour ride every week, probably two days before the race. You could do half before and half after work with 30 minutes of time trialling included. Try to arrange a motorbike for an hour one evening and go at around 50kph (31mph) after warming up for 15 minutes at 40kph (25mph).

Another ride of up to two hours, should include one hour full of 20-second bursts flat out, with five minutes in between each. These bursts use ATP (Adenosine Tri-Phosphate), which is direct energy. ATP is used before muscle energy but it only lasts for about 20 seconds. When you have climbed a flight of stairs and you feel dead at the top, your ATP has been used and your muscle energy is about to begin. The good thing about these bursts is that ATP causes no build-up of lactic acid and after five minutes has been replaced again. This type of training also improves your resistance levels, by increasing your heart beat, and can be

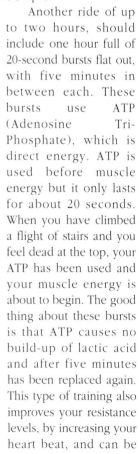

incorporated into a normal week of training. If you work during the week and race on Sundays, try to ride an extra hour or two after the race. This is very worthwhile when you are building up to a period of peak condition, because you are extending your limits.

Remember that for rides of over two hours you should take food and drink. During training you sweat and lose liquids, and these must be replaced. Your body is also busy cleaning itself while training: the kidneys work harder to eliminate toxins, helping the body to function better under the stress of riding. Once your stomach is empty you begin to use reserves of energy you need to train and race with. By eating you can replace some of this energy. Try to take quality food with you; Formula 1 engines do not run on diesel.

Cycling gloves should have reinforced palms and not be too bulky.

Neoprene overshoes keep feet warm and dry in winter.

Clothing

It does not matter if you do not have a long-sleeved team jersey or thermal leg warmers; the important thing is to be

Bib shorts with built-in braces are comfortable to wear and cover the lower back more effectively than conventional shorts.

aware of your body temperature and keep it stable. In the last few years cycle clothing has evolved greatly. Neoprene gloves and overshoes will keep your hands and feet warm. When the weather is cold and wet, you can feel the water getting warm inside the neoprene. It is not so good in dry weather because you perspire too much. Thermal suits, jackets and arm and leg warmers are great for keeping out the cold and help to maintain the temperature level in the rain. Gore-tex rain capes have also made life easier because you can wear one and, unlike with the old plastic variety, still ride hard without overheating. All of these articles of clothing are expensive, but well worth saving for. When it is raining my only real concern is my hands getting cold and losing their grip. With neoprene, I am safe.

The most important thing about clothing is that it should keep the body temperature up so as not to impede endurance and also to avoid muscle or tendon trouble. When the muscles get cold they do not function properly and it is easy to overload them and cause an injury. If you are too warm you can always remove clothing, but if you are cold to the bone then you are lost.

Bunch riding requires nerve and skill and can only come with experience. Training in a small group is a useful way of learning the basic skills.

There is no excuse for getting too cold, except in really atrocious weather.

Heat distribution is worth thinking about. In really cold races you see a lot of riders wearing two or three jerseys and a cape, but no leg warmers. It seems silly to me that the top of the body can be so well protected and the lower half open to let the heat fly out. Some riders complain of difficulty racing with leg warmers and say they get wet anyway. The important thing is that the wind is kept off the skin and muscles. Rain is not as bad as wind, and wind is even worse when the weather is wet. The main areas from which the body loses heat are the head, hands, feet and groin. When it is really cold, wearing a woollen cap under your crash hat makes an amazing amount of difference. This is one advantage of hard-shell helmets: they are warmer when it is cold.

Keep your clothing washed and looked after and it will last a lot longer. Sweaty clothing is a haven for bacteria, and shorts, especially, should be washed at least after every second ride. Chamois inserts should be dried carefully, not in direct sunlight, and kept soft with chamois cream if they start to feel dry and stiff.

Riding in the bunch

My first three years with the professionals were a difficult time when it came to bunch riding, especially on short, sharp hills or cobbled sections, where you can be left behind if there are falls or the bunch splits. I used to marvel at how some riders could make the first ten in the last 200m (220 yards) before a crucial moment, when they had not been near the front in the preceding kilometres. Fighting with 200 riders for position has many pitfalls. Good positioning can save a lot of energy because you will not have to chase if the bunch splits or if a group rides away. The bunches you ride in as an amateur may not be as hectic as the bunch that approaches a stretch of cobbles at 60kph (37mph) in Paris-Roubaix, but if you remember a few of the following tips you might make the race-winning break.

As a young professional I could never figure out why, when I moved up the side of the bunch to the front, I would end up at the back via the middle. The middle of the bunch is nowhere, unless you are Stephen Roche, who can find room between another rider's handlebars! Move to the front and stay on the side of the bunch behind the second or third rider. When someone passes you, drop in behind him and follow him as he moves towards the head of the bunch. In this way you can move up and back along the side of the bunch, but are always sheltered from the wind. It takes practice to get it right but if the bunch starts to ride hard in a side wind you will be ready. When the bunch is riding hard, move up on the wind side if you cannot follow someone else up. By taking the sheltered side you will not get room on the road. Using the wind side will get you there quickly. It may cost you a little energy, but you will have the position you want at the front.

If there is a strong side wind and the bunch is grouped tightly together you can use either the wind side or the sheltered side of the bunch. If the pace is high the best position is the sheltered side on the edge of the road, and let nobody through to put you out of place. Holding a good position takes a lot of concentration because everybody wants to be where you are. Learning to control your bike comes with practice. Over the years, by trial and error, you can learn all there is to know about racing. Keep your eyes and ears open and listen to everybody – even the ones that sound like fools! But in the end you must make your own decisions about how to ride.

Diet

In my opinion diet is the second biggest factor in cycling. If your body is not healthy you will not be able to train properly, let alone recover. It is my firm belief that when a professional rider's health is 100 per cent, his form must be good. By looking at a rider's face you can usually tell how his form is. Good diet is the foundation of a healthy body. Mind and body always work as two horses pulling one cart. With a good diet your mind has clarity, because the clearer your blood the better you feel. Diet, air and mental outlook all have big effects on our health. Diet is one thing we have full

Eat to win

Peiper's diet is as natural as he can make it – not an easy task when many of his meals are taken away from home in hotels and foreign countries.

Fresh fruit, oats, honey, lentils and pasta are all good basic foodstuffs both for training and racing.

On all but the shortest rides you should always take a drinking bottle along. Racers can get through several bottles per race.

control over in our daily lives.

The basis of a good diet is fruit and vegetables. The only differences between the good diet of a sportsman and the average person are the quantity and the carbohydrate intake. Fruit and vegetables are the prime sources of vitamins, minerals and fibre. The other foods added to a meal are carbohydrate and proteins for maintaining and building muscle. Raw fruit and vegetables are a living force, whereas meat is dead, although it is a good source of protein. If you were to live solely on meat your health would rapidly deteriorate, but a diet of fruit and vegetables would sustain you well under normal conditions. Fruit also cleanses the body, helping to eliminate the toxins that build up and can cause a loss of vitality and health. Meat causes the same toxic build-up and when we eat a steak we get the toxins as well as the protein. Fruit and vegetables generally help to balance out, clean and vitalize our bodies.

Over the past twelve years I have tried to adhere as closely as possible to a natural diet. It has been difficult being away from home so much, and I have had to compromise my beliefs to a great extent. But when I get home I eat as I like to: natural wholefoods. Spending 100 days a year in hotels, being served race food packed with refined sugar, was a problem for me but I have learnt to adjust as best as possible to any situation. I do eat meat now and then but I always stick to prime cuts of beef or lamb when away. At home I eat chicken and fish regularly, each about once a week. However, I will not eat chicken from the supermarket. How can you grow a chicken in thirty days? I try to eat deep-sea fish that has not been caught in sewage-infested waters.

The body works better and produces more energy when food and water are pure. In a 1990s diet, processed, de-nourished, take-away food is commonplace. Why not be generous to your body and give it food that makes you feel and ride better? The key is to focus on natural foods, the closer to nature the better. Read the labels on the food packets you buy. At many supermarkets you can buy, for the same price, foods without preservatives, stabilizers, colourings and conditioners. Instead of white bread, eat wholemeal; brown sugar rather than white. For every processed food there is an alternative. It is a big decision and a real test of character to change your lifestyle, but the results will be worth it. You need not change everything overnight. Aim to change slowly and you will still feel the benefits. The next time you want a can of lemonade, try a fruit juice. Instead of a bar of chocolate, eat an apple or a banana.

Breakfast for me usually consists of freshly squeezed grapefruit or orange juice mixed half and half with water, so that I only need one piece of fruit. My favourite breakfast is fresh fruit sliced and chopped with natural, unsweetened muesli, extra raisins, natural yoghurt, some chopped or ground nuts, soya or fresh milk and half a tablespoon of honey. It sounds like a lot but you just need a little bit of each. It contains all the energy needed for the day. If I have room I will have two pieces of wholemeal toast with butter and Vegemite. Every four days I have oat porridge cooked with raisins and chopped apple and topped with yoghurt and honey or brown sugar. If I am about to do a long ride I may have an egg on toast after one of these courses. These are my two favourite breakfasts.

On rides longer than two hours I always take food and a bottle filled with water. As training food I might have a wholemeal sandwich with cheese, jam or honey. I also eat muesli bars, bananas, dried figs or dates. I do not stop during training for either drink or food.

Lunch at home is always based around a salad. When I am tired from training or recovering from races I find a big mixed salad fills me up but does not slow me down. It allows me to recover a little because it is not heavy. By salad I mean raw vegetables. Usually we have between five and ten different vegetables, mixed, chopped, sliced or grated. It could be lettuce, white cabbage, grated carrot and beetroot, sliced red peppers and chopped celery with an olive-oil sauce, milk whey or apple-cider vinegar, salt, pepper and crushed garlic. It is an inexpensive meal but it does take a little time to prepare.

If you do not like to eat much salad you could start by having a small salad before your evening meal. This slowly adapts the body and the taste buds. The more you eat the more you will want. Always chop, slice and grate as finely as possible as it makes for less chewing and will help to prevent indigestion. With the salad I have a boiled egg, omelette, toasted cheese sandwich or wholemeal pasta with a cheese and tomato sauce. I try not to drink with meals as this waters down the digestive juices and makes life more difficult for the stomach.

Evening meals are cooked and usually based on rice. I use wholemeal rice, boiled slowly until the water has nearly evaporated. Sometimes I have rice and wheat in equal quantities, cooked the same way. Baked potatoes in their jackets are a fantastic food, and occasionally I have them mashed. I always eat butter, as it is natural. I love fish or chicken but very rarely eat red meat. It is not that I disagree with eating animals or dislike meat, but I do think we eat meat indiscriminately. I believe that people who do not play sports would be much healthier without meat. If I eat meat I always have it first because the digestive juices needed to deal with meat are much stronger than those needed for carbohydrates. Cooked vegetables I eat include carrots, peas, beans, pumpkin, spinach, eggplant and stuffed peppers. Occasionally I have a dessert of stewed apples with yoghurt. In the evening a cup of herb tea and a biscuit rounds off the day.

My wife is a vegetarian and makes many unusual dishes with lentils, millet and vegetables, as well as vegetarian lasagne, spaghetti or nut cutlets. We also eat vegetarian sausages, tofu (soyabean curd) and wheat protein. Make sure you always wash fruit and vegetables to clean off any sprays and coatings. A small coffee-grinder is ideal for grinding nuts, wheat, and sunflower seeds finely enough for the body to digest them without waste. These grains and seeds are full of life-giving force. To illustrate this point, grains of wheat 5000 years old were found under the pyramids – they were given a little water and they sprouted!

I hope this chapter has given you some insight into training and diet. Competitive cycling is a fantastic sport but there can be no half measures if you want to make it to the top. Change is what life is all about. Dare you take the positive steps that one day might produce a champion?

Develop your diet

Peiper's diet has evolved over a number of years and no one would expect a young racer to change his or her eating habits overnight. Elements of the Peiper diet, like eating more fresh fruit and vegetables and upping the carbohydrate intake, can be adopted straight away. Other aspects can be tried out on a longer-term basis.

Life as an amateur

Not every keen rider wants to become a full-time professional and, with the growth of international amateur racing, there is no need to. **Paul Kimmage**

Start young

Young cyclists can start racing at around fifteen years in the schoolboy or girl category. Serious racing, however, need not be contemplated for up to three or four years.

Young racers on the start line – above all else, competition at this stage should be fun and free from the pressure to win.

The attic of my home is decorated with memories of my youth. A big wooden desk with a portable computer and a printer fight for space with newspapers, match programmes and half an inch of coffee in a cup that should have been washed a couple of days ago. The sloping walls are covered with photographs of my years as a professional, press cuttings of my races as an amateur and faded prints of when I was a spotty-faced teenager with woollen shorts and a bicycle that was two sizes too big for me. When the creative juices are not flowing,

when the blank screen of the computer is stinging my eyes, it is comforting to lift my head and lose myself in the images on the walls – a youth of sore backsides and grazed elbows.

Where to begin? Life as a pro? What do I remember most? The descents from the mountains, speeding from one hairpin to the next, the grime of a day's racing on my legs, the wind blowing freely through my hair, the thrill of speeding towards the chequered flag at the end of a long day in a decent group with some good racers behind me on the mountain. The exhil-

aration that comes with fear: 50mph (80kph) on the mountain – one mistake and I'm gone. The next bend approaches. Size it up, ease off the brakes, then lean into it. Watch for gravel or traces of diesel left by the publicity caravan. The rims are starting to heat – time to alternate the braking. A touch with the front, a touch with the back – can't let the rims get too hot or the tyre will roll or blow. Last corner, a flat-out right. Made it.

Life as an amateur? More fear, a different kind of fear, standing on the start line of the world amateur road-race championship with the green of my country on my back. Shoulder to shoulder now with 200 of the world's hungriest bike riders as we await the explosion of the starter's gun for the biggest test of our lives. My heart thumping with excitement in my chest, the adrenalin flowing as it has never flowed before and everything, my whole existence, hinging on the outcome of the next four hours.

And then you hear it: the earth-shattering crack of the pistol, followed by the explosive burst from the start line and you're so nervous: 'Oh God if only I could be some place else.' And it starts, the journey into the unknown and four hours later, when it is over, you sit back and reflect that you would not swap the experience for the world.

Life as a boy? My first hunger knock. Strength evaporating with every pedal stroke from my body – should have eaten more for my breakfast, made sure I had more in my pockets when I set out from the house. Too late now, 5 miles (8km) to go, Dad pushing me home, barely able to lift my head to keep the bike in a straight line. I must have food, any food – steak, fruit cake, apple tart, anything. Never again. I will never ride this damn bike again – at least not until next time.

Looking back I realize that it was a giant ladder that had to be climbed one step at a time: schoolboy to junior to second-category senior to first-category senior to continental amateur to professional. In a way, I suppose it was a bit like growing up, learning to crawl before you walk and run.

Thank goodness that cycling is in no way as complicated as other sports. A young man in his first race can definitely feel like the champion – Merckx as it was in my time; Induraín, Bugno, or LeMond as it probably is now. I must return to my own experience as an example. I remember my second road race. I was ten years old and it was a handicap event over a 5-mile (8km) loop just outside Dublin on the Navan road. There were five, perhaps six of us in the race. I set off first with another lad of the same age and we were followed a couple of minutes later by the 'elite'. It was largely as a result of my better equipment that I managed to leave my partner on a railway bridge about ½ mile (0.8km) after the start and I can still feel the elation of those first pedal strokes of freedom. I wasn't Paul Kimmage, a spotty ten-year-old puffing and panting to hold 12mph (19kph) as I headed for victory in a handicap event. No, for that wonderful moment I was Eddy Merckx

Every cycling nation is represented at the annual world championships, where the size of the field and the variation in ability make for an unpredictable race.

At whatever level you race, the effort and experience can be as intense as any. Young riders should not over train or race too frequently, however, as the effects can have a lasting physical and mental effect.

heading for glory in Milan – San Remo.

I could hear the television commentator calling out my name and it was magic. In the second race of my cycling career I had discovered one of the great thrills of bike racing – the thrill of breaking away, of being in front. A powerful imagination is a good thing for a young lad starting off. When I was fourteen years old my parents owned a caravan 35 miles (56km) from our home. On summer weekends I would cycle down and, in my imagination, divide that distance into seven different stages of the Tour de France. There was never a dull moment – sprinting, hill climbing and time trialling, and always a desperate last-day chase to hold on to the yellow jersey.

Today, coaching manuals and books leave me a little cold – probably because I think I know it all. As I write, I feel conscious of the need to make my *own* message, or advice, as simple and as readable as possible. For me, the lessons of racing and training are basically a matter of common sense and I have no wish to complicate them with theory and science.

Why race? Competition is in the blood. You are either competitive by nature or not at all. It's not something you can coach, or a magic formula you can buy from a chemist. You either want to or don't want to – it's as simple as that. I suppose the most frustrating thing for any young person who decides he wants to race is the severity of it. Imagine a typical seventeen-year-old – let's call him Dave – on his first day of two-wheeled competition. He is fuelled by great enthusiasm and his general fitness keeps him in touch for 15 miles (24km), but then suddenly his legs go and he loses concentration and tips the wheel of the guy in front. He crashes, slides along a hard, gravelly road, which cuts a chunk out of his expensive shorts and removes most of the skin from his back. Then, writhing from a stinging pain he has never felt before, he crawls to his feet to find his front wheel is now square and the fine paintwork on his frame has been filed with a tarmac rasp. And straight away the harsh realities of bike racing will hit home and he will ask himself the question that, depending on his response, will determine whether he will stay in the sport or not: 'They didn't tell me about this. How much do I really want to race?'

Bike racing is a hard and physically cruel sport and it is only through full acceptance of this that you can begin to enjoy it. Some people race to win, others simply for the fun of competition, but both must endure pain. In this sport pain and pleasure go hand in hand – you can't have one without the other. So, to return to the unfortunate Dave (and he really is unfortunate; I wouldn't wish that first-race experience on anybody); he knocks on my door, tells me he wants to be a champion and asks for advice. So I show him the ladder, the steps he must climb, and begin to teach him to crawl.

The first lesson will be teaching him the skills of keeping his machine between the hedges. Crashes are a harsh reality of cycling life from the beginner right through to the professional and it is only through falling off that we learn to stay upright. There is no compensation for 'hours in the saddle': climbing, descending and cornering until you are at one with your machine, and feel confident on it. Cyclo-cross is perhaps the best way of acquiring bike control – much better than mountain biking, where fat tyres and suspension forks are moving this aspect of cycle sport into a distinct category of its own.

So, having learned the basics of staying upright, and with a fitness gained from a solid winter of regular and sensible training spins, Dave is ready to race. Whether he makes it as a champion depends on his mentality and his athletic ability. I have always believed that winning in bike racing is a question of mind over matter; that mental strength is more than a match for natural talent. I prefer to give credit to the less talented guy who worked hard and stuck it out and fought tooth and nail but got to the top. Of one thing, however, there is no doubt. The mentally strong with mediocre talent can become champions. The mentally

Grazes to the elbows and hips are the cyclist's most common injuries

strong with natural talent can become super-champions.

I can never adequately emphasize the importance of sitting down after each race and having a long, hard think about everything that happened during it. In my own time this was done at Mass on a Sunday evening, or during school on a Monday morning – it used to take me at least two days to get the race out of my system. During physical exercise – racing and training – our bodies are constantly sending us messages. If we are to improve, it is vitally important to spend a little time after each effort trying to decode and interpret these messages. As a simple example, let us imagine for a moment that Dave is really struggling for the first hour of the divisional championship and an important break develops and he is left behind. He feels really angry when it's over. He felt fine for the second and third hour but at

that stage it was too late. What went wrong? The question Dave must ask himself is why was he performing badly in the first hour. Was it because:

1   There was a hard hill at the start and he doesn't climb well?
2   He ate his breakfast two hours before the race and developed a stitch?
3   He had trained really hard two days before the race but rain prevented him from getting out the day before?
4   He had arrived late, taken the bike out of the car, and not had sufficient time to warm up?
5   It was cold and wet. He had forgotten the proper embrocation and started with just a light covering of oil on his legs and his joints were cold?

You would be amazed at the amount

Left: The world championships and the Olympics are the number one goal for an amateur cyclist.
Below: Winter cyclo-cross is a great way to pick up essential bike-handling skills.

Above: Do not expect to race in the sun all the time. Races in Britain, northern Europe and America, as these British women demonstrate, can often be held in cold and wet conditions.

Far right: Pro-am racing is popular in countries with a small professional class. Paul Kimmage (seventh from left) wears the climber's jersey in an early 1980s edition of the Sealink International in the UK.

of guys who would go on race after race thinking that faults like not being able to start quickly are something they inherited from their parents and can do nothing about! There is an answer for every weakness. We just have to look for it.

The modern Formula 1 car is fitted with a 'management system' not unlike the 'black box' that records and stores flight information in jet aircraft. At the end of each practice session an engineer hooks a portable computer into the management system and is fed all the relevant data of the thirty or forty practice laps: speed at each corner, rev counts, gear changes, the vibration and movement of the shock absorbers and so on. When the information has been thoroughly analyzed, the team owner, his engineer and the driver in question all sit down together to discuss how to implement the required changes.

So how is this relevant to our own sport? Well, just think about it. Wouldn't it be wonderful if we could

WORLD AMATEUR CHAMPIONSHIP

SENIOR MEN

1921 G. Skol (Sweden) 190km
1922 D. Marsh (UK) 161km
1923 L. Ferrario (Italy) 160km
1924 A. Leducq (France) 180km
1925 H. Hoevenaers (Belgium) 188km
1926 O. Dayen (France) 183km
1927 J. Aerts (Belgium) 182km
1928 A. Grandi (Italy) 200km
1929 P. Bertolazzo (Italy) 200km
1930 G. Martano (Italy) 194km
1931 H. Hansen (Denmark) 170km
1932 G. Martano (Italy) 137km
1933 P. Egli (Switzerland) 125km
1934 K. Pellenaars (Holland) 112km
1935 I. Mancini (Italy) 162km
1936 E. Buchwalder (Switzerland)145km
1937 A. Leoni (Italy) 204km
1938 H. Knecht (Switzerland) 170km
1946 H. Aubry (France) 189km
1948 H. Snell (Sweden) 186km
1949 H. Faanhof (Austria) 193km
1950 J. Hoobin (Austria) 175km
1951 G. Ghidini (Italy) 172.2km
1952 L. Ciancola (Italy) 175km
1953 R. Filippi (Italy) 180km
1954 E. Van Cauter (Belgium) 150km
1955 S. Ranucci (Italy) 188km
1956 F. Mahn (Holland) 194km
1957 L. Proost (Belgium) 190.4km

1958 G. A. Schur (East Germany) 177.9km
1959 G. A. Schur (East Germany) 189.2km
1960 B. Eckstein(East Germany) 174.6km
1961 J. Jourden (France) 181.5km
1962 R. Boncioni (Italy) 179.3km
1963 F. Vicentini (Italy) 197km
1964 E. Merckx (Belgium) 185,6km
1965 J. Botherel (France) 171.9km
1966 E. Dolman (Holland) 182.4km
1967 G. Webb (GB) 198.8km
1968 V. Marcelli (Italy) 200km
1969 L. Mortensen (Denmark) 180.2km
1970 J. Schmidt (Denmark) 180.3km
1971 R. Ovion (France) 168km
1973 R. Szurkowski (Poland) 162km
1974 J. Kowalski (Poland) 175km
1975 A. Gevoz (Holland) 182km
1977 C. Corti (Italy) 170km
1978 G. Glaus (Switzerland) 182.4km
1979 G. Giacomini (Italy) 178.8km
1981 A. Vedernikov (USSR) 187.6km
1982 B. Drogan (East Germany) 182.4km
1983 U. Raab(East Germany) 179.9km
1985 L. Piasecki (Poland) 177km
1986 U. Ampler (East Germany) 169.4km
1987 R. Vivien (France) 180km
1989 J. Halupczok (Poland) 185.2km
1990 M. Gualdi (Italy) 174km
1991 V. Rjaksinski (USSR) 158km
1993 J. Ullrich (Germany) 184km
Titles not awarded during Olympic years 1972 on.

Raod racing is not the only option for the keen amateur – track competition can be just as exciting and rewarding.

hook one of those 'management systems' into the mind of the frustrated racer who makes the same mistakes week in, week out, and always seems to be chasing his tail? And show him in black and white where he is going wrong. Not that we need to, of course – we were all created with our own management system and a portable computer to analyze it. It's called a brain. How unfortunate then that the average bike racer hasn't realized this simple fact yet.

I cannot overstress the importance of self-analysis after competition. The need to ask yourself: 'Why did I lose that race? What did I do that was positive and negative?' There is no aspect of performance that cannot be improved with work. A second opinion is often valuable and it isn't a bad thing to sometimes seek the advice of a local coach of experienced racing man. But their word should never be taken as Gospel. As individuals we all differ and what's good for one is not necessarily good for another. When Stephen Roche was coming up through the amateur ranks in Ireland, the question he asked most of the many experienced coaches and racing men was: 'And what do you think?' He would take a little of every-

MEN'S OLYMPIC ROAD-RACE CHAMPIONSHIP

SENIOR MEN
1896 Athens, A. Konstantinides (Greece) 87km
1906 Athens, B. Vast (France) 84km
1912 Stockholm, Rud Lewis (South Africa) 320km*
1920 Antwerp, H. Stencquist (Sweden) 175km*
1924 Paris, A. Blanchonnet (France) 188km*
1928 Amsterdam, H. Hansen (Denmark) 168km*
1932 Los Angeles, Attilio Pavesi (Italy) 100km*
1936 Berlin, R.Charpentier (France) 100km*
1948 London, José Beyaert (France) 194.6km
1952 Helsinki, André Noyelle (Belgium) 190.4km

1956 Melbourne, Ercole Baldini (Italy) 187.7km
1960 Rome, Viktor Kapitanov (USSR) 175.3km
1964 Tokyo, Mario Zanin (Italy) 194.8km
1968 Mexico, Pierfranco Vianelli (Italy) 196.2km
1972 Munich, Hennie Kuiper (Holland) 182.4km
1976 Montreal, Bernt Johansson (Sweden) 175km
1980 Moscow, Sergei Soukhorouchenkov (USSR)
1984 Los Angeles, Alexi Grewal (USA) 190.2km
1988 Seoul, Olaf Ludwig (East Germany) 196.8km
1992 Barcelona, Fabio Casartelli (Italy) 194.4km
       *Time trial

thing he was told and apply it to his racing and training.

Success in racing has always been a matter of '*la tête et les jambes*' (the head and the legs). In this modern age of digital speedometers, pulse meters and training schedules, isotonic drinks and liquid food it is very easy to lose sight of the basics and get caught up in the technical. An impression of the current state of amateur cycling in Ireland is that dedication and application have been pushed down the list of priorities, so that, it seems, looking like the champion is easier and more important than racing like him. By contrast, when I was starting out, the formula of success was train hard, eat sensibly and go to bed early. Weaknesses in learning to sprint, working on the climbs, concentrating in time trials were worked on until they became strengths.

I have stressed the importance of a positive mental attitude and in this regard fear of failure can be a terrible handicap. I have witnessed several schoolboy and junior races this year, watched them buzzing around the circuits in one compact group, and the one thing that stands out is that there are so few attacks – they are all content to play follow the leader like a pack of bleating sheep until the final sprint; content to be beaten but part of the group.

There is a misplaced shame about being left behind, about being dropped. The only real shame is in not trying.

During the recent Nissan Classic I had an interesting conversation with Alasdair McLennon, a Scotsman who holds the post of national director of racing in Ireland. He told me the following story about his compatriot Robert Millar, with whom he had raced in his youth.

'Millar used to turn up at every race and go from the line – attack right from the drop of the flag. And we would laugh because he would often be dangling 15 seconds in front for mile after mile. And we would leave him there, reel him in and then leave him behind. But then one day Robert attacked and we never saw him again.'

I suppose the moral of the tale is try and you succeed (try cleverly and you succeed even faster). There is no shame in defeat, no shame in being left behind by the sheep so long as you try. And trying can be fun. There is a wonderful thrill about being in front, either alone or as part of a group. I will never forget my first Tour de France, in 1986. As we moved into the last hour of the seventh stage from Cherbourg to St-Hilaire-du-Harcouët I latched on to an attack by an unknown but immensely strong young Spaniard

Peace race

The Peace Race started in 1948 and until recently was the number one showcase for East European amateurs. Recent winners like Olaf Ludwig, Uwe Ampler and Lech Piasecki, have all gone on to enjoy successful professional careers.

If you can't win against international opposition there is little point in considering a professional career.

called Miguel Induraín. We were joined, in ones and twos, by ten others in what was to be the winning move of the stage. The exhilaration of being in front that day was something I had never experienced before. The buzz of the helicopter overhead, the cheering from the roadside, the attention from the television motorbikes as they moved closer to beam the images of my 'exploit' all around the globe made the long and difficult road to professionalism more than worthwhile.

Although there are no television cameras or screaming roadside supporters at many of the amateur races, the exhilaration of being in front never

changes. It's the thrill of Jerry being chased by Tom and represents for me the true joy of racing. More often than not you will be caught, but the inner satisfaction of going for it more than compensates.

Getting back to our friend, Dave, let's take it that he is dedicated, racing well, has worked his way up the ladder to the rung of the elite or first-category amateur, and wants to become a professional. The first thing he must realize is that he is not alone – in France, Belgium and Spain there will be hundreds of fame-hungry young men just like him. There aren't enough places for all of them. Is he good enough to succeed?

Hard work and ambition have taken him this far but now is the time for honest self-appraisal. He must examine his career and ask himself, 'Can I improve? Am I really good enough? Can I move up the two gears I will need to be a professional?'

There is a cancer eating away at amateur cycling. It's all to do with the star system that has grown up in recent years. It starts with a fifteen-year-old boy smitten by a wild urge to race after seeing his heroes in the Tour de France on television. He buys a bike, wins a few races and within the space of a couple of years his whole life has become cycling. He doesn't want to know about responsibility – school, exams or getting a job! No, he's going to go to Europe to become an international star.

He leaves for France fired with hope and ambition, but it's harder than he imagined – a different language, a strange culture, no English-language television and a spiteful little Frenchman who calls himself a *directeur sportif* and makes his life a misery. Some last for a year,

Riders from the old Soviet Union used to dominate amateur racing. The break-up of the USSR, however, has greatly reduced the pool of riders that can be called upon to race at international level.

others stick it out for two before returning home with nothing but shattered dreams. And they don't want to race in Europe for a while.

When the idea of professionalism gets a hold on you, it is important to take stock, to confront the realities and answer honestly the questions that arise. There is nothing wrong with ambition. Every youngster should aspire to reach the top of the cycling ladder but there comes a time when this aspiration must be tempered with reality. In the last couple of years I have seen young lads in Ireland who are incapable of winning a race at home, leaving to join amateur clubs in France in the hope that eating croissants for breakfast will transform them into Bernard Hinault. It won't.

No amateur who is incapable of winning at international level should even think about turning professional – not that he will be given the opportunity anyway. With the recession biting hard into the European economy, team sponsors are being forced to cut back and make other areas their priority. As I write, there are only three or four professional teams in France sure to start the 1992 season. Given that each team comprises a maximum of eighteen riders, there isn't a lot for an ambitious young amateur, French or otherwise, to be optimistic about. This isn't to say he should abandon the sport. *Au contraire*, turning professional isn't the be all and end all of cycling. Representing one's country at international level is an achievement of considerable merit and one to be proud of.

So if I had any advice for a young amateur with the urge and determination to become a professional, it would be this: Go to Europe, and use the high-quality racing scene there to improve yourself, but always make racing for your country your priority. The professional team directors are no longer looking to their own domestic racing scene for their recruitment. Success in the world championship and the Olympic Games is the key.

Dream on. Every young rider wants to be a world champion – most settle for an amateur career which puts enjoyment before ambition.

You don't have to race

Few cyclists start out as racers – most take-up cycling for fresh air and fitness reasons. There are many alternatives to racing, and some, in their own way, are just as challenging. **Tim Hughes**

Mountain biking has broadened the appeal of leisure cycling in the last ten years, introducing many new converts to the sport and offering a refreshing alternative to those seeking sanctuary from busy roads.

R acing is far from the only type of cycling. Even in organized cycling clubs probably no more than 20 per cent of members race, and these are themselves only a tiny proportion of all cyclists. It is estimated that in Britain alone there are between thirteen and fifteen million bicycles, and well over a million are sold each year. Census figures show that more than a quarter of all bicycles in Britain are used at least once a week: that is over three million cyclists, compared with the few thousand who hold racing licences or ride time trials. It was as a means of personal transport that the bicycle's first inventors, back in the 1860s, saw the new machine; it would give the individual an alternative to the mass travel of the already developed railways. For the majority of riders, the bicycle remains just this convenient means of transport, but for a sizeable number it is the key to leisure travel and enjoyable, non-competitive exercise.

Even if you are not consciously following a training programme, regular steady cycling still confers health benefits. In most assessments it is surpassed only by swimming as an all-round exercise that improves breathing, circulation and general strength and stamina. Its only failings are in the areas of suppleness and to some extent failure to exercise the upper body to the same extent as the lower. At the same time the bicycle allows you to ride so much farther than you can walk because you do not have to expend energy in supporting the body upright – the bicycle bears most of your weight. Leisure cycling lets you exploit this advantage in the way you enjoy most. You can stick to quiet roads in open country, ride through woodland, or tackle hills and even mountains, always travelling at a pace to suit you, and with the knowledge

that you are causing little disturbance and creating virtually no pollution.

Leisure cycling covers an enormous range of endeavour, from a gentle afternoon ride in the country – a sort of bike-borne after-lunch stroll – to some very strenuous riding indeed. Perhaps the neatest summing up is the one French cyclists use, in terms that hardly need translation: cyclists who see the bicycle as a sporting machine for eating up the kilometres and bagging mountain passes are *cyclo-sportifs;* those whose more gentle progress gives them time to look around and explore are affectionately labelled *contemplatifs.* In recent years the explosive advent of the mountain bike has taken both types of rider into the different dimension of off-road riding (though of course cyclists have been riding bicycles off the roads ever since bicycles were first built).

There is no reason why you should not take part in both sport and 'contemplation', as the mood seizes you. Between the extremes of the rider straining to be among the first to complete the prestigious Paris-Brest-Paris ride and the family riding out for a country picnic, there is surely a bit of both creeds in most cyclists.

Sport cycling is necessarily the more structured end of leisure cycling. Virtually all events are promoted by cycling clubs or local groups of (in the UK) the Cyclists' Touring Club (CTC), although unattached riders may take part (often with a small surcharge on the entry fee to cover insurance – membership of organizations such as the CTC or British Cycling Federation includes such cover). While none of these events is a race, many, particularly the longer ones, can pose quite a tough personal challenge. Indeed it is taking up the challenge posed by the weather, the terrain and your own bodily and mental limits that is part of the appeal of these rides.

In the UK most of these events, frequently referred to as *randonnées,* are promoted under the banner of the organization Audax UK, which has codified some perhaps rather lengthy rules for their conduct. Riders follow a prescribed route that they must cover within time limits. Another part of the popularity of this type of ride derives from the wide range of abilities these limits cater for. Accordingly, average speeds from about 15kph (9.3mph) to 30kph (18.6mph) qualify for the appropriate certificate or medal. (The lowest qualifying speed is progressively reduced as the event distance increases.) Riders' progress is regulated by the opening and closing times of the various *contrôles* (checkpoints) along the route. (Because the organization is based largely on French practice, Audax UK uses many such French terms.) As events become longer, so the challenge offered by the highest permitted speed increases, and maintaining the fastest allowed average over the longer distances calls for near-racing fitness.

The course to be followed is described in detail on a route sheet and riders' progress is authenticated at the *contrôles,* which include one or more unannounced secret ones to ensure that everyone covers the full distance. Participants may ride alone or in, say, a club group as they choose. In practice, small groups tend to form spontaneously during the ride as participants

Touring is head-up riding – it can still be hard work, but the visual rewards are often more than worth the effort.

Reliability trial

In Britain many racing cyclists take part in early-season reliability trials as a sociable way of getting fit. Riders are set off in groups and cover a variety of set routes, usually up to 100 miles (160km). Time limits are also set, with each group aiming to complete the course within the specified time. A high level of fitness is required for the faster times.

Wide choice

Audax-style events are common in Europe, where there is a wide choice of rides to suit riders of varying abilities.

Access to some of the remotest, and often prettiest, areas of countryside is best gained on a mountain bike.

of comparable ability find themselves riding together. The Audax standard formula covers rides with set distances from 100km (62 miles) upwards, the commonest rides being this distance, 200km (124 miles), 300km (186 miles) and 400km (249 miles). Less often the rides are 600km (373 miles) or longer. As these *randonnées* are not races there is therefore no published finishing order. Most riders use normal touring bikes, often with tyres and wheels at the lighter end of the range. The rules insist on certain minimum equipment standards and naturally require lights to be fitted for any events that might involve night riding.

Similar events are common in France, Belgium and Holland, but with some differences. There is a clearer distinction between the harder-riding events and those organized by clubs who have devised an often ingenious route (or routes) to show off their region at its best. These latter often have picturesque names, and I am not sure if our club would have taken part in some of them if we hadn't been intrigued by such titles as the Toboggan des Côtes du Rhône and the Randonnée de la Montagne de Reims (in an area conspicuously short of mountains). A *toboggan*, as we were to discover, is a decidedly switchback

route, and the *montagne* above Reims is the hill where the champagne-producing grapes grow. So that families and children, as well as stronger riders, can take part, organizers frequently offer a choice of routes of widely differing length – 25-170km (15.5-106 miles), for example – often cleverly arranged so that the *contrôle* common to all is the one with refreshments on offer.

As a way of meeting French touring cyclists and becoming acquainted with little roads and bits of rural France that may not even figure on the map, these events are unsurpassed. Little formality is called for to join them, and most are listed in the annual guide, *Ou irons-nous?* (*Where Shall We Go?*), of the Fédération Française de Cyclotourisme (FFCT). When you are in France you can also find them listed in the local bike shop or on the town noticeboard. Local or regional daily papers (France has virtually no national daily press) often list events under the rubric *Cyclotourisme*. Look out in Thursday's paper for the following Sunday's rides. In areas that are off the tourist track, be prepared to be an object of some interest. We have had to give interviews to local papers and once won an extremely large cup (embarrassingly so, since we were on a cycle-camping holiday at the time) as the 'foreign club travelling the greatest distance to take part'!

At the other end of the scale, some of the bigger and more prestigious rides are quite athletic feats. For example, the classic Brevet du Randonneur des Alpes, based on Grenoble, climbs three passes higher than 2000m (6562ft) in its 250-km (155 miles) or so extent, plus some smaller ones *en route*, and there is a longer version for those who feel they have not done enough. This event regularly draws several thousand par-

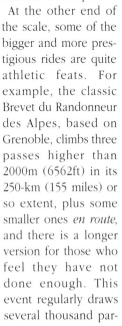

ticipants, enough to be a logistical nightmare to the organizers. For these more strenuous events French, Belgian and Dutch riders tend to use machines that are closer to road-racing bikes, though sensibly they have lower bottom gears, often down to 28 x 26 (27in/68.6cm). Possibly to some degree because of the weather, bicycles used in *randonnées* seem to become more and more like outright stripped-down racing machines the nearer you are to the Mediterranean.

Away from the mountains, the most prestigious event is the 1200-km (746 miles) Paris-Brest-Paris ride, which takes place every four years. Originally a professional race, the event was relaunched as a 'tourist' ride when interest in very long-distance racing waned. Would-be participants have to qualify to take part by riding a graduated series of increasingly long events, and places in 'P-B-P' are much sought after. Several other events follow roughly the routes of some of the classic races – there is even a 'tourist' version of the notorious Paris-Roubaix.

The USA also has its *sportif* rides. The classic, and one that originated long before the bike boom of the last few years, is known universally as TOSRV. The Tour of the Scioto River Valley is a two-day trip every May from Columbus to Portsmouth, Ohio, and back – up one side of the river and back down the other. From modest family beginnings in 1962, this 210-mile (378km) ride grew to attract 3500 riders, at which number the organizers set a limit. Other rides have grown from it – for example, TOSRV West, which follows Montana's Swan River valley.

Many bicycle clubs in the USA run challenging 'century' rides – 100-mile (160km) round trips to be covered at whatever speed the participant chooses. In addition the League of American Wheelmen (LAW) runs a 'National Century Month' during which riders completing the distance in any one of a series of nominated events qualify for a commemorative certificate. LAW sees the rides as demonstrating the legitimate position of the cyclist on

America's roads as well as offering a personal challenge.

Less athletically daunting are some of the mass rides, often termed 'fun' rides, organized to offer both a mild challenge to people who would not consider themselves dedicated cyclists and to demonstrate the actual and potential strength of cycling. Most also encourage participants to obtain sponsorship to benefit a charity. The best known and largest in Britain is the London to Brighton ride every June in which over 10,000 riders tackle the roughly 50 miles (80km) (the exact starting-point varies). Nearly every spring and summer weekend sees rides of varying distance and scale of organization in most parts of Britain. They are publicized in the cycling press as well as in local newspapers.

Surprisingly, the palm for the best-supported ride of the kind is not held by one of the major cycling countries, such as France, Belgium or Italy, or even the USA or Britain, but by Canada. The annual Tour de l'Ile de Montréal, which is held under the auspices of Vélo Québec, attracts an amazing 16,000 or so riders to its 50-km (31 miles) route early every summer.

Not everybody who likes a cycling challenge can fit in with the dates of

Winter riding, with a group of friends for company, can give as much pleasure as cycling at any time of the year.

organized events. Popular in France for a long time and increasingly elsewhere are *randonnées permanentes*. These are set-route rides that individuals or small groups can conveniently follow at any time, either, if of the *sportif* tendency, within a set time limit, or over a longer period. These to a degree bridge the gap between structured events and gentler leisure riding, by covering both strenuous long-distance place-to-place rides and quite gentle scenic circular routes taking in places of interest.

Among the tougher challenges, both Britain and France now have their *diagonales* – rides from corner to corner of the respective countries. Surprisingly, considering that France is Western Europe's largest country, Britain's 839-mile (1350km) 'End-to-End', Land's End to John o'Groats, is a longer ride than France's longest, which links the port of Brest on Brittany's Atlantic coast with Menton on the Mediterranean near the Italian border.

To some degree similar in concept, though with a distinctly American flavour, are some of the routes offered by the US organization Bikecentennial. These, supplied in the form of specially drawn cyclists' maps and information on accommodation, food and emergency procedures, are intended more to lead cyclists to discover the USA than to be set-time challenges. Bikecentennial was set up in the early 1970s when a small group conceived the idea of celebrating the forthcoming (1976) bicentenary of the Declaration of Independence by organizing a mass bike ride right across the country. Some 2000 cyclists made the trip from Astoria in Oregon on the Pacific coast to Yorktown, Virginia, on the Atlantic seaboard. Nowadays, Bikecentennial offers its members thirty-nine fully mapped routes, including two across the USA – a northern one in addition to the classic 1976 version, these soon to be joined by a southern variant; Pacific and Atlantic coastal routes; and a leg into Canada (and eventually Alaska) through the Rocky Mountains.

Events of any kind, however, are far from the thoughts of most people who ride bicycles for leisure. They just want to see places by bike – what is generally known as 'cycle touring' – probably travelling alone or with one or two friends, rather than a large group.

Cycle touring for more than single-day rides can include any type of stopping place – from five-star hotel to camp-site, according to your whim and your

Long, switchback climbs in France may not be very steep but they can go on for 10 miles (16km) or more.

financial situation. Camping obviously calls for a greater initial outlay but costs relatively little from then on. Lightweight camping is a subject too specialized to be dealt with in detail here, but equipment bulk and weight are the main problems. Specialist advice on camping is available to members from the major cycling organizations.

If you prefer to have transit and accommodation arrangements made for you, many organizations offer complete cycle holidays. The CTC, FFCT and Bikecentennial run tours programmes for their members, while a large number of private organizations now offer cycle trips in Britain and elsewhere, often in a package with air or sea travel. Cycling magazines carry listings, usually in issues around the turn of the year. This type of cycling holiday can be a good introduction to cycle touring, particularly in countries where you might be hesitant about cycling alone for the first time.

In addition there are many designated cycle routes. In Britain, local authorities, tourist boards and others have researched routes for cyclists, waymarked them on the ground and produced explanatory leaflets. Examples include the Cumbria, Lancashire, Cheshire, Oxfordshire and Wiltshire Cycleways – signed routes using minor roads and devised to take in places of interest as well as offering pleasant cycling. Bikecentennial's American routes have already been mentioned. Both the CTC and the FFCT also have a wide range of detailed routes available. All three organizations offer this information to members only.

Half the fun of any sort of travel lies in the anticipation. So, even if you are following others' routes on your trips, it is worth learning how to devise a route for yourself. This means using a suitable map. The detail a map can show is determined by its scale; the British maps most useful to cyclists have scales in the range 1:25 000 (2.5in to the mile/4cm to the kilometre) to 1:50 000 (1.25in to the mile/2cm to the kilometre). Maps at scales of 1:25 000 or 1:50 000 are detailed enough to show virtu-

ally every road and track, as well as details of villages, towns, churches, farms, woodland, streams, lakes and rivers and other landmarks. The larger 1:25 000 scale can be particularly useful for off-road riding. However, the bigger the scale, the more maps you need, so your choice of maps has to be a practical compromise.

Probably the cyclist's ideal scale for on-road riding is 1:100 000 (0.625in to the mile/1cm to the kilometre), and most European countries (oddly, Britain lacks a 1:100 000) have official maps at this and the two larger scales. The British Ordnance Survey, French IGN, Swiss National Map and official maps of the German *Lände* are reliable and in many cases beautiful examples of the cartographer's art. In the more highly settled European countries smaller scales are most useful for pretrip planning (although Michelin's 1:200 000 (0.3in to the mile/0.5cm to the kilometre) series of France and parts of nearby countries is very easy to follow on the road). Where there is less detail, a scale of 1:250 000 (0.25in to the mile/0.4cm to the kilometre) is adequate, and this is the scale Bikecentennial has chosen for its cyclists' strip maps of the USA.

All maps differentiate between main roads (usually red) and minor ones (usually yellow or uncoloured) – an essential distinction because it is on the minor roads that cycling is most pleasant. It is nearly always worth while to accept the slightly slower and possibly slightly longer by-road in preference to the direct and busier main route.

Maps convey a great deal more information than just roads, of course, and

How else but on a mountain bike could you end up with a four-legged fellow traveller?

Cycling through a dramatic stone tunnel adds a thrill to this ride in Provence, in the south of France .

layers of meaning are revealed as you become familiar with them, including the all-important information on relief. This may be shown by changes of colouring, by contour lines (imaginary lines linking points at the same height), or by 'spot heights', which show the height above sea level of a particular point. You will soon develop the ability to judge how much effort is called for to climb, say, a 50-m (164ft) height difference. Some maps show roads going up steep hills by arrow marks or chevrons. These can mean very different things on different maps, even to the extent of pointing uphill on some and downhill on others, so study carefully the key to the symbols.

Armed with this information, you can quite easily work out on the map a

simple route that follows minor roads, preferably crossing main roads rather than following them, and one that is not too hilly. You will soon get the feel for how far a given length on the map feels on the road. You may find a cycle computer helpful to indicate when you have covered the distance the map tells you should bring you to the next check or turning, particularly in wild or rather featureless country.

There are several ways of carrying maps on a bicycle. Map carriers are available that clip to the handlebars and hold the opened and folded map, while most handlebar bags have a transparent pocket on top for a map or route instructions. Or of course you can carry your map in a pocket.

Leisure cycling is a long way from

racing but even so you are using energy. You will find it a great deal more enjoyable if you ride within your capabilities – which will increase rapidly with experience. This means not trying to travel too fast or too far to begin with, but starting off with trips you are sure you can manage easily and then working up. Trying to go too fast can make any road hard, so ride gently, in a gear low enough so that your legs are turning steadily at around seventy or so revolutions per minute, or perhaps up to ninety if you are a supple pedaller. You will soon find that you have a natural easy cruising speed (and hence gear) at which you feel comfortable on flattish roads. This speed and your preferred pedalling rate will probably increase with practice.

Riders' natural abilities differ widely, and nowhere do they show up more than on hills. It is of course possible to walk where it is steep, but gears that are low enough make it easier to ride up almost anything than to walk, even at little more than walking pace. On longer and perhaps less steep hills you will find that it is uncomfortable to try to go faster than your natural speed and probably irksome to go much slower. If you are with other people whose natural speeds are different it is best for each to travel at his or her chosen pace and to meet again at the top (or at intervals on a long mountain pass).

It is quite common to get very hungry and thirsty when cycling. The evaporating cooling effect of the passing air means that in warm weather you can be steadily perspiring quite heavily without realizing

it. Even in winter you lose a lot of moisture. Plain water and some simple carbohydrate sources such as fruit bars or biscuits are best for immediate replenishment. It is better to make fairly frequent stops for small meals or snacks than to stop infrequently and eat a lot.

The golden rule about luggage is that the bicycle should carry it (although some mountain-bike riders prefer small rucksacks for off-road use). You will need some sort of purpose-made bag and usually a carrier or rack to support it. For light loads a small handlebar bag is recommended. This fits in front of the handlebars, preferably on a small carrier to keep it clear both of the part of the bars you might want to hold and also of the mudguard. Some handlebar bags and carriers are not easy to fit to mountain bikes.

For larger loads you have the choice of a saddle-bag, which fits behind and below the saddle and above the rear carrier, or panniers. Both have advantages and disadvantages. Saddle-bags

Many touring riders like to cycle in a group since in this way they can make new friends and take advantage of a little shelter from the wheel in front.

Mountain biking can be as tough as you want to make it . However, planning a route carefully is always advisable.

carriers are those that are triangulated in three dimensions.

Panniers can fit beside the back or front wheel; in the latter case they are best mounted low down on an appropriate carrier, when they help to counterbalance rear loads. Tests suggest that a weight distribution of two thirds at the rear and one third at the front gives the best stability. Some mountain-bike users report problems when panniers that are too large or too low-mounted are used when cycling on rough or rutted ground.

It is increasingly difficult to find places where cyclists have not been. Even the members of a much-publicized trip to the highest mountain in the Atlas range in North Africa found that others had been to the top before them!

A common belief among non-cyclists is that flat country is ideal for cycling. Up to a point it is true

have limited capacity, need packing carefully if they are not to sag lopsidedly, and carry the weight a little high but mostly within the wheelbase. They are also easy to put on and take off and sit well clear of road dirt. Panniers comprise two separate bags, ranging from modest to enormous, which are clipped or strapped on either side of the carrier. They carry the load well down, which helps keep the bicycle's centre of gravity low, but can cause the bicycle to shake, or 'shimmy', particularly if the carrier is not rigid (although the ultimate cause of this odd vibration is rather more complex). The most rigid

that flat country is easy, but broad, flat horizons take a long time to change. Holland does offer some very attractive cycling (and an extensive network of cycle paths) but the attraction is mostly in the intimate juxtaposition of land, water and the small towns and villages. For beginners, gently rolling country makes a good start. Eastern England – East Anglia and Lincolnshire – has pleasing landscapes. Hillier, rolling country is also attractive (with your mileage ambitions appropriately trimmed): the Cotswold hills, Dorset, the counties of Hereford and Worcester, Shropshire and Cheshire, bordering Wales, and the Leicestershire Wolds all offer superb cycling. About the same level of cycling effort is required in much of northern France and some of the foothills of the mountain ranges, such as the Limousin, near the centre of the country, and, conveniently, many of the wine areas. Ireland, Denmark, southern Norway and Sweden, and much of central Germany also fall into this category.

Inevitably, as you get fitter you will be attracted to mountain regions, if perhaps first to the gentler ones. In Britain, good areas for the beginner are south and central Wales, much of the Peak District and Pennines, and most of Scotland. Hilly islands, too, have their appeal: the Hebrides, Inner and Outer, offer very fine cycling, and bicycles travel free on the ferries. The foothills of the French Alps – the Vercors, the Chartreuse and the mountains of Haute Provence – the Massif Central and the hill country running up to the Pyrenees give a fine introduction to mountain riding. Similarly, the hills of Bavaria in Germany, of Italy's Apennines, and of most of the Iberian peninsula, plus the USA's Appalachians and Adirondacks, come into this category.

From then on, you will be ready to ride anywhere in the world: the high Alps and Pyrenees, the Sierra Nevada, the Rockies, the Andes – even the majestic Himalayas.

The rise of the mountain bike has led to widespread interest in off-road routes. In England and Wales cyclists are specifically permitted to ride on paths classified as bridleways (giving way to walkers and horse-riders where necessary), while unsurfaced byways open to all traffic may also be cycled on. The OS 1:50 000 and 1:25 000 maps give details of these public rights of way. Matters are different under Scottish law, where right of way can depend on evidence of continuous usage. The CTC publication *Cycling Off-road and the Law* by Neil Horton, gives more detail on this. Certain long-distance trails incorporate long stretches of cyclable off-road route, notably the bridleway of the South Downs Way and the section of the Ridgeway Path west of the River Thames. There are further plans afoot for other routes, including a bridleway following the Pennine Way.

In addition to rights of way there are so-called permissive routes such as canal towpaths (for which a permit has to be bought) and some forest trails in Forestry Commission woodland. Many forest regions are opening up their routes to cyclists: early in the 1990s, for example, some 200 miles (322km) were opened up in the Galloway Forest in south-west Scotland.

A number of urban routes have been created specifically as cycle routes, many of them offering traffic-free routes out of large towns, such as the Bath-

Wherever you ride off-road, always check on a map that the routes taken are legal rights of way.

Bristol path or the routes out of Glasgow. Quite a few such routes follow the beds of former railway branches. In the Peak National Park two such routes are the Tissington and High Peak Trails, which wind an almost level way into the hills.

It is not necessary to own a mountain bike to be able to follow many of these routes, which cyclists have been using for many years. The mountain bike comes into its own on the rougher, stickier or looser-surfaced paths. This ability of mountain-bike riders to penetrate wilder places initially caused some conflict between them and walkers on some popular routes. Involved organizations in Britain have now published an advisory Mountain Bike Code intended to inform new mountain-bike owners of the rights of way open to them and to give some practical advice on travel in wild places.

In less densely populated parts of Europe there is generally less conflict, and several countries have developed mountain-bike trails, which have become something of a summer speciality of cross-country ski resorts. In most countries, forest tracks and unsurfaced paths and trails are cyclable provided that they are not obviously private roads leading to, for example, farms. In the USA, however, some of the disputes between mountain bikers and conservationists have not been so easily resolved and some wilderness areas now have mountain-bike bans. On a more positive note, organizations such as Bikecentennial are cooperating with forest authorities to develop and publicize mountain-bike routes in less sensitive areas.

The real attraction of all off-the-beaten-track routes is that they can lead into remote and solitary places – they reach the parts that other roads cannot reach. The off-road cyclist should give them the respect they deserve and treat them with great care.

Off-road riding in remote areas should never be done alone as a fall or injury could leave you dangerously isolated.

CHAPTER FOUR

FACTS AND FIGURES

race results and
cycling organizations

MILAN-SAN REMO (Italy)

INDIVIDUAL SUCCESSES	DISTANCE (km)
1907 Lucien Petit-Breton (France)	281
1908 Cyrille Van Hauwaert (Belgium)	281
1909 Luigi Ganna (Italy)	281
1910 Eugène Christophe (France)	281
1911 Gustave Garrigou (France)	281
1912 Henri Pelissier (France)	281
1913 Odiel Defraeve (Belgium)	281
1914 Ugo Agostini (Italy)	281
1915 Enzio Corlaita (Italy)	281
1916 Not held	
1917 Gaetano Belloni (Italy)	281
1918 Costante Girardengo (Italy)	281
1919 Angelo Gremo (Italy)	281
1920 Gaetano Belloni (Italy)	281
1921 Costante Girardengo (Italy)	281
1922 Giovanni Brunero (Italy)	281
1923 Costante Girardengo (Italy)	281
1924 Pietro Linari (Italy)	281
1925 Costante Girardengo (Italy)	281
1926 Costante Girardengo (Italy)	281
1927 Pietro Chesi (Italy)	281
1928 Costante Girardengo (Italy)	281
1929 Alfredo Binda (Italy)	281
1930 Michele Mara (Italy)	269
1931 Alfredo Binda (Italy)	281
1932 Alfredo Bovet (Italy)	281
1933 Learco Guerra (Italy)	281
1934 Jozef Demuysère (Belgium)	281
1935 Giuseppe Olmo (Italy)	281
1936 Angelo Varetto (Italy)	281
1937 Cesare De Cancia (Italy)	281
1938 Giuseppe Olmo (Italy)	281
1939 Gino Bartali (Italy)	281
1940 Gino Bartali (Italy)	286
1941 Pierino Favalli (Italy)	281
1942 Adolfo Leoni (Italy)	281
1943 Cino Cinelli (Italy)	281
1944 Not held	
1945 Not held	
1946 Fausto Coppi (Italy)	292
1947 Gino Bartali (Italy)	285
1948 Fausto Coppi (Italy)	281
1949 Fausto Coppi, (Italy)	290
1950 Gino Bartali (Italy)	282
1951 Louison Bobet (France)	282
1952 Loretto Petrucci (Italy)	282
1953 Loretto Petrucci (Italy)	282
1954 Rik Van Steenbergen (Belgium)	282
1955 Germain Derijcke (Belgium)	282
1956 Fred De Bruyne (Belgium)	281
1957 Miguel Poblet (Spain)	282
1958 Rik Van Looy (Belgium)	282
1959 Miguel Poblet (Spain)	281
1960 René Privat (France)	288
1961 Raymond Poulidor (France)	288
1962 Émile Daems (Belgium)	288
1963 Joseph Groussard (France)	288
1964 Tom Simpson (Great Britain)	288
1965 Arie Den Hartog (Holland)	287
1966 Eddy Merckx (Belgium)	288
1967 Eddy Merckx (Belgium)	288
1968 Rudi Altig (Germany)	288

1969 Eddy Merckx (Belgium)	288
1970 Michele Dancelli (Italy)	288
1971 Eddy Merckx (Belgium)	288
1972 Eddy Merckx (Belgium)	288
1973 Roger De Vlaeminck (Belgium)	288
1974 Felice Gimondi (Italy)	288
1975 Eddy Merckx (Belgium)	288
1976 Eddy Merckx (Belgium)	288
1977 Jan Raas (Holland)	288
1978 Roger De Vlaeminck (Belgium)	288
1979 Roger De Vlaeminck (Belgium)	288
1980 Pierino Gavazzi (Italy)	288
1981 Fons De Wolf (Belgium)	288
1982 Marc Gomez (France)	294
1983 Giuseppe Saronni (Italy)	294
1984 Francesco Moser (Italy)	294
1985 Hennie Kuiper (Holland)	294
1986 Sean Kelly (Ireland)	293
1987 Eric Maechler (Switzerland)	294
1988 Laurent Fignon (France)	294
1989 Laurent Fignon (France)	294
1990 Gianni Bugno (Italy)	294
1991 Claudio Chiappucci (Italy)	294

TOUR OF FLANDERS (Belgium)

INDIVIDUAL SUCCESSES	DISTANCE (km)
1913 Paul Deman (Belgium)	370
1914 Marcel Buysse (Belgium)	280
1915-18 Not held	
1919 Henri Van Lerberghe (Belgium)	203
1920 Jules Van Hevel (Belgium)	262
1921 René Vermandel (Belgium)	262
1922 Leon De Vos (Belgium)	253
1923 Henri Suter (Switzerland)	243
1924 Gérard Debaets (Belgium)	284
1925 Julien Delbecque (Belgium)	210
1926 Denis Verschueren (Belgium)	217
1927 Gérard Debaets (Belgium)	210
1928 Jan Mertens (Belgium)	225
1929 Jozef Dervaes (Belgium)	216
1930 Frans Bonduel (Belgium)	244
1931 Romain Gijssels (Belgium)	227
1932 Romain Gijssels (Belgium)	227
1933 Alfons Schepers (Belgium)	227
1934 Gaston Rebry (Belgium)	239
1935 Louis Duerloo (Belgium)	260
1936 Louis Hardiquest (Belgium)	250
1937 Michel Dhooghe (Belgium)	267
1938 Edgard De Caluwe (Belgium)	260
1939 Karel Kaers (Belgium)	230
1940 Achiel Buysse (Belgium)	211
1941 Achiel Buysse (Belgium)	198
1942 Brik Schotte (Belgium)	226
1943 Achiel Buysse (Belgium)	205
1944 Rik Van Steenbergen (Belgium)	220
1945 Sylvain Grysolle (Belgium)	222
1946 Rik Van Steenbergen (Belgium)	275
1947 Émile Faignaert (Belgium)	257
1948 Brik Schotte (Belgium)	257
1949 Fiorenzo Magni (Italy)	260
1950 Fiorenzo Magni (Italy)	275
1951 Fiorenzo Magni (Italy)	274

1952	Roger Decock (Belgium)	258
1953	Wim Van Est (Holland)	253
1954	Raymond Impanis (Belgium)	255
1955	Louison Bobet (France)	263
1956	Jean Forestier (France)	238
1957	Fred De Bruyne (Belgium)	242
1958	Germain Derijcke (Belgium)	230
1959	Rik Van Looy (Belgium)	242
1960	Arthur Decabooter (Belgium)	227
1961	Tom Simpson (Great Britain)	255
1962	Rik Van Looy (Belgium)	254
1963	Noel Fore (Belgium)	249
1964	Rudi Altig (Germany)	240
1965	Jo De Roo (Holland)	235
1966	Edward Sels (Belgium)	243
1967	Dino Zandegu (Italy)	245
1968	Walter Godefroot (Belgium)	249
1969	Eddy Merckx (Belgium)	259
1970	Eric Leman (Belgium)	265
1971	Evert Dolman (Holland)	268
1972	Eric Leman (Belgium)	250
1973	Eric Leman (Belgium)	263
1974	Cees Bal (Holland)	256
1975	Eddy Merckx (Belgium)	225
1976	Walter Planckaert (Belgium)	261
1977	Roger De Vlaeminck (Belgium)	264
1978	Walter Godefroot (Belgium)	260
1979	Jan Raas (Holland)	267
1980	Michel Pollentier (Belgium)	265
1981	Hennie Kuiper (Holland)	266
1982	Rene Martens (Belgium)	267
1983	Jan Raas (Holland)	272
1984	Johan Lammerts (Holland)	268
1985	Eric Vanderaerden (Belgium)	271
1986	Adri Van Der Poel (Holland)	275
1987	Claude Criquielion (Belgium)	274
1988	Eddy Planckaert (Belgium)	279
1989	Edwig Van Hooydonck (Belgium)	264
1990	Moreno Argentin (Italy)	262
1991	Edwig Van Hooydonck (Belgium)	261

PARIS-BREST-PARIS (France)

INDIVIDUAL SUCCESSES		DISTANCE (km)
1891	Charles Terront (France)	1196
1901	Maurice Garin (France)	1200
1911	Émile Georget (France)	1200
1921	Louis Mottiat (Belgium)	1200
1931	Hubert Opperman (Australia)	1186
1948	Albert Hendrickx (Belgium)	1182
1951	Maurice Diot (France)	1182

GHENT-WEVELGEM (Belgium)

INDIVIDUAL SUCCESSES		DISTANCE (km)
1934	Gustave Van Belle (Belgium)	–
1935	Albert Depreitere (Belgium)	–
1936	Robert Van Eenaeme (Belgium)	–
1937	Robert Van Eenaeme (Belgium)	–
1938	Hubert Godart (Belgium)	–

1939	Andre Declerckx (Belgium)	–
1940-44	Not held	
1945	Robert Van Eenaeme (Belgium)	200
1946	Ernest Sterckx (Belgium)	200
1947	Maurice Desimpelaere (Belgium)	230
1948	Valère Ollivier (Belgium)	276
1949	Marcel Kint (Belgium)	250
1950	Brik Schotte (Belgium)	255
1951	André Rosseel (Belgium)	250
1952	Raymond Impanis (Belgium	240
1953	Raymond Impanis (Belgium)	240
1954	Rolf Graf (Switzerland)	235
1955	Brik Schotte (Belgium)	232
1956	Rik Van Looy (Belgium)	228
1957	Rik Van Looy (Belgium)	207
1958	Noel Fore (Belgium)	231
1959	Leon Van Daele (Belgium)	221
1960	Frans Aerenhouts (Belgium)	253
1961	Frans Aerenhouts (Belgium)	231
1962	Rik Van Looy (Belgium)	237
1963	Benoni Behyt (Belgium)	231
1964	Jacques Anquetil (France)	233
1965	Noel De Pauw (Belgium)	235
1966	Herman Van Springel (Belgium)	251
1967	Eddy Merckx (Belgium)	242
1968	Walter Godefroot (Belgium)	246
1969	Willy Vekemans (Belgium)	250
1970	Eddy Merckx (Belgium)	233
1971	Georges Pintens (Belgium)	237
1972	Roger Swerts (Belgium)	245
1973	Eddy Merckx (Belgium)	250
1974	Barry Hoban (Great Britain)	244
1975	Freddy Maertens (Belgium)	250
1976	Freddy Maertens (Belgium)	262
1977	Bernard Hinault (France)	277
1978	Ferdi Van den Haute (Belgium)	245
1979	Francesco Moser (Italy)	252
1980	Henk Lubberding (Holland)	264
1981	Jan Raas (Holland)	254
1982	Frank Hoste (Belgium)	245
1983	Leo Van Vliet (Holland)	255
1984	Guido Bontempi (Italy)	255
1985	Eric Vanderaerden (Belgium)	262
1986	Guido Bontempi (Italy)	250
1987	Teun Van Vliet (Holland)	243
1988	Sean Kelly (Ireland)	275
1989	Gerrit Solleveld (Holland)	265
1990	Herman Frison (Belgium)	210
1991	Djamolidine Abdujaparov (USSR)	210

PARIS-ROUBAIX (France)

INDIVIDUAL SUCCESSES		DISTANCE (km)
1896	Jozef Fischer (Germany)	280
1897	Maurice Garin (France)	280
1898	Maurice Garin (France)	268
1899	Albert Champion (France)	268
1900	Émile Bouhours (France)	268
1901	Luc Lesna (France)	280
1902	Luc Lesna (France)	268
1903	Hippolyte Aucouturier (France)	268
1904	Hippolyte Aucouturier (France)	268
1905	Louis Trousselier (France)	268
1906	Henri Cornet (France)	270
1907	Georges Passerieu (France)	271

1908	Cyrille Van Hauwaert (Belgium)	271
1909	Octave Lapize (France)	276
1910	Octave Lapize (France)	266
1911	Octave Lapize (France)	266
1912	Charles Crupelandt (France)	266
1913	François Faber (Luxemburg)	265
1914	Charles Crupelandt (France)	274
1915-18	Not held	
1919	Henri Pelissier (France)	280
1920	Paul Deman (Belgium)	263
1921	Henri Pelissier (France)	263
1922	Albert Dejonghe (Belgium)	262
1923	Henri Suter (Switzerland)	270
1924	Jules Van Hevel (Belgium)	270
1925	Félix Sellier (Belgium)	260
1926	Julien Delbecque (Belgium)	270
1927	Georges Ronsse (Belgium)	260
1928	André Leducq (France)	260
1929	Charles Meunier (Belgium)	260
1930	Julien Vervaecke (Belgium)	255
1931	Gaston Rebry (Belgium)	255
1932	Romain Gijssels (Belgium)	255
1933	Sylveer Maes (Belgium)	255
1934	Gaston Rebry (Belgium)	255
1935	Gaston Rebry (Belgium)	255
1936	Georges Speicher (France)	262
1937	Jules Rossi (Italy)	255
1938	Lucien Storme (Belgium)	255
1939	Émile Masson (Belgium)	262
1940-42	Not held	
1943	Marcel Kint (Belgium)	250
1944	Maurice Desimpelaere (Belgium)	246
1945	Paul Maye (France)	246
1946	Georges Claes (Belgium)	246
1947	Georges Claes (Belgium)	246
1948	Rik Van Steenbergen (Belgium)	246
1949	André Mahé (France) and	
	Serse Coppi (Italy)	244
1950	Fausto Coppi (Italy)	247
1951	Ant. Bevilacqua (Italy)	247
1952	Rik Van Steenbergen (Belgium)	245
1953	Germain Derijcke (Belgium)	245
1954	Raymond Impanis (Belgium)	246
1955	Jean Forestier (France)	249
1956	Louison Bobet (France)	252
1957	Fred De Bruyne (Belgium)	252
1958	Leon Van Daele (Belgium)	269
1959	Noel Fore (Belgium)	202
1960	Pino Cerami (Belgium)	262
1961	Rik Van Looy (Belgium)	263
1962	Rik Van Looy (Belgium)	258
1963	Emile Daems (Belgium)	266
1964	Peter Post (Holland)	265
1965	Rik Van Looy (Belgium)	267
1966	Felice Gimondi (Italy)	262
1967	Jan Janssen (Holland)	263
1968	Eddy Merckx (Belgium)	262
1969	Walter Godefroot (Belgium)	264
1970	Eddy Merckx (Belgium)	266
1971	Roger Rosiers (Belgium)	266
1972	Roger De Vlaeminck (Belgium)	272
1973	Eddy Merckx (Belgium)	272
1974	Roger De Vlaeminck (Belgium)	274
1975	Roger De Vlaeminck (Belgium)	277
1976	Marc De Meyer (Belgium)	270
1977	Roger De Vlaeminck (Belgium)	250

1978	Francesco Moser (Italy)	263
1979	Francesco Moser (Italy)	259
1980	Francesco Moser (Italy)	264
1981	Bernard Hinault (France)	263
1982	Jan Raas (Holland)	270
1983	Hennie Kuiper (Holland)	274
1984	Sean Kelly (Ireland)	265
1985	Marc Madiot (France)	265
1986	Sean Kelly (Ireland)	268
1987	Eric Vanderaerden (Belgium)	264
1988	Dirk Demol (Belgium)	266
1989	Jean-Marie Wampers (Belgium)	265
1990	Eddy Plankaert (Belgium)	265
1991	Marc Madiot (France)	266

FLÈCHE-WALLONNE (Belgium)

INDIVIDUAL SUCCESSES		DISTANCE (km)
1936	Philippe Demeersman (Belgium)	236
1937	Adolf Braeckeveldt (Belgium)	291
1938	Émile Masson Jnr (Belgium)	300
1939	Edmond Delathouwer (Belgium)	285
1940	Not held	
1941	Sylvain Grysolle (Belgium)	205
1942	Karel Thijs (Belgium)	208
1943	Marcel Kint (Belgium)	208
1944	Marcel Kint (Belgium)	208
1945	Marcel Kint (Belgium)	213
1946	Désiré Keteleer (Belgium)	253
1947	Ernest Sterckx (Belgium)	276
1948	Fermo Camellini (Italy)	234
1949	Rik Van Steenbergen (Belgium)	231
1950	Fausto Coppi (Italy)	235
1951	Ferdi Kubler (Switzerland)	220
1952	Ferdi Kubler (Switzerland)	220
1953	Stan Ockers (Belgium)	220
1954	Germain Derijcke (Belgium)	220
1955	Stan Ockers (Belgium)	220
1956	Richard Van Genechten (Belgium)	221
1957	Raymond Impanis (Belgium)	226
1958	Rik Van Steenbergen (Belgium)	235
1959	Jos Hoevenaars (Belgium)	218
1960	Pino Cerami (Belgium)	208
1961	Willy Vannitsen (Belgium)	193
1962	Henri Dewolf (Belgium)	201
1963	Raymond Poulidor (France)	213
1964	Gilbert Desmet (Belgium)	215
1965	Roberto Poggiali (Italy)	214
1966	Michele Dancelli (Italy)	233
1967	Eddy Merckx (Belgium)	223
1968	Rik Van Looy (Belgium)	222
1969	Jos Huysmans (Belgium)	222
1970	Eddy Merckx (Belgium)	225
1971	Roger De Vlaeminck (Belgium)	225
1972	Eddy Merckx (Belgium)	249
1973	Andre Dierickx (Belgium)	249
1974	Frans Verbeeck (Belgium)	225
1975	Andre Dierickx (Belgium)	225
1976	Joop Zoetemelk (Holland)	227
1977	Francesco Moser (Italy)	223
1978	Michel Laurent (France)	223
1979	Bernard Hinault (France)	248
1980	Giuseppe Saronni (Italy)	248

1981	Daniel Willems (Belgium)	240
1982	Mario Beccia (Italy)	251
1983	Bernard Hinault (France)	248
1984	Kim Andersen (Denmark)	246
1985	Claude Criquielion (Belgium)	219
1986	Laurent Fignon (France)	248
1987	Jean-Claude Leclercq (France)	245
1988	Rolf Golz (Germany)	243
1989	Claude Criquielion (Belgium)	253
1990	Moreno Argentin (Italy)	208
1991	Moreno Argentin (Italy)	207

LIÈGE-BASTOGNE-LIÈGE (Belgium)

INDIVIDUAL SUCCESSES		DISTANCE (km)
1894	Léon Houa (Belgium)	223
1895-1911	Not held	
1912	Omer Verschoore (Belgium)	257
1913-18	Not held	
1919	Léon Devos (Belgium)	237
1920	Léon Scieur (Belgium)	245
1921	Louis Mottiat (Belgium)	209
1922	Louis Mottiat (Belgium)	218
1923	René Vermandel (Belgium)	218
1924	René Vermandel (Belgium)	245
1925-9	Not held	
1930	Herman Buse (Germany)	231
1931	Alfons Schepers (Belgium)	213
1932	Marcel Houvoux (Belgium)	214
1933	Francois Gardier (Belgium)	213
1934	Theo Herckenrath (Belgium)	213
1935	Alfons Schepers (Belgium)	240
1936	Albert Beckaert (Belgium)	211
1937	Elio Meulenberg (Belgium)	211
1938	Alfons Deloor (Belgium)	211
1939	Albert Ritserveldt (Belgium)	211
1940-42	Not held	
1943	Richard Depoorter (Belgium)	211
1944	Not held	
1945	Jean Engels (Belgium)	204
1946	Prosp. Depredomme (Belgium)	205
1947	Richard Depoorter (Belgium)	218
1948	Maurice Mollin (Belgium)	205
1949	Camille Danguillaume (France)	256
1950	Prosp. Depredomme (Belgium)	263
1951	Ferdi Kubler (Switzerland)	211
1952	Ferdi Kubler (Switzerland)	229
1953	Alois De Hertog (Belgium)	236
1954	Marcel Ernzer (Luxemburg)	236
1955	Stan Ockers (Belgium)	238
1956	Fred De Bruyne (Belgium)	247
1957	Frans Schouben (Belgium) and Germain Derycke (Belgium)	255
1958	Fred De Bruyne (Belgium)	246
1959	Fred De Bruyne (Belgium)	240
1960	Albert Geldermans (Holland)	248
1961	Rik Van Looy (Belgium)	251
1962	Jos Planckaert (Belgium)	254
1963	Frans Melckenbeeck (Belgium)	237
1964	Willy Bocklant (Belgium)	245
1965	Carmine Preziosi (Italy)	253
1966	Jacques Anquetil (France)	253
1967	Walter Godefroot (Belgium)	256

1968	Valeer Van Sweefelt (Belgium)	268
1969	Eddy Merckx (Belgium)	253
1970	Roger De Vlaeminck (Belgium)	235
1971	Eddy Merckx (Belgium)	251
1972	Eddy Merckx (Belgium)	239
1973	Eddy Merckx (Belgium)	236
1974	Georges Pintens (Belgium)	246
1975	Eddy Merckx (Belgium)	246
1976	Jos Bruyère (Belgium)	246
1977	Bernard Hinault (France)	243
1978	Jos Bruyère (Belgium)	241
1979	Dietrich Thurau (Germany)	241
1980	Bernard Hinault (France)	244
1981	Joseph Fuchs (Switzerland)	244
1982	Silvano Contini (Italy)	244
1983	Steven Rooks (Holland)	246
1984	Sean Kelly (Ireland)	246
1985	Moreno Argentin (Italy)	245
1986	Moreno Argentin (Italy)	252
1987	Moreno Argentin (Italy)	258
1988	Adri Van De Poel (Holland)	260
1989	Sean Kelly (Ireland)	268
1990	Eric Van Lancker (Belgium)	256
1991	Moreno Argentin (Italy)	267

AMSTEL GOLD RACE (Holland)

INDIVIDUAL SUCCESSES		DISTANCE (km)
1966	Jean Stablinski (France)	302
1967	Arie Den Hartog (Holland)	213
1968	Harry Steevens (Holland)	245
1969	Guido Reybrouck (Belgium)	259
1970	Georges Pintens (Belgium)	240
1971	Frans Verbeeck (Belgium)	233
1972	Walter Planckaert (Belgium)	237
1973	Eddy Merckx (Belgium)	238
1974	Gerrie Knetemann (Holland)	238
1975	Eddy Merckx (Belgium)	238
1976	Freddy Maertens (Belgium)	230
1977	Jan Raas (Holland)	230
1978	Jan Raas (Holland)	230
1979	Jan Raas (Holland)	237
1980	Jan Raas (Holland)	238
1981	Bernard Hinault (France)	237
1982	Jan Raas (Holland)	237
1983	Phil Anderson (Australia)	242
1984	Jacques Hanegraaf (Holland)	247
1985	Gerrie Knetemann (Holland)	242
1986	Steven Rooks (Holland)	242
1987	Joop Zoetemelk (Holland)	242
1988	Jelle Nijdam (Holland)	242
1989	Eric Van Lancker (Belgium)	242
1990	Adri Van Der Poel (Holland)	249
1991	Frans Maassen (Holland)	244

BORDEAUX-PARIS (France)

INDIVIDUAL SUCCESSES		DISTANCE (km)
1892	Auguste Stéphane (France)	572
1893	Louis Cottereau (France)	572
1894	Lucien Lesna (France)	572
1895	Charles Meyer (Denmark)	592

BORDEAUX-PARIS (France)

INDIVIDUAL SUCCESSES		DISTANCE (km)
1892	Auguste Stéphane (France)	572
1893	Louis Cottereau (France)	572
1894	Lucien Lesna (France)	572
1895	Charles Meyer (Denmark)	592
1896	Arthur Linton (Great Britain) and	
	Gaston Rivierre (France)	592
1897	Gaston Rivierre (France)	592
1898	Gaston Rivierre (France)	592
1899	Constant Huret (France)	594
1900	Josef Fischer (Germany)	594
1901	Lucien Lesna (France	594
1902	Édouard Wattelier (France)	575
	Maurice Garin (France)	575
1903	Hippolyte Aucouturier (France)	575
1904	Fernand Augereau (France)	575
1905	Hippolyte Aucouturier (France)	575
1906	Marcel Cadolle (France)	592
1907	Cyrille Van Hauwaert (Belgium)	592
1908	Louis Trousselier (France)	593
1909	Cyrille Van Hauwaert (Belgium)	592
1910	Émile Georget (France)	592
1911	François Faber (Luxemburg)	592
1912	Émile Georget (France)	592
1913	Louis Mottiat (Belgium)	592
1914	Paul Deman (Belgium)	592
1915-18	Not held	
1919	Henri Pelissier (France)	587
1920	Eugène Christophe (France)	592
1921	Eugène Christophe (France)	587
1922	Francis Pelissier (France)	587
1923	Émile Masson (Belgium)	587
1924	Francis Pelissier (France	587
1925	Henri Suter (Switzerland)	587
1926	Adelin Benoît (Belgium)	587
1927	Georges Ronsse (Belgium)	587
1928	Hector Martin (Belgium)	597
1929	Georges Ronsse (Belgium)	589
1930	Georges Ronsse (Belgium)	598
1931	Bernard Van Rysselberghe (Belgium)	600
1932	Romain Gijssels (Belgium)	601
1933	Fernand Mithouard (France)	588
1934	Jean Noret (France)	571
1935	Edgard De Caluwe (Belgium)	578
1936	Paul Chocque (France)	586
1937	Joseph Somers (Belgium)	572
1938	Marcel Laurent (France)	572
1939	Marcel Laurent (France)	572
1940-45	Not held	
1946	Émile Masson Jnr (Belgium)	588
1947	Joseph Somers (Belgium)	596
1948	Ange Le Strat (France)	588
1949	Jesus Moujica (France)	586
1950	Wim Van Est (Holland)	586
1951	Bernard Gauthier (France)	586
1952	Wim Van Est (Holland)	586
1953	Ferdi Kubler (Switzerland)	572
1954	Bernard Gauthier (France)	572
1955	Not held	
1956	Bernard Gauthier (France)	551
1957	Bernard Gauthier (France)	551
1958	Jean-Marie Cieleska (France)	552
1959	Louison Bobet (France)	552
1960	Marcel Janssens (Belgium)	557

1961	Wim Van Est (Holland)	557
1962	Jo De Roo (Holland)	557
1963	Tom Simpson (Great Britain)	557
1964	Michel Nedelec (France)	557
1965	Jacques Anquetil (France)	557
1966	Jan Janssen (Holland)	557
1967	Georges Vanconingsloo (Belgium)	557
1968	Émile Bodart (Belgium)	554
1969	Walter Godefroot (Belgium)	579
1970	Hermann Van Springel (Belgium)	620
1972	Not held	
1973	Enzo Mattioda (France)	562
1974	Hermann Van Springel (Belgium) and	
	Régis Delépine (France)	593
1975	Hermann Van Springel (Belgium)	559
1976	Walter Godefroot (Belgium)	557
1977	Hermann Van Springel (Belgium)	597
1978	Hermann Van Springel (Belgium)	601
1979	André Chalmel (France)	584
1980	Hermann Van Springel (Belgium)	588
1981	Hermann Van Springel (Belgium)	594
1982	Marcel Tinazzi (France)	584
1983	Gilbert Duclos-Lassalle (France)	588
1984	Hubert Linard (France)	582
1985	René Martens (Belgium)	585
1986	Gilbert Glaus (Switzerland)	588
1987	Bernard Vallet (France)	619
1988	Jean-François Rault (France)	608

WINCANTON CLASSIC

INDIVIDUAL SUCCESSES		DISTANCE (km)
1989	Frans Maassen (Holland)	236
1990	Gianni Bugno (Italy)	239
1991	Eric Van Lancker (Belgium)	235
1992	Massimo Ghirotto (Italy)	236
1993	Alberto Volpi (Italy)	232

GRAND PRIX DES AMÉRIQUES

INDIVIDUAL SUCCESSES		DISTANCE (km)
1988	Steve Bauer (Canada)	192
1989	Jorg Müller (Switzerland)	224
1990	Franco Ballerini (Italy)	224
1991	Eric Van Lancker (Belgium)	224
1992	Federico Echave (Spain)	224
1993	Not held	

* Retitled **Grand Prix Teleglobe**

SAN SEBASTIÁN (Spain)

INDIVIDUAL SUCCESSES		DISTANCE (km)
1981	Marino Lejarreta (Spain)	230
1982	Marino Lejarreta (Spain)	229
1983	Claude Criquielion (Belgium)	244
1984	Niki Ruttimann (Switzerland)	244
1985	Adri Van Der Poel (Holland)	244
1986	Inaki Gaston (Spain)	244
1987	Marino Lejarreta (Spain)	244
1988	Gert-Jan Theunisse (Holland)	244
1989	Gerhard Zadrobilek (Austria)	244
1990	Miguel Induraín (Spain)	248

1991	Gianni Bugno (Italy)	238
1992	Raul Alcala (Mexico)	234
1993	Claudio Chiappucci (Italy)	238

PARIS-BRUSSELS (France and Belgium)

INDIVIDUAL SUCCESSES		DISTANCE (km)
1893	André Henry (Belgium)	–
1894-1905 Not held		
1906	Albert Dupont (Belgium)	–
1907	Gustave Garrigou (France)	405
1908	Lucien Petit-Breton (France)	420
1909	François Faber (Luxemburg)	405
1910	Maurice Brocco (France)	405
1911	Octave Lapize (France)	405
1912	Octave Lapize (France)	425
1913	Octave Lapize (France)	440
1914	Louis Mottiat (Belgium)	440
1915-18 Not held		
1919	Alexis Michiels (Belgium)	417
1920	Henri Pelissier (France)	420
1921	Robert Reboul (France)	412
1922	Félix Sellier (Belgium)	410
1923	Félix Sellier (Belgium)	406
1924	Félix Sellier (Belgium)	424
1925	Gérard Debaets (Belgium)	407
1926	Denis Verschureren (Belgium)	402
1927	Nicolas Frantz (Luxemburg)	388
1928	Georges Ronsse (Belgium)	366
1929	Pe Verhaegen (Belgium)	377
1930	Ernest Mottard (Belgium)	366
1931	Jean Aerts (Belgium)	347
1932	Julien Vervaecke (Belgium)	376
1933	Albert Barthelemy (France)	378
1934	Frans Bonduel (Belgium)	393
1935	Edgard De Caluwe (Belgium)	380
1936	Eloi Meulenbergh (Belgium)	380
1937	Albert Beckaert (Belgium)	380
1938	Marcel Kint (Belgium)	400
1939	Frans Bonduel (Belgium)	318
1940-45 Not held		
1946	Brik Schotte (Belgium)	320
1947	Ernest Sterckx (Belgium)	325
1948	Lode Poels (Belgium)	325
1949	Maurice Diot (France)	326
1950	Rik Van Steenbergen (Belgium)	326
1951	Jean Gueguen (France)	326
1952	Brik Schotte (Belgium)	295
1953	Loretto Petrucci (Italy)	302
1954	Marcel Hendrickx (Belgium)	302
1955	Marcel Hendrickx (Belgium)	307
1956	Rik Van Looy (Belgium)	291
1957	Leon Van Daele (Belgium)	295
1958	Rik Van Looy (Belgium)	287
1959	Frans Schoubben (Belgium)	289
1960	Pierre Everaert (France)	289
1961	Pino Cerami (Belgium)	291
1962	Jos Wouters (Belgium)	289
1963	Jean Stablinski (France)	289
1964	Georges Vanconingsloo (Belgium)	286
1965	Ward Sels (Belgium)	288
1966	Felice Gimondi (Italy)	286
1967-72 Not held		
1973	Eddy Merckx (Belgium)	294

1974	Marc Demeyer (Belgium)	287
1975	Freddy Maertens (Belgium)	285
1976	Felice Gimondi (Italy)	312
1977	Ludo Peeters (Belgium)	286
1978	Jan Raas (Holland)	194
1979	Ludo Peeters (Belgium)	286
1980	Pierino Gavazzi (Italy)	286
1981	Roger De Vlaeminck (Belgium)	286
1982	Jacques Hanegraaf (Holland)	286
1983	Tommy Prim (Sweden)	301
1984	Eric Vanderaerden (Belgium)	301
1985	Adri Van Der Poel (Holland)	313
1986	Guido Bontempi (Italy)	301
1987	Wim Arras (Belgium)	309
1988	Rolf Golz (Germany)	293
1989	Jelle Nijdam (Holland)	294
1990	Franco Ballerini (Italy)	246
1991	Brian Holm (Denmark)	246
1992	Rolf Sorensen (Denmark)	258
1993	Francis Moreau (France)	258

PARIS-TOURS (France)

INDIVIDUAL SUCCESSES		DISTANCE (km)
1901	Jean Fischer (France)	253
1902-5 Not held		
1906	Louis Petit-Breton (France)	234
1907	Georges Passerieu (France)	245
1908	Omer Beaugendre (France)	248
1909	François Faber (Luxemburg)	248
1910	François Faber (Luxemburg)	248
1911	Octave Lapize (France)	248
1912	Louis Heusghem (Belgium)	246
1913	Charles Crupelandt (France)	246
1914	Oscar Egg (Switzerland)	316
1915-16 Not held		
1917	Philippe Thijs (Belgium)	246
1918	Charles Mantelet (France)	248
1919	Hector Thiberghien (Belgium)	342
1920	Eugène Christophe (France)	342
1921	Francis Pelissier (France)	342
1922	Henri Pelissier (France)	342
1923	Paul Deman (Belgium)	342
1924	Louis Mottiat (France)	342
1925	Denis Verschueren (Belgium)	342
1926	Henri Suter (Switzerland)	324
1927	Henri Suter (Switzerland)	253
1928	Denis Verschueren (Belgium)	253
1929	Nicolas Frantz (Luxemburg)	253
1930	Jean Maréchal (France)	253
1931	André Leducq (France)	240
1932	Julien Moineau (France)	253
1933	Jules Merviel (France)	243
1934	Gustaaf Danneels (Belgium)	243
1935	René Le Greves (France)	251
1936	Gustaaf Danneels (Belgium)	251
1937	Gustaaf Danneels (Belgium)	251
1938	Jules Rossi (Italy)	251
1939	Frans Bonduel (Belgium)	251
1940	Not held	
1941	Paul Maye (France)	249
1942	Paul Maye (France)	248
1943	Gaby Gaudin (France)	241
1944	Lucien Teisseire (France)	253
1945	Paul Maye (France)	253
1946	Brik Schotte (Belgium)	251

1947	Brik Schotte (Belgium)	251
1948	Louis Caput (France)	251
1949	Albert Ramon (France)	251
1950	André Mahé (France)	251
1951	Jacques Dupont (France)	251
1952	Raymond Geugan (France)	253
1953	Jozef Schils (Belgium)	253
1954	Gilbert Scodeller (France)	253
1955	Jacques Dupont (France)	253
1956	Albert Bouvet (France)	251
1957	Fred De Bruyne (Belgium)	251
1958	Gilbert De Smet (Belgium)	251
1959	Rik Van Looy (Belgium)	267
1960	Jo De Haan (Holland)	267
1961	Jos Wouters (Belgium)	267
1962	Jo De Roo (Holland)	267
1963	Jo De Roo (Holland)	255
1964	Guido Reybrouck (Belgium)	248
1965	Gerben Karstens (Holland)	246
1966	Guido Reybrouck (Belgium)	249
1967	Rik Van Looy (Belgium)	249
1969	Guido Reybrouck (Belgium)	249
1969	Hermann van Springel (Belgium)	286
1970	Jurgen Tschan (Germany)	286
1971	Rik Van Linden (Belgium)	285
1972	Noel Van Tyghem (Belgium)	292
1973	Rik Van Linden (Belgium)	264
1974-87	Not held	
1988	Peter Pieters (Holland)	290
1989	Jelle Nijdam (Holland)	283
1990	Rolf Sorensen (Denmark)	283
1991	Johan Capiot (Belgium)	283
1992	Hendrik Redant (Belgium)	286
1993	Johan Museeuw (Belgium)	251

TOUR OF LOMBARDY (Italy)

INDIVIDUAL SUCCESSES		DISTANCE (km)
1905	Giovanni Gerbi (Italy)	230
1906	Giovanni Brambilla (Italy)	197
1907	Gustave Garrigou (France)	210
1908	François Faber (Luxemburg)	210
1909	Giovanni Cuniolo (Italy)	193
1910	Giovanni Micheletto (Italy)	232
1911	Henri Pelissier (France)	232
1912	Carlo Oriani (Italy)	235
1913	Henri Pelissier (France)	235
1914	Lauro Bordin (Italy)	235
1915	Gaetano Belloni (Italy)	190
1916	Leopoldo Torricelli (Italy)	232
1917	Philippe Thijs (Belgium)	204
1918	Gaetano Belloni (Italy)	190
1919	Costante Girardengo (Italy)	256
1920	Henri Pelissier (France)	241
1921	Costante Girardengo (Italy)	261
1922	Costante Girardengo (Italy)	246
1923	Giovanni Brunero (Italy)	250
1924	Giovanni Brunero (Italy)	250
1925	Alfredo Binda (Italy)	251
1926	Alfredo Binda (Italy)	251
1927	Alfredo Binda (Italy)	252
1928	Gaetano Belloni (Italy)	248
1929	Piero Fossati (italy)	238
1930	Michele Mara (Italy)	237
1931	Alfredo Binda (Italy)	234
1932	Antonio Negrini (Italy)	265

1933	Domenico Piemontesi (Italy)	230
1934	Learco Guerra (Italy)	245
1935	Enrico Mollo (Italy)	238
1936	Gino Bartali (Italy)	241
1937	Aldo Bini (Italy)	252
1938	Cino Cinelli (Italy)	232
1939	Gino Bartali (Italy)	231
1940	Gino Bartali (Italy)	225
1941	Mario Ricci (Italy)	217
1942	Aldo Bini (Italy)	184
1943-4	Not held	
1945	Mario Ricci (Italy)	222
1946	Fausto Coppi (Italy)	231
1947	Fausto Coppi (Italy)	222
1948	Fausto Coppi (Italy)	222
1949	Fausto Coppi (Italy)	222
1950	Renzo Soldani (Italy)	222
1951	Louison Bobet (France)	226
1952	Giuseppe Minardi (Italy)	226
1953	Bruno Landi (Italy)	222
1954	Fausto Coppi (Italy)	222
1955	Cleto Maule (Italy)	222
1956	André Darrigade (France)	238
1957	Diego Ronchini (Italy)	240
1958	Nino Defilippis (Italy)	243
1959	Rik Van Looy (Belgium)	240
1960	Emile Daems (Belgium)	226
1961	Vito Taccone (Italy)	253
1962	Jo De Roo (Holland)	253
1963	Jo De Roo (Holland)	263
1964	Gianni Motta (Italy)	266
1965	Tom Simpson (Great Britain)	266
1966	Felice Gimondi (Italy)	266
1967	Franco Bitossi (Italy)	266
1968	Herman Van Springel (Belgium)	266
1969	Jean-Pierre Monsere (Italy)	266
1970	Franco Bitossi (Italy)	266
1971	Eddy Merckx (Belgium)	266
1972	Eddy Merckx (Belgium)	266
1973	Felice Gimondi (Italy)	266
1974	Roger De Vlaeminck (Belgium)	266
1975	Francesco Moser (Italy)	266
1976	Roger De Vlaeminck (Belgium)	253
1977	Gian. Baronchelli (Italy)	257
1978	Francesco Moser (Italy)	266
1979	Bernard Hinault (France)	251
1980	Fons de Wolf (Belgium)	255
1981	Hennie Kuiper (Holland)	259
1982	Giuseppe Saronni (Italy)	248
1983	Sean Kelly (Ireland)	253
1984	Bernard Hinault (France)	251
1985	Sean Kelly (Ireland)	255
1986	Gian. Baronchelli (Italy)	262
1987	Moreno Argentin (Italy)	265
1988	Charly Mottet (France)	260
1989	Toni Rominger (Switzerland)	260
1990	Giles Delion (France)	246
1991	Sean Kelly (Ireland)	242
1992	Tony Rominger (Switzerland)	241
1993	Pascal Richard (Switzerland)	242

PROFESSIONAL WORLD CHAMPIONSHIP

INDIVIDUAL SUCCESSES		DISTANCE (km)
1927	Nürburgring, Germany	
	Alfredo Binda (Italy)	182
1928	Budapest, Hungary	
	Georges Ronsse (Belgium)	192
1929	Zurich, Switzerland	
	Georges Ronsse (Belgium)	200
1930	Liège, Belgium	
	Alfredo Binda (Italy)	210
1931	Copenhagen,Denmark	
	Learco Guerra (Italy)	172
1932	Rome, Italy	
	Alfredo Binda (Italy)	206
1933	Montlhéry, France	
	Georges Speicher (France)	250
1934	Leipzig, Germany	
	Karel Kaers (Belgium)	225
1935	Floreffe, Belgium	
	Jean Aerts (Belgium)	216
1936	Berne, Switzerland	
	Antonin Magne (France)	218
1937	Copenhagen, Denmark	
	Eloi Meulenberg (Belgium)	297
1938	Valkenburg, Holland	
	Marcel Kint (Belgium)	273
1939-45	Not held	
1946	Zurich, Switzerland	
	Hans Knecht (Switzerland)	270
1947	Reims, France	
	Theo Middelkamp (Holland)	274
1948	Valkenburg, Holland	
	Brik Schotte (Belgium)	266
1949	Copenhagen, Denmark	
	Rik Van Steenbergen (Belgium)	290
1950	Moorslede, Belgium	
	Brik Schotte (Belgium)	284
1951	Varese, Italy	
	Ferdi Kubler (Switzerland)	295
1952	Luxemburg	
	Heinz Müller (Germany)	280
1953	Lugano, Switzerland	
	Fausto Coppi (Italy)	270
1954	Solingen, West Germany	
	Louison Bobet (France)	240
1955	Frascati, Italy	
	Stan Ockers (Belgium)	193
1956	Ballerup, Denmark	
	Rik Van Steenbergen (Belgium)	285
1957	Waregem, Belgium	
	Rik Van Steenbergen (Belgium)	285
1958	Reims, France	
	Ercole Baldini (Italy)	277
1959	Zandvoort, Holland	
	André Darrigade (France)	292
1960	Sachsenring, East Germany	
	Rik Van Looy (Belgium)	279
1961	Berne, Switzerland	
	Rik Van Looy (Belgium)	285
1962	Salo, Italy	
	Jean Stablinski (France)	296
1963	Ronse, Belgium	
	Benoni Beheyt (Belgium)	279
1964	Sallanches, France	
	Jan Janssen (Holland)	290
1965	Lasarte, Spain	
	Tom Simpson (Great Britain)	267
1966	Nürburgring, West Germany	
	Rudi Altig (West Germany)	273
1967	Heerlen, Holland	
	Eddy Merckx (Belgium)	265
1968	Imola, Italy	
	Vittorio Adorni (Italy)	277
1969	Zolder, Belgium	
	Harm Ottenbros (Holland)	263
1970	Leicester, England	
	Jean-Pierre Monsere (Belgium)	272
1971	Mendrisio, Switzerland	
	Eddy Merckx (Belgium)	269
1972	Gap, France	
	Marino Basso (Italy)	272
1973	Montjuich, Spain	
	Felice Gimondi (Italy)	249
1974	Montreal, Canada	
	Eddy Merckx (Belgium)	262
1975	Yvoir, Belgium	
	Hennie Kuiper (Holland)	266
1976	Ostuni, Italy	
	Freddy Maertens (Belgium)	288
1977	San Cristóbal,Venezuela	
	Francesco Moser (Italy)	255
1978	Nürburgring, West Germany	
	Gerrie Knetemann (Holland)	273
1979	Valkenburg, Holland	
	Jan Raas (Holland)	275
1980	Sallanches, France	
	Bernard Hinault (France)	268
1981	Prague, Czechoslovakia	
	Freddy Maertens (Belgium)	281
1982	Goodwood, England	
	Giuseppe Saronni (Italy)	275
1983	Altenrhein, Switzerland	
	Greg LeMond (USA)	270
1984	Barcelona, Spain	
	Claude Criquielion (Belgium)	255
1985	Montello, Italy	
	Joop Zoetemelk (Holland)	265
1986	Colorado Springs, USA	
	Moreno Argentin (Italy)	261
1987	Villach, Austria	
	Stephen Roche (Ireland)	276
1988	Ronse, Belgium	
	Maurizio Fondriest (Italy)	274
1989	Chambéry, France	
	Greg LeMond (USA)	259
1990	Utsunomiya, Japan	
	Rudy Dhaenens (Belgium)	261
1991	Stuttgart, Germany	
	Gianni Bugno (Italy)	253
1992	Benidorm, Spain	
	Gianni Bugno (Italy)	261
1993	Oslo, Norway	
	Lance Armstrong (USA)	257

WOMEN'S WORLD CHAMPIONSHIP

INDIVIDUAL SUCCESSES	DISTANCE (km)
1958 Reims, France	
Elsie Jacobs (Luxemburg)	59
1959 Rotheux, France	
Yvonne Reynders (Belgium)	72
1960 Leipzig, East Germany	
Beryl Burton (Great Britain)	61
1961 Douglas, Isle of Man	
Yvonne Reynders (Belgium)	61
1962 Salo, Italy	
Marie-Rose Gaillard (Belgium)	64
1963 Ronse, Belgium	
Yvonne Reynders (Belgium)	66
1964 Sallanches, France	
Em. Sonka (USSR)	58
1965 Lasarte, Spain	
El. Eicholz (West Germany)	52
1966 Nürburgring (Germany)	
Yvonne Reynders (Belgium)	47
1967 Heerlen, Holland	
Beryl Burton (Great Britain)	53
1968 Imola, Italy	
Cornilia Hage (Holland)	55
1969 Brno, Czechoslovakia	
Audrey McElmury (USA)	70
1970 Leicester, Great Britain	
Anna Konkina (USSR)	60
1971 Mendrisio, Switzerland	
Anna Konkina (USSR)	50
1972 Gap, France	
Geneviéve Gambillon (France)	60
1973 Montjuich, Spain	
Nicola Vandenbroeck (Belgium)	55
1974 Montreal, Canada	
Geneviéve Gambillon (France)	60
1975 Mettet, Belgium	
Tineke Fopma (Holland)	54
1976 Ostuni, Italy	
Cornilia Hage (Holland)	62
1977 San Cristobal, Venezuela	
Josiane Bost (France)	49
1978 Brauweiler, Germany	
Beate Habetz (Germany)	70
1979 Valkenburg, Holland	
Petra De Bruin (Holland)	64
1980 Sallanches, France	
Beth Heiden (USA)	53
1981 Prague, Czechoslovakia	
Ute Enzenauer (Germany)	53
1982 Goodwood, Great Britain	
Mandy Jones (Great Britain)	61
1983 Altenrhein, Switzerland	
Marianne Berglund (Sweden)	60
1985 Montello, Italy	
Jeannie Longo (France)	74
1986 Colorado Springs, USA	
Jeannie Longo (France)	62
1987 Villach, Austria	
Jeannie Longo (France)	72
1989 Chambéry, France	
Jeannie Longo (France)	74
1990 Utsunomiya, Japan	
Catherine Marsal (France)	72
1991 Stuttgart, Germany	
Leontien Van Moorsel (Holland)	89
1993 Oslo, Norway	
Leontien Van Moorsel (Holland)	92

OLYMPIC GAMES

INDIVIDUAL SUCCESSES	DISTANCE (km)
1984 Mission Viejo, USA	
Connie Carpenter (USA)	79
1988 Seoul, Korea	
Monique Knol (Holland)	82
1992 Barcelona, Spain	
Kathryn Watt (Australia)	81

CORE STATES USA OPEN CHAMPIONSHIP

INDIVIDUAL SUCCESSES	DISTANCE (km)
1985 Eric Heiden (USA)	251
1986 Tom Prehn (USA)	250
1987 Tom Schuler (USA)	251
1988 Roberto Gaggioli (Italy)	250
1989 Greg Oravetz (USA)	252
1990 Paolo Cimini (Italy)	250
1991 Michel Zanoli (Holland)	251
1992 Bart Owen (USA)	253
1993 Lance Armstrong (USA)	251

KELLOGG'S TOUR (Great Britain)

INDIVIDUAL SUCCESSES	DISTANCE (km)
1987 Joey McLoughlin (Great Britain)	990
1988 Malcolm Elliott (Great Britain)	1081
1989 Robert Millar (Great Britain)	804
1990 Michel Dernies (Belgium)	1086
1991 Phil Anderson (Australia)	970
1992 Max Sciandri (Italy)	840
1993 Phil Anderson (Australia)	912

NISSAN CLASSIC

INDIVIDUAL SUCCESSES	DISTANCE (km)
1985 Sean Kelly (Ireland)	813
1986 Sean Kelly (Ireland)	840
1987 Sean Kelly (Ireland)	941
1988 Rolf Golz (Germany)	935
1989 Eric Vanderaerden (Belgium)	924
1990 Erik Breukink (Holland)	917
1991 Sean Kelly (Ireland)	864
1992 Phil Anderson (Australia)	841
1993 Not held	

TOUR DUPONT (USA)

INDIVIDUAL SUCCESSES	DISTANCE (km)
1989 Dag-Otto Lauritzen (Norway)	1257 *
1990 Raul Alcala (Mexico)	1768 *

1991	Erik Breukink (Holland)	1600
1992	Greg LeMond (USA)	1622
1993	Raul Alcala (Mexico)	1769

* These two events were called the Tour de Trump, being sponsored by the American entrepreneur Donald Trump.

TOUR DE FRANCE

INDIVIDUAL SUCCESSES		DISTANCE (km)
1903	Maurice Garin (France)	2428
1904	Henri Cornet (France)	2388
1905	Louise Trousselier (France)	2975
1906	René Pottier (France)	4637
1907	Lucien Petit-Breton (France)	4488
1908	Lucien Petit-Breton (France)	4488
1909	François Faber (Luxemburg)	4497
1910	Octave Lapize (France)	4700
1911	Gustave Garrigou (France)	5544
1912	Odile Defraye (Belgium)	5229
1913	Philippe Thijs (Belgium)	5387
1914	Philippe Thijs (Belgium)	5414
1915-18	Not held	
1919	Firmin Lambot (Belgium)	5560
1920	Philippe Thijs (Belgium)	5503
1921	Léon Scieur (Belgium)	5484
1922	Firmin Lambot (Belgium)	5375
1923	Henri Pelissier (France)	5386
1924	Ottavio Bottecchia (Italy)	5427
1925	Ottavio Bottecchia (Italy)	5430
1926	Lucien Buysse (Belgium)	5745
1927	Nicolas Frantz (Luxemburg)	5321
1928	Nicolas Frantz (Luxemburg)	5377
1929	Maurice Dewaele (Belgium)	5288
1930	André Leducq (France)	4818
1931	Antonin Magne (France)	5095
1932	André Leducq (France)	4502
1933	Georges Speicher (France)	4395
1934	Antonin Magne (France)	4363
1935	Romain Maes (Belgium)	4302
1936	Sylvère Maes (Belgium)	4442
1937	Roger Lapebie (France)	4415
1938	Gino Bartali (Italy)	4694
1939	Sylvère Maes (Belgium)	4224
1940-46	Not held	
1947	Jean Robic (France)	4640
1948	Gino Bartali (Italy)	4922
1949	Fausto Coppi (Italy)	4813
1950	Ferdi Kubler (Switzerland)	4776
1951	Hugo Koblet (Switzerland)	4474
1952	Fausto Coppi (Italy)	4801
1953	Louison Bobet (France)	4479
1954	Louison Bobet (France)	4855
1955	Louison Bobet (France)	4495
1956	Roger Walkowiak (France)	4528
1957	Jacques Anquetil (France)	4555
1958	Charly Gaul (Luxemburg)	4319
1959	Federico Bahamontes (Spain)	4363
1960	Gastone Nencini (Italy)	4272
1961	Jacques Anquetil (France)	4394
1962	Jacques Anquetil (France)	4272
1963	Jacques Anquetil (France)	4140
1964	Jacques Anquetil (France)	4505
1965	Felice Gimondi (Italy)	4175
1966	Lucien Aimar (France)	4329
1967	Roger Pingeon (France)	4780
1968	Jan Janssen (Holland)	4662

1969	Eddy Merckx (Belgium)	4102
1970	Eddy Merckx (Belgium)	4367
1971	Eddy Merckx (Belgium)	3690
1972	Eddy Merckx (Belgium)	3847
1973	Luis Ocaña (Spain)	4140
1974	Eddy Merckx (Belgium)	4098
1975	Bernard Thévenet (France)	3999
1976	Lucien Van Impe (Belgium)	4016
1877	Bernard Thévenet (France)	4093
1978	Bernard Hinault (France)	3914
1979	Bernard Hinault (France)	3720
1980	Joop Zoetemelk (Holland)	3945
1981	Bernard Hinault (France)	3757
1982	Bernard Hinault (France)	3512
1983	Laurent Fignon (France)	3962
1984	Laurent Fignon (France)	4021
1985	Bernard Hinault (France)	4127
1986	Greg LeMond (USA)	4083
1987	Stephen Roche (Ireland)	4231
1988	Pedro Delgado (Spain)	3281
1989	Greg LeMond (USA)	3285
1990	Greg LeMond (USA)	3449
1991	Miguel Induraín (Spain)	3918
1992	Miguel Indurain (Spain)	3983
1993	Miguel Indurain (Spain)	3700

TOUR OF ITALY

INDIVIDUAL SUCCESSES		DISTANCE (km)
1909	Luigi Ganna (Italy)	2448
1910	Carlo Galetti (Italy)	2987
1911	Carlo Galetti (Italy)	3530
1912	'ATALA' (Italy)	2439
1913	Carlo Oriani (Italy)	2932
1914	Alfonso Calzolari (Italy)	3162
1919	Costante Girardengo (Italy)	2964
1920	Gaetano Belloni (Italy)	2632
1921	Giovanni Brunero (Italy)	3107
1922	Giovanni Brunero (Italy)	3095
1923	Costante Girardengo (Italy)	3202
1924	Giuseppe Enrici (Italy)	3613
1925	Alfredo Binda (Italy)	3250
1926	Giovanni Brunero (Italy)	3429
1927	Alfredo Binda (Italy)	3758
1928	Alfredo Binda (Italy)	3044
1929	Alfredo Binda (Italy)	2920
1930	Luigi Marchisio (Italy)	3097
1931	Francesco Camusso (Italy)	3012
1932	Antonio Pesenti (Italy)	3235
1933	Alfredo Binda (Italy)	3343
1934	Learco Guerra (Italy)	3706
1935	Vasco Bergamaschi (Italy)	3577
1936	Gino Bartali (Italy)	3756
1937	Gino Bartali (Italy)	3840
1938	Giovanni Valetti (Italy)	3645
1939	Giovanni Valetti (Italy)	3011
1940	Fausto Coppi (Italy)	3574
1941-5	Not held	
1946	Gino Bartali (Italy)	3039
1947	Fausto Coppi (Italy)	3843
1948	Fiorenzo Magni (Italy)	4164
1949	Fausto Coppi (Italy)	4088
1950	Hugo Koblet (Switzerland)	3981
1951	Fiorenzo Magni (Italy)	4153
1952	Fausto Coppi (Italy)	3964
1953	Fausto Coppi (Italy)	4035

1954	Carlo Clerici (Switzerland)	4337
1955	Fiorenzo Magni (Italy)	3871
1958	Charly Gaul (Luxemburg)	3523
1957	Gastone Nencini (Italy)	3926
1958	Ercole Baldini (Italy)	3341
1959	Charly Gaul (Luxemburg)	3657
1960	Jacques Anquetil (France)	3481
1961	Arnaldo Pambianco (Italy)	4004
1962	Franco Balmamion (Italy)	4180
1963	Franco Balmamion (Italy)	4063
1964	Jacques Anquetil (France)	4119
1965	Vittorio Adorni (Italy)	4151
1966	Gianni Motta (Italy)	3976
1967	Felice Gimondi (Italy)	3816
1968	Eddy Merckx (Belgium)	3917
1969	Felice Gimondi (Italy)	3731
1970	Eddy Merckx (Belgium)	3292
1971	Gosta Pettersson (Sweden)	3567
1972	Eddy Merckx (Belgium)	3725
1973	Eddy Merckx (Belgium)	3796
1974	Eddy Merckx (Belgium)	4001
1975	Fausto Bertoglio (Italy)	3963
1976	Felice Gimondi (Italy)	4161
1977	Michel Pollentier (Belgium)	3868
1978	Johan De Muynck (Belgium)	3610
1979	Giuseppe Saronni (Italy)	3301
1980	Bernard Hinault (France)	4025
1981	Giovanni Battaglin (Italy)	3895
1982	Bernard Hinault (France)	4010
1983	Giuseppe Saronni (Italy)	3922
1984	Francesco Moser (Italy)	3808
1985	Bernard Hinault (France)	3998
1986	Roberto Visentini (Italy)	3858
1987	Stephen Roche (Ireland)	3915
1988	Andrew Hampsten (USA)	3597
1989	Laurent Fignon (France)	3418
1990	Gianni Bugno (Italy)	3450
1991	Franco Chioccioli (Italy)	3724
1992	Miguel Indurain (Spain)	3843
1993	Miguel Indurain (Spain)	3777

TOUR OF SPAIN

INDIVIDUAL SUCCESSES		DISTANCE (km)
1935	Gustave Deloor (Belgium)	3431
1936	Gustave Deloor (Belgium)	4349
1941	J. Berrendero (Spain)	4442
1942	J. Berrendero (Spain)	3634
1943-4	Not held	
1945	Del. Rodríguez (Spain)	3723
1946	Dal. Langarica (Spain)	3847
1947	Edw. Van Dijck (Belgium)	3818
1948	Bernardo Ruíz (Spain)	4090
1950	Em. Rodríguez (Spain)	3924
1955	Jean Dotto (France)	2735
1956	Angelo Conterno (Italy)	3204
1957	Jesús Lorono (Spain)	2943
1958	Jean Stablinski (France)	3276
1959	Antonio Suárez (Spain)	3060
1960	Frans De Mulder (Belgium)	3368
1961	Antonio Soler (Spain)	2818
1962	Rudi Altig (West Germany)	2843
1963	Jacques Anquetil (France)	2419
1964	Raymond Poulidor (France)	2865
1965	Rolf Wolfshohl (West Germany)	3409
1966	Franc. Gabica (Spain)	2950

1967	Jan Janssen (Holland)	2941
1968	Felice Gimondi (Italy)	2981
1969	Roger Pingeon (France)	2921
1970	Luis Ocaña (Spain)	3560
1971	Ferdinand Bracke (Belgium)	2793
1972	José-M. Fuente (Spain)	3078
1973	Eddy Merckx (Belgium)	3056
1974	José-M. Fuente (Spain)	2987
1975	Agust. Tamames (Spain)	3075
1976	J. Pessarodona (Spain)	3343
1977	Freddy Maertens (Belgium)	2785
1978	Bernard Hinault (France)	2990
1979	Joop Zoetemelk (Holland)	3373
1980	Faust. Ruperez (Spain)	3216
1981	Giovanni Battaglin (Italy)	3446
1982	Marino Lejarreta (Spain)	3456
1983	Bernard Hinault (France)	3398
1984	Eric Caritoux (France)	3593
1985	Pedro Delgado (Spain)	3474
1986	Alvaro Pino (Italy)	3666
1987	Luis Herrera (Colombia)	3921
1988	Sean Kelly (Ireland)	3428
1989	Pedro Delgado (Spain)	3683
1990	Marco Giovannetti (Italy)	3711
1991	Melchior Mauri (Spain)	3393
1992	Tony Rominger (Switzerland)	3395
1993	Tony Rominger (Switzerland)	3465

In 1992 the Union Cyclists Internationale (UCI) voted to alter the conditions required for breaking a World Record, moving away from allowing one rider on the track to also include competition between riders at all major championships. British riders Chris Boardman and Graeme Obree both benefited from this, setting 4,000 meters pursuit records in the 1992 Olympic Games and 1993 World Championships, respectively.

The UCI also decided to streamline the World Record list, selecting only three to survive from the many previously accepted (these are indicated in **bold** type), and decided not to differentiate between sea level and altitude record attempts. Shown here is the new definitive list along with the records that have passed into history.

New Men's Records

4000m Standing Start   Graeme Obree (Great Britain)
Viking Ship Indoor Vel, Norway   4:20.894 (19 Aug 1993)
4000m Team Standing Start   Australia
Brett Aitken/Stuart O'Grady /
Tim O'Shannessy/Billy Joe Shearsby
Viking Ship Indoor Vel, Norway   4:03.840 (20 Aug 1993)
Hour Standing Start   Chris Boardman (Great Britain)
Bordeaux le Lac Ind. Stad., Fr.   52.270km (23 July 1993)

New Women's Records

200m Flying Start   Olga Sliusareva (Russian)
Moscow Olympic Indoor Vel.   10.831 (25 April 1993)
500m Flying Start   Erika Saloumiaee (Est)
Moscow Olympic Indoor Vel.   29.655 (6 Aug 1993)
500m Standing Start   Felicia Ballanger (France)
Bordeaux le Lac Ind. Stad., Fr.   35.190 (28 July 1993)
3000m Standing Start   Rebecca Twigg (USA)
Viking Ship Indoor Vel, Norway   3:37.347 (20 Aug 1993)
Hour Standing Start   Jeannie Longo (France)
Mexico City   46.352km (1 Oct 1993)

Original Records

PROFESSIONAL: OPEN-AIR VELODROMES

UNPACED STANDING START

1km	D. Rueda Efrain (Colombia)	1:05.100 (15 Dec 1986)
5km	Gregor Braun (Germany)	5:44.700 (12 Jan 1986)
10km	F. Moser (Italy)	11:39.720 (19 Jan 1984)
20km	F. Moser (Italy)	23:21.592 (23 Jan 1984)
100km	Ole Ritter (Denmark)	2:14.02.510 (18 Nov 1971)
Hour:		
Below 600m:	F. Moser (Italy)	49.80193km (3 Oct 1986)
Above 600m:	F. Moser (Italy)	51.51350km (23 Jan 1984)

UNPACED FLYING START

200m	John Kennedy (Australia)	10.405 (24 August 1991)
500m	D. Rueda Efrain (Colombia)	27.432 (12 Dec 1986)
1km	D. Rueda Efrain (Colombia)	58.269 (13 Dec 1986)

PACED STANDING START

100km	G. Renosto (Italy)	1:10.29.420 (16 Sept 1988)
Hour	G. Renosto (Italy)	85.067km (16 Sept 1988)

PROFESSIONAL: INDOOR VELODROMES

UNPACED STANDING START

1km	Stephen Pate (Australia)	1:04.147 (19 Mar 1989)
5km	Francis Moreau (France)	5:40.617 (17 Aug 1991)
10km	F. Moser (Italy)	11:50.360 (13 May 1988)
20km	F. Moser (Italy)	24:12.280 (16 Oct 1987)
Hour	F. Moser (Italy)	50.644km (21 May 1988)

UNPACED FLYING START

200m	Michael Hubner (Germany)	10:345 (20 Aug 1990)
500m	Michael Hubner (Germany)	27:350 (18 Jan 1992)
1km	Stephen Pate (Australia)	59:893 (17 Mar 1990)

PACED STANDING START

100km	Fred Rompelberg (Holl)	1:10:14.363 (30 Oct 1986)
Hour	Fred Rompelberg (Holl)	86.449km (30 Oct 1986)

AMATEUR: OPEN-AIR VELODROMES

UNPACED STANDING START

1km	**Maik Melchow (Ger.)**	**1:02.091 (28 Aug 1986)**
4km	Gintautas Umaras (USSR)	4:31.160 (18 Sept 1987)
5km	Chris Boardman (GB) 5:38.083	(22 Sept 1992)
10km	Hans-Henrik Oersted (Den.)	11:54.906 (31 Oct 1979)
20km	John Frey (USA)	23:53.436 (10 Oct 1991)
100km	Kent Bostick (USA)	2:09:11.312 (13 Oct 1989)
Hour:		
Below 600m:	E. Baldini (Italy)	46.39361km (19 Sept 1956)
Above 600m:	John Frey (USA)	49.946622km (10 Oct 1991)
4km	Team Germany: Michael Glockner/Jens Lehman/ Guido Fulst/Stefan Steinweg	4:08.791 (31 July 1992)

UNPACED FLYING START

200m	Michael Hubner (Germany)	10.118 (27 Aug 1986)
500m	Rory O'Reilly (USA)	26.993 (23 Nov 1985)
1km	Rory O'Reilly (USA)	58.510 (23 Nov 1985)

STANDING START WITH TRAINER

50km	Al. Romanov (USSR)	35:21.108 (6 May 1987)
100km	Al. Romanov (USSR)	1:10:50.940 (6 May 1987)
Hour	Al. Romanov (USSR)	84.710km (6 May 1987)

AMATEUR: INDOOR VELODROMES

UNPACED STANDING START

1km	Alex. Kiritchenko (USSR)	1:2.576 (2 Aug 1989)
4km	Viat. Ekimov (USSR)	4:28.900 (20 Sept 1986)
4km	Team Germany: Michael Glochner/Jens Lehman/ Stefan Steinweg/Andreas Walzer	4:08.064 (16 Aug 1991)
5km	Viat. Ekimov (USSR)	5:43.514 (21 Aug 1987)
10km	Viat. Ekimov (USSR)	11:31.968 (7 Jan 1989)
20km	Viat. Ekimov (USSR)	23:14.553 (3 Feb 1989)
100km	B. Meister (Switz)	2:10:08.287 (22 Sept 1989)
Hour	Viat. Ekimov (USSR)	49.672km (27 Oct 1986)

PACED STANDING START

50km	Al. Romanov (USSR)	32:56.746 (21 Feb 1987)
100km	Al. Romanov (USSR)	1:05:58.031 (21 Feb 1987)
Hour	Al. Romanov (USSR)	91.131km (21 Feb 1987)

UNPACED FLYING START

200m	**V. Adamachvili (USSR)**	**10:099 (6 Aug 1990)**
500m	**Alex. Kirichenko (USSR)**	**26.649 (29 Oct 1988)**
1km	Alex. Kirichenko (USSR)	57.260 (25 Apr 1989)

WOMEN: OPEN-AIR VELODROMES

UNPACED STANDING START

1km	Jane Eickhoff (USA)	1:12.298 (14 June 1991)
3km	Jeannie Longo (France)	3:38.190 (5 Oct 1989)
5km	Jeannie Longo (France)	6:14.135 (27 Sept 1989)
10km	Jeannie Longo (France)	12.59.435 (1 Oct 1989)
20km	Jeannie Longo (France)	25:59.883 (1 Oct 1989)
100km	Franc. Galli (Italy)	2:28:26.259 (26 Oct 1987)
Hour:		
Below 600m:	J. Longo (France)	43.58789km (30 Sept 1986)
Above 600m:	J. Longo (France)	46.35270km (1 Oct 1989)

UNPACED FLYING START

200m	Galini Enukhina (USSR)	11.101 (4 July 1992)
500m	Isobelle Gautheron (France)	30.590 (14 Sept 1986)
1km	Erica Saloumiaee (USSR)	1:10.463 (15 May 1984)

WOMEN: INDOOR VELODROMES

UNPACED STANDING START

1km	Magali Humbert (France)	1:11.503 (23 May 1992)
3km	J. Longo-Ciprelli (France)	3:40.264 (2 Nov 1992)
5km	J. Longo-Ciprelli (France)	6:17.608 (1 Nov 1991)
10km	J. Longo (France)	12:54.250 (19 Oct 1989)
20km	J. Longo (France)	26:51.222 (29 Oct 1989)
100km	Tea Vikstedt-Nyman (Fin.)	2:24:57.618 (30 Oct 1990)
Hour	Jeannie Longo (France)	45.016km (29 Oct 1989)

UNPACED FLYING START

200m	Galina Enukhina (USSR)	11.164 (6 Aug 1990)
500m	Erica Saloumiaee (USSR)	29.655 (6 Aug 1987)
1km	Erica Saloumiaee (USSR)	1:05.232 (31 May 1987)

JUNIOR MEN: OPEN-AIR VELODROMES

UNPACED STANDING START

1km	Florian Rousseau (France)	1:04.585 (14 Sept 1992)
3km	Roman Saprykine (Russia)	3:23.7 (15 Sept 1992)
4km	Team Russia (Alexi Bjakov/Anton Chantyr/ Rol Saprykine/Igor Soloviev)	4:17.4 (17 Sept 1992)
5km	Cyril Sabatier (France)	6:30.157 (12 July 1989)
10km	P. Nardini (Italy)	13:07.293 (15 May 1988)

UNPACED FLYING START

200m	Roberto Chiappa (Italy)	10.274 (17 July 1991)
500m	Kai Melcher (Germany)	29.280 (13 Jul 1988)

JUNIOR MEN: INDOOR VELODROMES

UNPACED STANDING START

1km	Darryn Hill (Australia)	1:04.865 (15 Mar 1992)
5km	Dim. Neljubin (USSR)	5:46.415 (6 Jan 1989)
10km	Vassili Jakovlev (USSR)	12:00.251 (27 Oct 1990)

UNPACED FLYING START

200m	Viat. Dolguinov (USSR)	10.236 (1 Aug 1989)
500m	Alex. Khromyhe (USSR)	26.969 (9 Aug 1990)
1km	Alex. Khromyhe (USSR)	58.576 (10 Aug 1990)

JUNIOR WOMEN: OPEN-AIR VELODROMES

UNPACED STANDING START

500m	Jiang Cui-hui (China)	37.772 (1 Oct 1993)
2km	Hanka Kupfernagel (Ger.)	2:25.279 (4 Sept 1992)

UNPACED FLYING START

200m	Kathrin Freitag (Germany)	11.683 (18 July 1991)

JUNIOR WOMEN: INDOOR VELODROMES

UNPACED STANDING START

1km	Symeko Jochinke (Aust)	1:15.77 (15 Mar 1991)

UNPACED FLYING START

200m	Svetlana Potemkina (USSR)	11.367 (27 Oct 1991)
500m	Svetlana Potemkina (USSR)	30.230 (27 Oct 1991)

GLOSSARY

Bidon French for plastic water bottle.

Block Freewheel and gear cluster with up to eight sprockets (cogs).

Bottom bracket Main bearing unit at the bottom of the frame that supports the chainset and cranks.

Break Situation in which one or more riders are ahead of the main bunch in a road race.

Broom Wagon A vehicle that follows a road race, picking up riders who have quit and taking them to the finish.

Bunch The main group in a road race.

Chainset Pedal and toothed cog assembly with one (track), two (road), or three (mountain bike) chainrings (cogs).

Commissaire Official referee.

Crank Arm to which the pedals are attached.

Criterium Short-circuit race often held in a town centre.

Derailleur Mechanism that moves the chain up and down the block.

Directeur sportif Team manager and coach.

Disc wheel Solid-sided wheel with hollow or braced interior used in time trials.

Domestique Team rider who rides in support of a team leader by fetching and carrying drinks and clothing, and chases or defends the leader's position on the road.

Echelon Diagonal line-out of road riders to combat a cross-wind.

General classification System of determining overall race positions by the total time accumulated by each rider. The rider with the shortest time is the leader.

Giro Italian for tour.

Green jersey Award normally given to the leader of a road race on points – usually won by the most consistent sprinter rather than the overall leader.

Hot-spot sprint Sprint or series of sprints during a road race, either for points, time bonuses or as a separate competition within the race.

Index gears Method of shifting the gears by a click system of synchronized gear levers and derailleur. Known as SIS by Japanese manufacturer Shimano.

Kermesse Belgian criterium, longer and on bigger circuits than other criteriums.

King of the Mountains Title given to the best hill climber in a road race. In the Tour de France he wears a white jersey with red polka dots.

Low profile Term for 'droop snoop' time-trial bike, often fitted with a small front wheel and aerodynamic handlebars.

Maillot jaune French for the yellow jersey – the garment worn by the overall leader of many stage races.

Musette French for cloth feeding bag held up at feeding stations along the route of a road race.

Open race Race contested by professionals and amateurs.

Pavé French for a cobblestone – made famous by the cobbled stretches of road in the Paris-Roubaix one-day race.

Peloton French for bunch.

Prime French for prize awarded at the top of a hill or for an intermediate sprint.

Shoeplate Plastic plate that engages, or clips into the pedal, allowing the rider to pull up and back as well as push down.

Sit on To follow another rider in his slipstream.

Soigneur French for masseur and coach.

Stage Daily race in a stage race.

Stem Alloy bar that holds the handlebars.

Time trial Individual race against the clock.

Triathlon bars Narrow bars that are bolted onto normal handlebars, enabling the rider to assume an elbows-in position for time trialling.

Toe clips Metal clips mounted on the pedals into which the foot slips. Less common among professional road racers nowadays as most use quick-release pedals.

Tubular Lightweight racing tyre that is completely round and sealed, with stitching and glue. Usually known as a 'tub'.

UCI Union Cycliste Internationale – cycling's governing body.

Velodrome Banked circuit for track racing, made from wood, concrete or asphalt.

Vuelta Spanish for tour.

USEFUL ADDRESSES

CYCLING FEDERATIONS
(amateur and professional)

Argentina
Federación Ciclista Argentina
Código Postal 1233
Avda San Juan 3078, Piso 1
Buenos Aires

Australia
Australian Cycling Federation
68 Boadway, Sydney NSW 2007

Austria
Österreichischer Radsport Verband
Prinz Eugenstrasse 12
1040 Vienna

Belgium
Royale Ligue Vélocipédique Belge
49 Avenue du Globe
1190 Bruxelles

Canada
Association Cycliste Canadienne
1600 Promenade James Naismith
Drive
Gloucester
Ontario K1B 5NF

Colombia
Federación Colombiana de
Ciclismo
Diag. 109 No 15-35
Bogotá D.E.

Czechoslovakia
Repub. Czech. Cycling Federation
Velodrome Nad Trebesinem III
100 00 Praha 10 – Strasnice

Denmark
Dansk Professionelt Cykle
Forbund
Vaargyvelvej 43
DK 2690 Karlslunde

France
Fédération Française de Cyclisme
ZAC de Nanteuil

I.J. Monnet
5 Rue de Rome
93561 Rosny-Sous-Bois (Cedex)

Germany
Bund Deutscher Radfahrer eV
Otto-Fleck-Schneise 4
60528 Frankfurt S.Main 71

Great Britain
British Cycling Federation
(including British Mountain Bike
Federation)
36 Rockingham Road
Kettering
Northants NN16 8HG

Holland
Koninklijke Nederlandsche
Wielren
Unie
Postbus 136
Polanerbaan 15
3447 GN Woerden

India
Indian Professional Cyclists'
Association
C/O Homi Bhathena
802-D, Sonal Villa
Dr Ambedkar Road
Dadar Bombay 400014

Ireland
Federation of Irish Cyclists
Halston Street
Dublin 7

Italy
Federazione Ciclistica Italiana
Stadio Olimpico – Curva Nord
Cancello L – Porta 91
00194 Rome

Japan
Japanese Professional Cycling
Federation
2-1 Hasune 2- Chome
Itabashi-ku
Tokyo

Liechtenstein
Liechtensteiner Radfahrerverband
Postfach 319
9491 Ruggell

Luxemburg
Fédération du Sport Cycliste
Luxembourgeois
Case Postale 2253
L-1022 Luxemburg

Monaco
Fédération Monégasque de
Cyclisme
12 Avenue des Castellans
98000 – Monaco

Norway
Norges Cykleforbund
Hauger Skolevei 1
1351 Rud-Oslo 1

New Zealand
New Zealand Cycling Association
PO Box 35-048
Christchurch

Poland
Polski Zwiazek Kolarski
1 Plac, Zelaznej Bramy
00136 Varsovie

Portugal
Federacao Portuguesa de Ciclismo
Rua Barros Queiros 39-10
1100 Lisbonne

Puerto Rico
Federación Puertorriqueña de
Ciclismo
Apartado Postal 4674
San Juan
PR 00919-4674

San Marino
Federazione Ciclistica Sanmarinese
Via XXV Marzo
47031 Domagnano

Spain
Federación Española de Ciclismo
Ferraz 16-5
28008 Madrid

Sweden
Svenska Cykelforbundet
Drakslingan 1
19340 Sigtuna

Russia
Cycling Union of Russia
119270
Quai Loujnetscaya 8
Moscow

Switzerland
National Committee for Cycling
Industriestrasse 47
Case Postale
8152 Glattbrugg

USA
United States Cycling Federation
1750 East Boulder Street
Colorado Springs
Co. 80909

Venezuela
Federación Venezolana de
Ciclismo
Velodrome Teo Caprile
La Vega – Caracus

Touring Organizations

Austria
Österreichischer Fahrradverband
Hasnerstrasse 10
1170 Vienna

Finland
Finnish Cycling Association
Radrokatu 12
PL27 00241 Helsinki

France
Fédération Française de Cyclotourisme
8 Rue Jean-Marie Jégo
75013 Paris

Great Britain
Cyclists' Touring Club
Cotterell House
69 Meadrow
Godalming
Surrey GU7 3HS

Audax UK
P.E. Hanson
Corner Cottage
7 Prosper Hill
Gwithian
Cornwall TR27 5BW

Sustrans (cycle paths, many
following disused railways)
35 King Street
Bristol BS1 4DZ

Holland
Nederlandse Rijwiel Toer Unie
Vendelier 27
PB 326, 3900
Veenendaal

Italy
Touring Club Italiano
Corsa Italia 10
20122 Milan

Sweden
Cykelframjandet
Stora Nygatan 41-43
103-12 Stockholm

USA
United States Cycling Federation
1750 East Boulder Street
Colorado Springs
Colo. 80909

National Off Road Bicycle
Association (NORBA)
PO Box 1901
Chandler
AZ 85244

League of American Wheelmen
PO Box 988
MD 21203

Bikecentennial
PO Box 8308
Missoula
MT 59807

PICTURE CREDITS

Stewart Clarke: 23, 78/9, 79, 80, 81, 83, 85, 87a, 160,
Cycling Weekly: 7b, 16, 33, 36, 37, 38, 40, 41, 45, 48, 49, 70, 72, 77, 90, 91, 92, 100, 102, 105, 110, 111, 112, 113, 114, 143b, 145, 148, 149, 151,
Tim Hughes: 31, 167, 169, 170, 172, 173
Alan McFaden: 10, 12, 13, 14, 17, 18, 20, 21, 22, 24, 25, 26, 28, 29, 30, 32
Phil O'Connor: 6b, 8b, 68/9, 71, 74, 75, 76, 97, 107, 109, 115, 117, 118, 119, 120, 122, 127, 128, 129, 134, 137, 138, 140, 143a, 144, 147, 150, 152, 154, 156, 157, 159, 161, 164,
Photosport International: 82, 84, 86, 87b, 132,
Presse Sports: 104,
Raleigh Cycles: 6a, 8a, 126, 131, 166, 168, 171, 174, 175, 176
Bernard Thompson: 73, 101,
US Bicycling Hall of Fame: 69
Graham Watson: 1, 2, 7a, 11, 15, 19, 27, 34/5, 35, 39, 42, 43, 44, 46, 47, 50, 51, 52, 53, 54, 55, 56, 57, 58/9, 59, 60, 61, 62, 63, 64, 65, 66, 67, 88/9, 89, 93, 94, 95, 96, 98/9, 99, 103, 106, 108, 116, 121, 123, 124, 125, 130, 135, 136, 141, 142, 155, 158, 162, 163, 165, 176

12   8   99